1984

From ENIAC to UNIVAC

*An Appraisal of the
Eckert-Mauchly Computers*

Digital Press History of Computing Series

From ENIAC to UNIVAC

An Appraisal of the Eckert-Mauchly Computers

NANCY STERN

Digital Press

Copyright © 1981 by Digital Equipment Corporation.

Design by David Ford
Printed in U.S.A.
10 9 8 7 6 5 4 3 2
Documentation number EY-AX013-DP
ISBN 0-932376-14-2

UNIVAC and UNISERVO are registered trademarks of the Sperry Corporation.

The text was created on a DEC Word Processing System and, via a translation
program, was automatically typeset on the DECset-8000 Typesetting System.

Library of Congress Cataloging in Publication Data

Stern, Nancy B.
    From ENIAC to UNIVAC

    (Digital Press history of computing series)
    Bibliography: p.
    Includes index.
    1. Electronic digital computers—History.   2. Computer industry–United
states—History.   I. Title.   II. Title: Eckert-Mauchly computers.   III. Series.
QA76.5.S775   001.64'09   81-3280
                      AACR2

Preface

My purpose in writing about the Eckert-Mauchly computers is threefold. First, I wanted to focus on the process of development in the burgeoning computer field. The work of J. Presper Eckert and John W. Mauchly on four computers, each in some manner a "first," afforded ample opportunity to study an evolving technology.

Second, I wanted to analyze the social forces, especially the institutional ones, influencing the development process. In the instance of the Eckert-Mauchly computers, the interaction and changing roles of the academic, government, and commercial spheres clearly invited such analysis.

Finally, I was prompted to study the achievements of two men whose work has given rise to much controversy and to try to place these achievements in the appropriate historical context. Some of my conclusions differ radically from those of other writers in the field. I have attempted to remain as objective as possible, to base my interpretations firmly on the evidence available to me, and to maintain a consistent point of view.

I wish to express my gratitude for the generous assistance of the late John Mauchly, who, despite his illness, was willing to spend long hours discussing events relating to his work. Though he did not always agree with my analysis, he was a tireless supporter of my research project. I am also grateful to Presper Eckert, who, though less often available for interviews, provided invaluable assistance. His direct and uncompromising views helped me define the major issues.

Many pioneers in the field of computer development were extremely helpful in furnishing interviews and directing me to appropriate source material. Those interviewed are listed in the Bibliography, and I extend thanks to them all. I would like to express particular thanks to Arthur W. Burks and Herman H. Goldstine.

I must also acknowledge the support and advice of many scholars who read the manuscript: I. Bernard Cohen, Ruth Schwartz Cohen, Elizabeth

Garber, Melvin Kranzberg, Robert Multhauf, Mina Rees, Saul Rosen, Thomas M. Smith, Henry Tropp, and Fred Weinstein.

I would like to express my appreciation to the following people for providing me with photographs: John V. Atanasoff; Joseph Chapline; Uta C. Merzbach, curator, Section of Mathematics, Smithsonian Institution; and Louis D. Wilson.

I am grateful to the National Science Foundation for a grant that enabled me to undertake the research for this study. I wish also to express my appreciation to Digital Press for all the production and editorial assistance that was provided and to Richard Rubinstein for compiling the table in Chapter 6.

But most of all, I must acknowledge the encouragement and understanding of my children, Lori and Melanie, and my husband, Bob, without whose support this book would simply not have been written.

Nancy Stern

Contents

Illustrations

Introduction

Between the years 1943 and 1951, John Presper Eckert, Jr., and John William Mauchly developed four electronic digital computers. (1) The ENIAC was the first fully operational large-scale electronic digital computer. It was constructed at the University of Pennsylvania's Moore School of Electrical Engineering under an Army Ordnance Department contract during the years 1943–1946. (2) The EDVAC was the first electronic digital computer to incorporate the stored-program concept. Conceived in 1944 and funded as a supplement to the ENIAC contract, it was not actually completed until 1951, five years after Eckert and Mauchly left the Moore School to form their own company. (3) The BINAC was the first electronic digital computer with stored-program capability to be completed in the United States. Begun in 1947, a year after Eckert and Mauchly formed their business partnership, the BINAC was completed in August 1949, just a few months after the British unveiled the EDSAC, the world's first fully operational stored-program electronic digital computer. The EDSAC was modeled after the EDVAC. (4) The UNIVAC was the first general-purpose electronic digital computer designed for commercial use. Begun by Eckert and Mauchly's firm in 1946 and completed in 1951, the UNIVAC was initially funded by several government and private contracts.

Eckert, Mauchly, and their associates built the ENIAC and began the design of the EDVAC as employees of the Moore School of Electrical Engineering. Both projects were supported by wartime government funding. Consequently the design features incorporated in the machines and the direction taken by the inventors were significantly influenced by academic and governmental forces. Indeed, Eckert and Mauchly's decision to undertake commercial production of the BINAC and UNIVAC was, in large part, a response to these academic and governmental influences.

Industrial organizations also had a significant impact on Eckert and Mauchly. During the war, the Bell Telephone Laboratories and the Radio Corporation of America, among others, were actively engaged in government work; employees from these organizations were frequently called upon to assess the computational work at the Moore School and in some instances to provide assistance.

Later, when Eckert and Mauchly formed their own company, they received contracts for UNIVACs from the A. C. Nielsen Company and the Prudential Insurance Company, as well as from the government, and also obtained financial support from the American Totalisator Company. Even with this funding, the two inventors could not sustain their organization long enough to complete the UNIVAC. Faced with bankruptcy in 1950 as a direct result of the loss of American Totalisator support, they sold their corporation to Remington Rand, which later merged with the Sperry Gyroscope Company to form Sperry Rand.

The commercial forces affecting Eckert and Mauchly provide insight into their problems as small businessmen undertaking a major development project in a high-technology field. The constraints imposed upon them by the government and also by Nielsen and Prudential were typical constraints within which large corporations must operate. Contractual requirements and funding policies, to name just two, were a constant source of concern for the two men. Because of their financial difficulties, Eckert and Mauchly simply could not function within these constraints and eventually were forced to sell their company.

Remington Rand's acquisition of the Eckert-Mauchly Computer Corporation marked the emergence of large commercial organizations into the computing field. One focus of this book is to consider, along with institutional forces affecting Eckert and Mauchly, the reasons why companies like Remington Rand and IBM were so late in realizing the commercial potential of electronic digital computers.

The relationship of Eckert and Mauchly to each other and to others with whom they worked is also of historical significance. Eckert was an electrical engineer with great inventive capabilities. Mauchly was a physicist who was extremely innovative in his ideas about computers and their applications to the sciences. They were a unique team, hybrid in a sense; the contributions of each man to the development of their computers, the dynamics of their relationship, and the applications of their machines to scientific problems illuminate the interaction between science and technology.

This relationship between science and technology was a critical factor in the origins of electronic digital computers. John von Neumann was a significant catalyst in fostering that interaction. When he became an integral part of the Eckert-Mauchly work at the Moore School in 1944, von Neumann had already received acclaim as an eminent mathematician. During World War II, he had shifted his interest from pure to applied mathematics and to computers, partly in response to wartime needs and partly as a result of the

Moore School computational work. Von Neumann was instrumental in familiarizing the Los Alamos Scientific Laboratory with the capabilities of the ENIAC. The use of the ENIAC to test the feasibility of some aspects of the hydrogen bomb for Los Alamos became the first test run of the computer. Along with the Eckert-Mauchly team, von Neumann was also instrumental in developing and formalizing the stored-program concept.

After the war, however, von Neumann's scientific orientation came into direct conflict with the engineering and commercial orientation of Eckert and Mauchly. This led to a bifurcation in computer technology, with some machines being developed exclusively for commercial use and others for scientific use. This duality in the history of electronic digital computers will be explored in detail in the chapters that follow.

In recent years, Eckert and Mauchly and their computers have been the subject of considerable controversy, largely as a result of the 1971–1973 litigation between Honeywell and Sperry Rand over the ENIAC patent. The *Honeywell* v. *Sperry Rand* trial has great significance for the history of computing in general and for a study of the Eckert and Mauchly organization in particular.

The ENIAC patent was filed on June 16, 1947, but largely as a result of numerous patent interference proceedings was not actually issued by the government until February 4, 1964. The ENIAC patent, as issued, consisted of over 200 pages of text with 148 claims relating to the principles of electronic digital computers.

Patent law stipulates that a patentee or his or her assignee retains the rights to a patent for a period of 17 years, during which time the patentee has the right to exclude others from making, using, or selling the invention defined by the patent. Accordingly, other persons or organizations wanting to use such an invention must obtain permission from the patentee, normally through payment of royalties, or face litigation for patent infringement.

Hence, Sperry Rand, the company that had purchased the Eckert-Mauchly firm in 1950 and held the ENIAC patents in 1964, had hoped to derive great financial benefit from these patents. As an alternative to the payment of royalties, IBM and Sperry Rand, the two major tabulating equipment manufacturers, entered cross license agreements under which money and patent rights of both parties were exchanged. This occurred while the ENIAC was still in patent application form. Other companies, however, were faced with the problem of paying large royalties for use of the technology covered by the ENIAC patent. When Sperry Rand sued Honeywell for patent infringement, the latter set out to find grounds on which to file a countersuit. Honeywell hired the Minneapolis law firm of Dorset, Windhorst, Hannaford, Whitney and Halladay to determine if there were any grounds for declaring the ENIAC patent invalid. In June 1971, Henry Halladay, chief counsel for Honeywell in this matter, filed a countersuit in Minneapolis, Minnesota, charging that the ENIAC patent was invalid and that Sperry Rand was in violation of antitrust laws. The defendants named were Sperry Rand and the Illinois Scientific Development Company, a wholly owned subsidiary of Sperry Rand that held the ENIAC patent.

One of the major claims on which the Honeywell suit rested was that Eckert and Mauchly were not the true inventors of the first electronic digital computer. The claim held that they derived their ideas from John Vincent Atanasoff, an associate professor of physics and mathematics at Iowa State College, which later became the University of Iowa. Atanasoff had designed a vacuum-tube computer to solve linear simultaneous equations. During the 1940s Atanasoff invited Mauchly to see his computer and thereafter the two men had some correspondence.

As part of its case, Honeywell also claimed that the ENIAC was put into public use more than one year prior to the June 16, 1947, patent filing date. If this claim could be proven, the ENIAC patent would be invalid because the ideas would have entered the public domain.

The trial continued for almost ten months with expert testimony provided by many key pioneers in computing on behalf of both the plaintiff and the defendant; still more pioneers gave their affidavits. Honeywell entered 30,000 documents into the record, Sperry entered 6,000. When the proceedings were finally over on March 13, 1972, there were 50,000 pages of trial transcript.

On October 19, 1973, the presiding judge handed down his verdict in a 319-page document entitled "Findings of Fact, Conclusions of Law, and Order for Judgment." Although he did not find Sperry Rand in violation of antitrust laws, he declared the ENIAC patent invalid, stating, among many other things, that "Eckert and Mauchly did not themselves first invent the automatic electronic digital computer, but instead derived the subject matter from one Dr. John Vincent Atanasoff."[1] This opinion was somewhat contradictory since the judge also stated that Eckert and Mauchly were the inventors of the ENIAC and the ENIAC patent claims did not rest on Atanasoff's work.

The findings of the court have not been challenged or appealed by Sperry Rand. Thus, the verdict represents a judgment about the history of electronic digital computing in the United States that must be analyzed and assessed. A major objective of this book is to provide such an assessment.

Several priority issues relating to the court case are also examined in the chapters that follow. The relationship between John Mauchly and John Vincent Atanasoff is considered in an effort to shed some light on the ideas that were exchanged between the two men. The first problem run on the ENIAC is discussed in an effort to clarify whether it was a test run as the defendants claimed during the trial or an actual run as was claimed by the plaintiff. And finally the relationship between Eckert and Mauchly, on the one hand, and the Moore School engineers on the other, is examined to determine whether the ENIAC is best described as the invention of two men or rather as a group effort.

This book, then, is a case study in the history of electronic digital computing focusing on two men who made very significant technical contributions to the field and on the institutional, technological, scientific, and economic problems they faced along the way. Such a study is well-timed for two reasons. Many of the participants in early computer development are approaching advanced age; their recollections and records must be examined and placed in perspective to provide an adequate and accurate record of events in this field. Further, because technology today is no longer unquestionably correlated with progress, the need to justify research and development projects, both past and present, has become a matter of increasing concern. The electronic digital computer is precisely the sort of technological advance that requires historical assessment to provide a better understanding of its social and intellectual impact.

ABBREVIATIONS USED IN THIS BOOK

ACM	Association for Computing Machinery
AIEE	American Institute of Electrical Engineers
AIRE	American Institute of Radio Engineers
AMP	Applied Mathematics Panel
BRL	Ballistics Research Laboratory
ECC	Electronic Control Company
EMCC	Eckert-Mauchly Computer Corporation
ERA	Engineering Research Associates, Inc.
IAS	Institute for Advanced Study
IBM	International Business Machines Corporation
IEE	Institute of Electrical Engineers
IEEE	Institute of Electrical and Electronics Engineers
IRE	Institute of Radio Engineers
JvN Papers	John von Neumann Papers
MIT	Massachusetts Institute of Technology
NBS	National Bureau of Standards
NCR	National Cash Register Corporation
NDRC	National Defense Research Committee
ONR	Office of Naval Research
RCA	Radio Corporation of America
SHCP	Smithsonian History of Computing Project
SUA	Sperry-Univac Archives
UPA	University of Pennsylvania Archives

1

The ENIAC: Genesis of a Computer

The development of the ENIAC really begins with John William Mauchly. Mauchly was born in Cincinnati, Ohio, in 1907. During his school years, he assumed that he would attend the University of Cincinnati, where his father had received his Ph.D. and where a "cooperative course" that combined "theory and practice" by allowing students to spend part of their time working in industry appealed to his interests. When he was ready for college, however, his family was living in Maryland. He enrolled instead at the Johns Hopkins University in Baltimore, initially as an engineering student, but later transferred to physics. He received a Ph.D. in physics from Hopkins in 1932.[1]

Mauchly's interest in both engineering and science was not uncommon among computer pioneers. It may well be that this kind of interdisciplinary background served to foster invention by integrating, or synthesizing, both a scientific and a technological perspective.

After receiving his doctorate, Mauchly became instructor, then professor, of physics at Ursinus College, a small school near Philadelphia. He was fortunate to secure this position, since these were the depression years when academic jobs were difficult to find. Mauchly's decision to follow an academic career and his interest in science and technology were both greatly influenced by his father, who served as chairman of the department of terrestrial magnetism at the Carnegie Institution in Washington, D.C. Like his father, Mauchly was interested in meteorology and especially in applying statistical methods to weather forecasting. Because of the vast amounts of data associated with weather forecasting, Mauchly explored the possibility of using existing mechanical tabulating equipment for statistical computations.[2] Unsatisfied with the speed of these calculating devices, he set out to develop a harmonic analyzer that could be used for weather forecasting.

"While I was at Ursinus College I began thinking about electronic means of calculation," Mauchly stated in the early 1970s; "I wanted the rapidity and flexibility of electrical circuits to do more complex calculations with less

The Moore School differential analyzer, operated by Doris Blumberg, Betty Pollsky, and Lucy Mott. Courtesy Joseph Chapline.

error and greater speed than can be obtained by use of commercial mechanical computing machines."[3] Sometime in the late 1930s, Mauchly began to explore the use of vacuum tubes in high-speed counters. "I started buying my own vacuum tubes, and putting things together in a laboratory, and showing that you could generate counts and use these counting devices with vacuum tubes in them; not gears and wheels like all the traditional calculators had," he recalled in 1976, and added: "You could do all this if you just had enough money."[4] Because vacuum tubes were expensive, Mauchly experimented with neon tubes. He became increasingly convinced that an electronic digital calculator was a feasible device, but he lacked the engineering skills and the money to bring his ideas to fruition.

The 1973 decision in *Honeywell* v. *Sperry Rand* minimized the significance of Mauchly's early work by stating that he derived his ideas from John Vincent Atanasoff, whom he met in 1940 (see below, Chapter 2).[5] Since Mauchly never published any papers in the 1930s describing his proposed invention, he had no way of actually proving that he had conceived the idea for an electronic digital computer prior to his meeting with Atanasoff. Although Joseph Chapline, one of Mauchly's students at Ursinus and later a contributor to the ENIAC, knew of Mauchly's early work in vacuum-tube computers, the judge in *Honeywell* v. *Sperry Rand,* in the absence of documentation or an actual device, was not convinced of Mauchly's pioneering efforts.[6]

Mauchly at the Moore School

Mauchly's interest in electronic computation became even more intense during the early war years. In 1941 he enrolled in a summer war-training course at the Moore School of Electrical Engineering at the University of Pennsylvania. The school's "Engineering, Science, Management War Training Course" was designed to provide career training in electronics and other subjects that might prove useful for the war effort. The Moore School at that time had an undergraduate enrollment of about a hundred students and a senior staff of about a dozen.

Mauchly's skills and quick mind impressed the Moore School staff, particularly Carl C. Chambers and John Grist Brainerd, two of the school's three directors of research. Brainerd offered Mauchly a position as assistant professor. Since Mauchly was eager to pursue his interest in electronics and to explore the feasibility of his device with some of the engineers at the school, he accepted.[7]

During the war, the Moore School established a reputation not only in electronics but in the construction and use of computational devices as well. In 1939, the school had built the country's second differential analyzer, modeled on the analyzer invented by Vannevar Bush at the Massachusetts Institute of Technology.[8] The Moore School's device was actually more powerful than Bush's MIT machine, since it had more integrators. Eventually the Moore School's adaptation of the MIT analyzer and the school's subsequent computational work was to become a source of tension between the two institutions.[9]

The Moore School's construction of the differential analyzer also led to a close relationship between the school and the Ballistics Research Laboratory (BRL) operated by the Army Ordnance Department at the Aberdeen Proving Ground in Aberdeen, Maryland. According to the recollections of Brainerd, "Early in 1940, Col. Zornig, then director of the Ballistics Research Laboratory, came to the Moore School to discuss the use of the differential analyzer." Dean Harold Pender of the Moore School then asked Brainerd "to arrange an agreement with BRL" for its use. "Within a year," Brainerd recalled, "not only was the Moore School's differential analyzer being used by BRL, but in addition Col. Leslie Simon, the new director of BRL succeeding Zornig, asked the Moore School to cooperate by providing a staff of human computers."[10] It was this close relationship between the Moore School and BRL during World War II that provided the incentive for the design and construction of both the ENIAC and the EDVAC.

Eckert, Mauchly and the ENIAC

In 1941 Mauchly discussed his ideas for an electronic digital computer with Chambers, Brainerd, and many other engineers at the Moore School. But the person who was to have the major role in the design and development of the ENIAC was John Presper Eckert, Jr., then a graduate student at the Moore School. Eckert was born in Philadelphia in 1919, the son of a real estate developer. Like Mauchly, Eckert was greatly influenced by his father. In an interview in 1977, Eckert commented on his and Mauchly's origins:

John had a different background. His father was a theoretician. My father was the guy whose mother died when he was 15; he went to high school for one day and he got his high school education by mail order. He got his college and law degree by going to night school. He started in business with $50. One time in his life he was a millionaire . . . He fits the definition of an engineer although he wasn't an engineer.[11]

Mauchly pursued a career in pure science, as his father had; Eckert, like his father, was far more interested in business-related projects.[12] Eckert was serving as a laboratory assistant for one of the Moore School's war-training courses when he first met Mauchly in 1941. Mauchly discussed his proposed device with Eckert, who agreed that it was indeed feasible.[13] According to Herman Goldstine, Eckert, who was "undoubtedly the best electronic engineer in the Moore School . . . immediately, as was his wont, immersed himself in the meager literature on counting circuits and rapidly became an expert in the field."[14]

IBM tabulating equipment in use. Courtesy Smithsonian Institution.

The engineer par excellence, Eckert was considered brilliant by faculty and peers alike. He took a "no nonsense" approach to his subject and was highly respected. His somewhat intimidating personality stood in sharp contrast to Mauchly's amicable and outgoing one. The two men became a complementary team: Mauchly the visionary and Eckert the consummate engineer.

Other individuals at the Moore School during this period made significant contributions to the design of the ENIAC, among them Arthur W. Burks, John Davis, Thomas Kite Sharpless, and Robert Shaw. All except Burks were engineers. Burks was a mathematician and logician; like Mauchly, he had enrolled in the war-training course at the Moore School and was then offered a position as an engineer.

But the man who was in large part responsible for convincing the Army of the feasibility of the proposed computer was Herman Heine Goldstine, a mathematician who had studied ballistics and worked with Gilbert A. Bliss at the University of Chicago during the 1930s. After the University of Chicago, Goldstine went to the University of Michigan as an assistant professor. In 1942, when Goldstine was called to active duty as a first lieutenant, Bliss was instrumental in having him assigned to the Ballistics Research Laboratory at Aberdeen to assist in the Army's ballistics work. There, Goldstine was personally responsible for bringing Mauchly's ideas for a high-speed computational device to the attention of the Army Ordnance Department, which funded work at the laboratory.[15]

Factors Leading to a Government Contract

The Army's Ballistics Research Laboratory had primary responsibility for solving ballistics problems. During the war, new weapons were being developed in increasing numbers, and BRL was required to produce range tables that would furnish gunners with information necessary for firing these weapons. As the war progressed, BRL's ability to provide such tables became a matter of concern.[16] Exterior ballistics, the field of applied mathematics used in determining trajectories and ranges for new weapons, deals with equations that incorporate atmospheric variables as well as those relating to speed and distance. Hence, preparation of the tables was both a mathematical and a labor-intensive task requiring solutions of numerous nonlinear differential equations in several variables.[17]

In addition to harnessing the skills of scientists (primarily mathematicians, physicists, and astronomers trained in ballistics), BRL employed approximately 200 human computers, most of them women, who, with the computational equipment available at the time, solved the necessary equations and prepared the firing tables.[18] Using standard desk-top commercial calculators, these computers could typically calculate trajectories for a weapon in

Human computers at the Moore School use desk calculators to prepare artillery range tables.
Courtesy Smithsonian Institution.

approximately three hours.[19] In addition to standard calculators, BRL used the Moore School's differential analyzer, which was ideally suited to solving ordinary differential equations. In fact, such equipment was not entirely suitable for ballistics problems, which required solutions to partial (nonlinear) differential equations. Nonetheless, with the use of this equipment, the time required to calculate a range table was reduced to approximately twenty minutes.

By 1943, even though it was using all its available machinery, BRL was falling far behind in providing firing tables for new artillery. The government needed faster and more suitable computational equipment. This need became the single most important impetus to technological development in the field of electronic digital computers in the United States.

BRL's computational requirements were not only a sufficient condition for development of the computer at that time, but a necessary condition as well. A year earlier, in August 1942, John Mauchly had written a proposal that outlined the main features of a high-speed vacuum-tube computer and focused on its technical feasibility. This report, "The Use of High Speed Vacuum Tube Devices for Calculating," submitted to the Moore School and the Army Ordnance Department, was at the time ignored by both.[20] It was not until the following year, when computation problems had reached a critical point at BRL, that Mauchly's 1942 proposal was resurrected and resubmitted to the same agency.

The factors surrounding the resubmittal of the proposal in 1943 are characteristic of government research and development policies during the war. First, as a result of wartime exigencies the government was often prepared to fund numerous and even parallel research and development efforts. In the hope that some solution to its diverse problems would be found, it frequently gave only minimal attention to economic factors and, as in this case, to technical feasibility. Second, the government was more likely to award contracts to those institutions with which it had had some previous association. The Moore School, as a result of its collaboration with BRL in designing the differential analyzer and training human computers for ballistics work, was viewed as a competent agent to help solve the laboratory's computational problems. In 1943, therefore, the Army's confidence in the Moore School served to assuage doubts concerning the success of the proposed vacuum-tube computer. Third, Herman Goldstine, who undertook to convince government officials of the feasibility of a large-scale electronic digital computer, was, unlike Mauchly, known to Army personnel and had earned the trust of BRL.[21]

BRL sent Goldstine to the Moore School to serve as liaison on the project to train human computers. There he came across Mauchly's original memorandum and asked Brainerd, who was then serving as liaison with the Army Ordnance Department, for further clarification. Brainerd had only recently read the proposal and had written to Mauchly: "Read with interest. It is easily conceivable that labor shortage may justify development work on this in the not too distant future."[22] Both Brainerd and Goldstine were sufficiently convinced of the technical feasibility of Mauchly's ideas and of the pressing need for ballistics information that they decided to prepare and promote a more comprehensive proposal.

The ENIAC Contract

On April 2, 1943, Brainerd submitted a "Report on an Electronic Diff. [sic] Analyzer," which included as an appendix Mauchly's original memorandum. Initial discussions with Army representatives and members of BRL began on April 9 and progressed rapidly.[23] By April 26, Brainerd confidently wrote Dean Harold Pender of the Moore School that a contract acceptable to both sides would be forthcoming:

As you know, we have had numerous conferences recently with representatives of the Ordnance Department of the Army concerning the possibility of developing and constructing an electronic difference analyzer and computer. These conversations have progressed unexpectedly rapidly, and I therefore want to place before you in writing the situation as it now stands. If the proposed project continues to move as swiftly as it has in the past month, there is a possibility that we might have a letter of intent within another month.[24]

Six weeks later the Army and the Moore School reached an agreement on contract terms. On May 17, 1943, a cost estimate for the first six-month period was prepared, calling for an initial expenditure of $61,700 and a total estimated development cost of $150,000. On June 5, the contract was signed. John Brainerd became the project supervisor; John Presper Eckert, Jr., the chief engineer; John Mauchly, the principal consultant; and Herman Goldstine, the technical liaison for BRL.[25]

The proposed device was called the Electronic Numerical Integrator and Computer, or ENIAC. Suggested by Colonel Paul Gillon of the Army Ordnance Department, who was also executive officer of BRL, the name for the device was to replace Brainerd's term, "electronic diff. analyzer." The ENIAC was to be designed with a special application in view. That is, it would be designed expressly for the solution of ballistics problems and for the printing of range tables, though, as originally envisioned by Mauchly, the device could have had wider applicability.

Questions about Reliability

The Army's decision to support the project was not a cautiously planned policy decision, but instead reflected the government's tendency to fund experienced institutions without paying too much attention to the technical nature of the proposal. In this case, the Army's confidence in the Moore School and in Brainerd and Goldstine were the important considerations influencing the decision.[26]

Brainerd's and Goldstine's own accounts of events leading to the ENIAC contract, as well as the accounts of others, suggest that the Army made no attempt to ascertain the technical feasibility of the proposed machine, but questions were raised in other circles about the technical feasibility and reliability of the proposed device. Brainerd's own cautious approach to the issue is demonstrated in his report of April 2, 1943:

> The disadvantages of the electronic diff. analyzer arise almost entirely from the fact that it is new. Although it appears reasonably certain that sufficient knowledge is available to develop and design each unit needed in the device, nevertheless it must be considered disadvantageous . . . (a) that no such analyzer had yet been built, hence there is no exact basis in experience on which to establish the problems which will arise in the construction of one, and (b) there is no store of knowledge concerning maintenance and upkeep.[27]

The ENIAC progress report of December 1943 was similarly cautious: "The most uncertain question concerning the ENIAC is its reliability."[28]

The Government's Science Advisors

After June 1943, the Moore School staff directed its efforts in part toward convincing prestigious scientists and engineers, serving as advisors to the government, of the technical feasibility of the device. This effort to legitimize the ENIAC is best understood in conjunction with the government's science policy during the war.

As early as 1939 American engineers and scientists were expressing concern about the technical capabilities of the various government agencies, particularly the military branches. With Vannevar Bush as their spokesman, they were influential in convincing President Franklin D. Roosevelt of the need for a central agency, directly responsible to the president, that would "bring the whole scientific resources of the country to bear on weapons research."[29] The National Defense Research Committee (NDRC) was created in 1940, and although it moved ahead rapidly, as the historian A. Hunter Dupree has pointed out, "it soon proved too narrow an organization for the emergency because its field was limited to weapons research. In June, 1941, FDR by an executive order established OSRD [Office of Scientific Research and Development] in response to shortcomings that scientists, especially Vannevar Bush, had observed."[30] As a result, NDRC was incorporated into a more inclusive research and development organization which was to provide technical assistance to government agencies by funding projects deemed beneficial to the war effort and by coordinating projects to facilitate the flow of information from one research center to another.[31]

Although in the spring of 1943 the Army Ordnance Department did not request electronics experts to pass judgment on the technical feasibility of the proposed ENIAC, members of NDRC did so, and with alacrity—an act that was to substantially affect the development of the ENIAC.

Communication between participants in the ENIAC project and members of NDRC began even before the contract was signed. As the nation's central scientific and technical agency which in 1941–1942 had funded research on several electronic counters, NDRC possessed information of potential import to the Moore School staff. As a funding agency, it was also a possible source of additional resources, specifically through its fire-control section. Finally, and most importantly, as an agency staffed by the country's most influential scientists and engineers, its approval would have lent special credence to the project.

From the outset, however, NDRC's reaction to the ENIAC was not at all enthusiastic. The committee consisted of reputable scientists and engineers who had already made significant contributions to science and technology. They were deeply committed, whether consciously or unconsciously, to the status quo.[32] By the nature of its task as well as the commitment of its members, NDRC often approached new advances in a conservative manner. James Conant, an active participant in the organization, wrote retrospectively: "Ideas that originated within the NDRC organization were more than once greeted at the start with skepticism."[33]

This conservative orientation was more evident in the area of computational equipment than in other research fields. As indicated earlier, Vannevar Bush, chairman of OSRD, was a major force in the development of the differential analyzer, which was a mechanical analog computer. Moreover, Samuel Caldwell and Harold Hazen, both of whom held key positions in NDRC, were, along with Bush, widely known for their work on analog devices, which were used extensively as computational instruments for scientific purposes. George Stibitz, also serving on NDRC, helped develop the Bell Telephone Laboratories' electromechanical relay computers, which by 1943 also had become effective scientific instruments. Thus it was not surprising that NDRC approached the ENIAC venture and its requisite expense with some reservations. Moreover, NDRC had previously funded several projects to develop electronic counters, the fundamental unit of an electronic digital computer, all of which had been abandoned.[34]

NDRC and the Moore School

It is reasonable to assume that a group such as NDRC, consisting of those who have come to be called "gatekeepers" or leaders of science, would have a deep commitment to the industrial organizations and academic institutions that had provided the setting for the group's own individual successes and would regard those institutions as the most likely environment for future technical advance.[35] Remarks from an interview in the Smithsonian History of Computing Project clearly illustrate the spirit of commitment and easy fellowship within this group. In 1972, Henry Tropp interviewed E. A. Andrews and George Stibitz of Bell Telephone Laboratories about their work on the Bell relay computers in the early 1940s:

Question: In the early period, what was it like in terms of the cooperation you got, the necessary funding and the general atmosphere in which you were working?

Andrews: Well, I'll answer it from my viewpoint. As far as funding, I'd go to George (Stibitz) and say, "I need another $17,000."

Stibitz: And that was just passed up to Warren Weaver. As I told you yesterday, Weaver was really responsible for the support that we got.[36]

This commitment is illustrated by the fact that the initial 1941 work on electronic fire-control devices, performed under the auspices of NDRC, was undertaken by Bell Telephone Laboratories, RCA, Eastman Kodak, and National Cash Register—all large, well-established firms. Moreover, NDRC's decision to support a Radiation Laboratory at MIT was similarly fostered by the committee members' close relationship with that institution.[37]

NDRC regarded the Moore School, an institution not nearly so prominent as MIT, as naive and pretentious. The failure of several major industrial organizations to successfully build electronic counters in previous years made the committee skeptical of the Moore School's success. That the project's protagonists were all young (in 1943 Mauchly was thirty-six, Goldstine thirty, Eckert twenty-four, and Brainerd thirty-nine) and relatively inexperienced served to increase the skepticism of the members of NDRC. The fact that most of the project's engineers lacked Ph.D. degrees did not help the situation.

NDRC became aware of the Moore School venture on April 14, 1943. A letter dated April 12, 1943, from Brainerd to Dr. Thomas Johnson, chief physicist of BRL, outlined the purpose, design features, and inherent advantages of the proposed "diff. analyzer."[38] Brainerd had employed the term "diff." to circumvent the expected disapproval of Hazen and Caldwell, who had been associated with the MIT differential analyzer. The ENIAC's proponents thought that if the device could be presented as a modification of the differential analyzer, it might be viewed more positively. The problem was that the ENIAC was digital and therefore solved differential equations by differencing, not differentiating. To use the term "differential," then, to describe the ENIAC would have been deceptive; but to use the term "diff.," which was really an abbreviation for "difference," was meant to suggest an appropriate alternative, one that would reinforce the similarity between the ENIAC and the differential analyzer. (Paradoxically, the differential analyzer solved differential equations by integrating, not differentiating.) Looking back many years later, Eckert explained that the term "diff." was coined to help sell the concept: "This was in part a matter of salesmanship because the people with whom we were dealing were accustomed to differential analyzers. So we gave the thing a name that tied it more closely with something with which they were familiar . . . We hoped by this method to encounter less sales resistance."[39]

Reactions of Established Scientists

On April 14, 1943, Johnson suggested to Harold L. Hazen, chief of Division 7, the fire-control division of NDRC, that Hazen's division might find the Brainerd proposal of interest. Hazen recorded his initial reaction to the proposed device in a diary entry on that date:

Regarding a proposed electronic differential analyzer, TJ [Tom Johnson] described in general terms a proposal, which as far as he knew, originated with Brainerd at the Moore School of the University of Pennsylvania. . . .

TJ indicated that the Aberdeen group thought this might be an interesting project for NDRC. There was a brief discussion on the technical phases of the subject in which it was agreed by TJ and HLH that the techniques proposed were sadly outdated and that NCR or the RCA development under the Division 7 contract just terminated should most certainly be taken into account if such a device were to be undertaken. . . .

HLH talked over the phone with SHC [Samuel H. Caldwell] who rightly emphasized the emergence of considerable new differential analyzer capacity in that the new differential analyzer at MIT is now actually doing ballistic solutions in shakedown operations. . . .

Should a new development be, by chance, indicated, the question would of course arise as to the most suitable contractor which, in view of the advanced nature of the work already done by RCA and NCR, might well be one of these agencies.

How's for some bright ideas as to how to get Moore School profitably occupied.[40]

Hazen did not deny the possibility that the proposed computer might in the end function properly, but he thought the device was based on obsolete technology and was unnecessary in light of MIT's highly classified work on the newly proposed Rockefeller Analyzer, an electronic differential analyzer.[41] Hazen also claimed that such a device could not be built in time to serve war needs; this was in fact an accurate assessment, since the testing of the ENIAC was not begun until the fall of 1945.

The rest of Hazen's statements, however, tend to demonstrate his skepticism about digital computers and to support the claims made above about the attitudes of gatekeepers.[42] Hazen's remarks, particularly the last paragraph, suggest that he looked at the Moore School as unsuitable for a project to construct the first electronic digital computer, especially since more prestigious organizations had already done work in this area.

Hazen's doubts about the ENIAC project were shared by his fellow NDRC member Samuel Caldwell, an associate professor of electrical engineering at MIT who had also made significant contributions to the development of analog computers. In October 1943, several months after the ENIAC project was initiated, Caldwell still questioned its feasibility in a letter to Hazen:

From the description given by Colonel Gillon, it would appear that the specifications of the equipment under development by the Ordnance Department substantially duplicate the specifications of the Rapid Arithmetical Machine program [a proposed electronic digital computer]. . . .

As far back as 1939, we realized that we could build a machine for electronic computation. But, although it was possible to build such a machine and possible to make it work, we did not consider it practical. The reliability of electronic equipment required great improvement before it could be used with confidence for computation purposes. . . .

I make the above comments merely to clarify my previous remarks and also to indicate our active interest in the Ordnance Department program because of its great similarity to the one which we have at present packed away in camphor balls.[43]

Hazen's and Caldwell's lack of enthusiasm for electronic digital computers in general was a deterrent to MIT's entry into the digital field. It was a major reason why the computer at MIT eventually called "Whirlwind" began as an analog device and was changed to digital only after a costly research effort had been undertaken.[44]

George Stibitz, the Bell Telephone Laboratories' mathematician who had developed electromechanical relay computers, also expressed reservations about the ENIAC project:

I see no reason for supposing that the relay device RDAFB [Bell's computer] is less broad in scope than the ENIAC, since each is a numerical calculator and can presumably perform exactly the same operations provided switching and storage problems in connection with the ENIAC can be solved. I think the ideal equipment would probably be a combination of relay and electronic devices, but I am very sure that the development time for the electronic equipment will be four to six times as long as that for relay equipment.[45]

NDRC's Commitments to Computing

Both Caldwell's and Stibitz's remarks were communicated to Colonel Gillon of BRL, who, with appropriate input from Brainerd and Goldstine, was able to point out that the proposed ENIAC would be a much faster device than Stibitz's RDAFB. It would also benefit from current wartime electronic technology, making it far more likely to succeed than MIT's prewar Rapid Arithmetical Machine. Since wartime exigencies gave rise to a government policy in which competitive research and development projects could be supported, it was possible, in the end, for the Army to fund both Stibitz's RDAFB and the Moore School's ENIAC.

Another possible reason for the hostility of the MIT members on NDRC toward the ENIAC was a more self-serving one. As a result of the ENIAC project, the Moore School found it necessary to terminate radar Project PL, undertaken in conjunction with MIT's Radiation Laboratory. Brainerd explained in later years: "We had to terminate Project PL despite the fact that the Radiation Laboratory wanted us to continue it. The most embarrassing thing was to tell the Rad. Lab. people we weren't going to keep going on their contract."[46]

Hazen's negativism may also have been related to the Moore School's recent success in building a more powerful differential analyzer than the one constructed by Hazen, Caldwell, and Bush at MIT. In a 1970 interview, Hazen noted that the Moore School failed to acknowledge adequately MIT's priority in this field and that the Moore School's work on analog devices was nothing more than an application of an existing technique:

Speaking of ENIAC . . . Aberdeen was interested in the beginning of the war and a little before that, in getting a duplicate of our machine. The University of Pennsylvania asked us, or I guess asked Aberdeen, if they could have a set of these drawings, so a set was made available to them, and they built their differential analyzer to these drawings. In their publicity they never once mentioned any indebtedness to MIT. . . . It [The Moore School analyzer] was a strict production from our drawings.[47]

Moreover, in 1943 the MIT people may well have seen the development work on the ENIAC to be in direct competition with their own classified work on the Rockefeller Analyzer.

In short, the government's central body of technical administrators, whose task it was to harness the scientific and technical resources of the nation for wartime use, was at best unenthusiastic and at worst hostile toward the computer development work undertaken at the Moore School. The reactions of men like Caldwell, Hazen, and Stibitz were, at least in part, tied to their own personal commitment to different technologies.

The Moore School's Response to NDRC

From the start, the ENIAC group was inhibited by the reluctance of NDRC to provide the Moore School with various reports on electronic counters. Letters from Jan Rajchman of RCA to Brainerd attest to this reluctance: "I regret to inform you that I have just received a note from Dr. G. R. Stibitz informing me that we cannot forward to you the documents in our possession which I thought might be of interest to you." In the same letter dated May 22, 1943, Rajchman continued, "My request had been transmitted to Dr. Weaver who referred it to Dr. H. L. Hazen and he suggested that you request the information through formal channels."[48] This was, after all, established procedure.

The success of the Moore School in finally obtaining the desired reports was primarily the result of two factors. First, the persistence of Colonel Gillon, a career officer with the Office of the Chief of Ordnance who served as liaison between the Moore School and NDRC, was important in legitimizing the project. The role of administrators in facilitating the flow of information and fostering the research effort is a factor often overlooked in technical development.[49] In the case of the ENIAC, it was of singular importance. Second, the NDRC administrators eventually subordinated their initial hostility to the ideal of wartime cooperation which they saw as their primary responsibility.

NDRC's unenthusiastic reaction served to foster a spirit of competition at the Moore School, specifically with MIT, which imbued the project with an added sense of purpose.[50] From the outset, the ENIAC participants and representatives from the Army as well reacted strongly to the committee's attitude. Gillon sent Goldstine a copy of a letter he had written to Hazen on October 7, 1943, with a note stating that he hoped this would "kill their impertinent interference once and for all."[51] Similar remarks characterized the Moore School's reaction to MIT throughout the ENIAC project. Gillon's correspondence with Goldstine indicates an intense desire to prove the committee wrong: "I am particularly anxious to learn about the status of the ENIAC. I surely hope it is progressing well in spite of the active hostility of

Protagonists of the ENIAC, *left to right*, Presper Eckert, John Grist Brainerd, Samuel Feltman of the Office of Chief of Ordnance, Herman Goldstine, John Mauchly, Dean Harold Pender, General Gladeon Barnes, and Colonel Paul Gillon, at the computer's dedication in February 1946. Courtesy Smithsonian Institution.

some of our friends."[52] Gillon's reaction is characteristic of that of many career officers during the war who felt that the new scientific agencies were ill-prepared to make recommendations on military matters. After returning from a visit to MIT in November 1944, Goldstine wrote of the computational facilities there: "It was, I think, a pretty sad spectacle of what the supermen at NDRC can do."[53]

In the end, both the elements of youth and the hostility of NDRC served to foster a greater commitment among the ENIAC staff than might otherwise have existed and thus actually enhanced the prospects for the project's success. That youth can be seen as a positive force has been suggested by Redmond and Smith in their study of Project Whirlwind: "The spirit of the laboratory was high, in part because it was the product of Professor Brown's inconspicuous leadership, but also in part because of such factors as the élan of the graduate student and research assistant determined to demonstrate his creative abilities and to find new worlds to conquer."[54]

It is possible to isolate clear and countervailing governmental influences on the ENIAC which were to persist in future Eckert-Mauchly computer work. On the one hand, the traditional military forces in the government were enthusiastic about the proposed device and were willing to provide funds for the project. On the other hand, the more technically proficient scientists and engineers who served as government advisors were outspoken in their skepticism. Thus what is beginning to emerge is a view of a more conservative scientific elite and a more venturesome and enterprising bureaucracy than is often depicted. Such tendencies were to manifest themselves in the EDVAC and UNIVAC projects as well.

2

ENIAC
Research
and
Development

The first year of development work on the ENIAC, from the summer of 1943 into the summer of 1944, proved to be the most significant. During this period, research on existing calculating equipment and electronic circuitry was undertaken and the technological ideas shaped; by June of 1944 the formal design of the computer was completed.[1]

The extraordinary speed with which this project proceeded is attributable, in large part, to the government's need. The war effort fostered a spirit of cooperation and a willingness on the part of the ENIAC engineers to subordinate their creative impulses and adapt existing technology, where feasible, rather than undertake independent invention. In later projects, when this wartime factor did not exist, the drive to invent resulted in significant delays in producing a final design.

Most of the early participants acknowledge that the ENIAC was to be an electronic analog of the desk calculator. Mauchly's original memorandum stated that the machine was to be "in every sense the electrical analogue of the mechanical adding, multiplying and dividing machines which are manufactured for ordinary arithmetic purposes."[2] In an historical analysis, Arthur Burks, a mathematician who served as a senior engineer on the ENIAC team, emphasized the parallels between the ENIAC and mechanical desk calculators: "The arithmetic design of ENIAC was influenced mainly by two kinds of calculators: mechanical desk calculators, electrically powered and hand-operated; electromechanical card-operated IBM machines."[3] Similarly, in *The Computer from Pascal to von Neumann*, Herman Goldstine emphasizes this aspect of the ENIAC's design.[4]

John Grist Brainerd's original proposal called for the design of the following units: cycling unit for controlling pulse sequences; initiating unit for starting and stopping the device; accumulator; multiplier; divider and square rooter; function table for storing numbers; constant transmitter for transmitting numbers to the computer; printer; and master programmer for con-

24

trolling operations to be performed.[5] From the start ideas from other technologies were incorporated in the design of each of these units. Engineers were assigned the task of evaluating existing devices and components, basing their evaluations on various NDRC reports.[6]

Elements of the ENIAC

During the first year, the project's team concentrated on the construction of two accumulators, the arithmetic units of the ENIAC, of which there were to be a total of twenty. In the beginning, research focused largely on an electronic counter, the major component of an accumulator and the fundamental counting unit of the ENIAC itself. Among the devices examined were the NCR thyratron counter, the RCA ring counter, and the Lewis ring counter.[7] At the same time, Eckert worked on a proposal for an entirely new decade ring counter in case existing technology proved to be inadequate. By December 1943 the staff had decided that Eckert's ring counter was the most feasible.[8]

Herman Goldstine describes the electronic ring counter by first explaining a flip-flop or trigger circuit:

This basic electronic memory device consists of a pair of vacuum tubes so interconnected that at each instant of time exactly one of the pair is conducting (i.e. current is flowing through the tube) and the other is non-conducting (no current is flowing). When one of the tubes is conducting we may say the flip-flop is in the "1" state and when the other is, the "0" state.

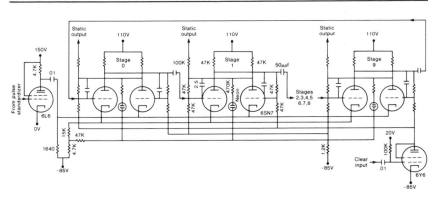

ENIAC decade ring counter. From Burks, "Electronic Computing Circuits of the ENIAC," *Proceedings of the IRE* 35: 746–767, © IRE (now IEEE), 1947. All rights reserved.

A counter in the ENIAC consisted of a linear array of flip-flops connected in such a fashion that at each instant (a) exactly one flip-flop of the array was in the "1" state, all the others being in the "0" state; (b) when a pulse was received by the counter this flip-flop was returned to the "0" state and its successor in the array was turned from the "0" to the "1" state; (c) there was a provision to reset the counter so that always a pre-assigned flip-flop, called the first stage, was set to the "1" state.

All the ENIAC counters were ring counters, which means simply that the first and last stages were so interconnected that whenever the counter was in its last stage and a pulse was received it cycled to its first stage, i.e. the successor of the last stage in the array was the first stage. This made a ring counter very like a counter wheel in principle of its action, but it was very much faster.[9]

In an earlier publication, Goldstine and his wife Adele described the completed ENIAC as follows:

The machine is a large U-shaped assemblage of 40 panels . . . which together contain approximately 18,000 vacuum tubes and 1,500 relays. These panels are grouped to form 30 units . . . each of which performs one or more of the functions requisite to an automatic computing machine.

The units concerned mainly with arithmetic operations are 20 accumulators (for addition and subtraction), a multiplier, and a combination divider and square rooter.

Numbers are introduced into the ENIAC by means of a unit called the constant transmitter which operates in conjunction with an IBM card reader. The reader scans standard punched cards (which hold up to 80 digits and 16 signs) and causes data from them to be stored in relays located in the constant transmitter. The constant transmitter makes these numbers available in the form of electrical signals as they are required. Similarly, results computed in the ENIAC may be punched on cards by the ENIAC's printer unit operating in conjunction with an IBM card punch. Tables can be automatically printed from the cards by means of an IBM tabulator.

The numerical memory requirements of the machine are met in several ways. Three function table units provide memory for tabular data. Each function table has associated with it a portable function matrix with switches on which can be set 12 digits and 2 signs for each of 104 values of an independent variable. While primarily designed for the storage of tabular functions, the function table memory can be utilized for any numbers known before a computation begins. Switches for 20 digits and 4 signs on the constant transmitter can also be used for such numbers. Numbers formed in the course of a computation and needed in subsequent parts of a computation can be stored in accumulators. Should the quantity of numbers formed during a computation and needed at a later time exceed the accumulator storage capacity, these numbers can be punched on cards and, later, can be reintroduced by means of the card reader and constant transmitter.

The ENIAC's programming memory (memory for instructions relevant to a particular computation) is chiefly local in nature, i.e. instructions are given to each unit. Sets of switches called program switches are located on the front faces of the various units. Before a computation begins these switches are set to specify which particular operations in a unit's repertoire are to be performed . . . A unit called the master programmer unit provides a certain amount of centralized programming memory . . . The remaining two units, the initiating and cycling units, govern the operation of the others. The initiating unit has controls for turning the power on and off, initiating a computation, clearing the machine, and incorporates certain testing features. The cycling unit supplies the fundamental signals upon which the various units operate, and synchronizes the machine.[10]

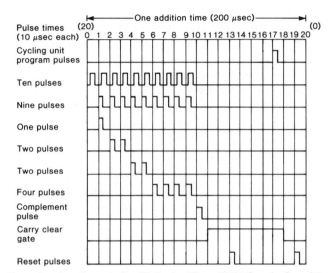

ENIAC cycling-unit pulses. From Arthur W. Burks, "From ENIAC to the Stored-Program Computer," *A History of Computing in the Twentieth Century*, edited by N. Metropolis, J. Howlett, Gian-Carlo Rota, P. 326.

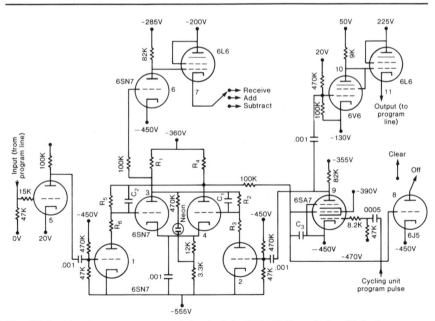

Simplified accumulator program control circuit of the ENIAC. From Arthur W. Burks, "Electronic Computing Circuits of the ENIAC," *Proceedings of the IRE* 35: 746–767.

Programming the ENIAC

Stored programming, in the later sense of the term, was not a feature of the ENIAC, largely as a result of the need to expedite construction. Although there has been a good deal of controversy over priority claims for the invention of the stored-program concept, there is evidence to suggest that the Moore School engineers did explore the possibility of incorporating automatic controls, but faced with the wartime need for ballistics information they chose to develop a less novel but more timely device.[11] That automatic controls were considered early in the project is implied in the December 31, 1943, progress report:

No attempt has been made to make provision for setting up a problem automatically. This is for the sake of simplicity and because it is anticipated that the ENIAC will be used primarily for problems of a type in which one setup will be used many times before another problem is placed on the machine.[12]

Similarly, in January 1944 Eckert wrote a disclosure that suggests his appreciation of the possible advantages of automatic programming:

A simplified method of constructing a numeric calculating machine is proposed in which some of the mechanical features of an ordinary mechanical calculating machine are retained and combined with certain electrical and magnetic features to produce a speedier, simpler machine . . . This disc could generate such pulse or electric signals as were required in time to control and initiate the operations required in the calculations. This is similar to the tone generating mechanism used in some electric organs and offers a permanent way of storing the basic signals required . . . If multiple shaft systems are used a great increase in the available facilities for allowing automatic programming of the facilities and processes involved may be made since longer time scales are provided. This greatly extends the usefulness and attractiveness of such a machine. This programming may be of the temporary type set up on alloy discs or of the permanent type on etched discs.[13]

The stored-program concept that became the basis for automatic control in all subsequent computers required the invention of a computer memory, a technological achievement that proved exceedingly difficult for postwar engineers. In short, the decision to build the ENIAC without a memory and without stored-program capability was one of those wartime decisions that sacrificed the creative impulses of the engineers for a more expedient device. Since the ENIAC was designed with a particular application in view and would, once initially set up, solve numerous ballistics problems, the overall setup time was not considered to be critical.

Input and Output

The question of input and output, like the question of automatic control, was eventually decided in favor of expediency. At the start, some thought was given to designing input and output units that would use electronic com-

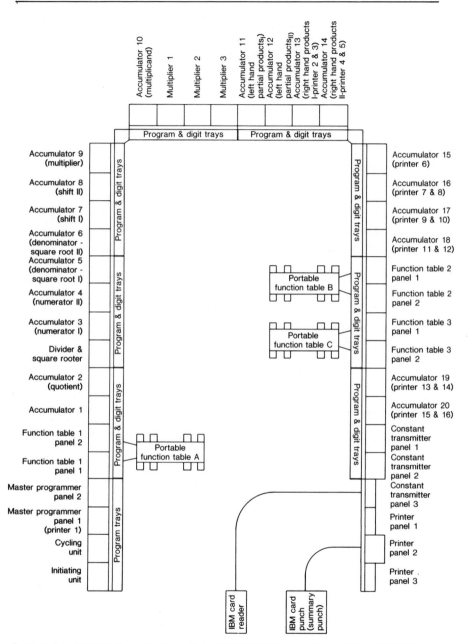

Layout of the ENIAC. From the Moore School's "ENIAC Progress Report," June 30, 1945. Courtesy University of Pennsylvania.

ponents. The first ENIAC progress report reflects the staff's indecision on this point: "At the time the project was started, the means of recording the results were left in abeyance. This is primarily a question to be resolved by the sponsors and the plans were being made at the date of this report to decide the form in which the results were desirous."[14] In the spring of 1944, the staff decided to use IBM electromechanical punch-card equipment for both input and output.[15] A card reader with a speed of 120 cards per minute served as the input unit and a card punch with a speed of 100 cards per minute was used as the output unit.[16] These peripheral units were considerably slower than the ENIAC's data processing elements and caused a decided reduction in the computer's overall efficiency. Here again the fact that these required minimal adaptation was considered by the group to be the most important factor.

The units necessary to ensure compatibility of the IBM devices with the electronic components of the ENIAC were the constant transmitter and the printer. The constant transmitter, as Goldstine pointed out, stored in relays punch-card data read by the IBM reader. This unit was constructed with the assistance of Bell Telephone Laboratories, an organization that had extensive experience with relays. The main feature of the unit was its ability to receive low-speed data and supply it to the computer at high speed. The printer similarly synchronized the flow of data from the accumulator to the low-speed output device. Both these units were designed by June 1944, but were not actually completed for another year.[17]

Vacuum Tube Reliability

Another concern during this first critical year was the issue of vacuum-tube reliability. The ENIAC was to have 18,000 vacuum tubes at a time when electronic devices of several hundred tubes were considered extraordinary. Because of the number of tubes to be used, many prominent engineers regarded the entire project as infeasible. They believed that the difficulties associated with tube reliability would be insurmountable. Indeed, Eckert himself recognized that a single defective tube could invalidate hours of computation.[18]

Once again the Moore School staff decided to adapt existing tubes rather than to produce their own. The RCA tubes used were operated at levels considerably below the standards established by the manufacturer and were systematically replaced according to specifications established by Eckert. His appreciation of the vacuum-tube problem and the measures he instituted to ensure a high degree of reliability contributed to the ultimate success of the project.[19]

Eckert's precision as an engineer was illustrated in his remarks in 1977:

Rear view of the ENIAC's racks, showing some of the computer's 18,000 vacuum tubes. Courtesy Smithsonian Institution.

Summary of Tube Failure in ENIAC

	Approx. number	Percent of 18,800	Number removed	Percent of 644 removed	General use
6SN7 Twin Triode	6,550	35.0	200	31.0	Trigger and pulse counting circuits; also normally-on amplifier
6L6 Beam Power	4,200	22.0	175	27.2	Pulse amplifier; transmission normally off, pulsed on
6SA7 Pentagrid Converter	2,600	14.1	50	7.8	Coincidence tube, normally off; turned on by pulsing both grids; called gate
6SJ7 Triple Grid Amplifier	1,500	8.0	20	3.1	Input pulse amplifier; normally off
6V6 Beam Power	1,300	7.0	25	3.9	Pulse-forming circuits; normally on, pulsed off
6L7 Pentagrid Mixer	1,200	6.5	35	5.4	Use similar to 6SA7
6AC7 Television Pentode	500	2.5	110	17.1	Normally on; input amplifier with critical cutoff
807 (Enlarged 6L6)	350	1.8	20	3.1	Power amplifier, high voltage swings; normally off
6J5 Detector Triode	300	1.6	2	0.3	Amplifier; normally on
6Y6 Beam Power	300	1.6	7	1.1	Amplifier; normally on
Total	18,800	100.0	644	100.0	

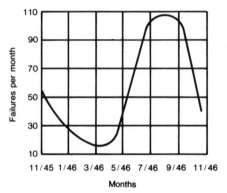

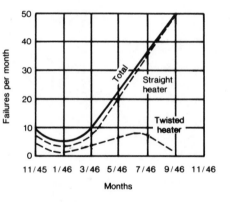

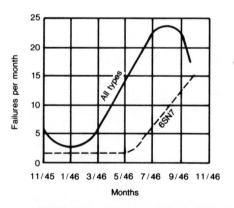

It's always been true that I was interested in the details of how you go about calculating the specific design pieces to make things work. In fact in the ENIAC I took every engineer's work and checked every calculation of every resistor in the machine to make sure that it was done correctly. Normally, I wouldn't want to have to do that. But this was the first for a machine with an order of 100 times as much stuff as anybody has ever built electronically. And if it was going to work, one had to be 100 times more careful.[20]

In summary, the design of the ENIAC incorporated features from a wide variety of sources owing to the government's overriding need and the war-related spirit of cooperation existing at the Moore School. To state that the ENIAC was heavily dependent on existing technology is not to deny its uniqueness or its contribution to electronic digital computer technology. The fact that the machine as designed employed vacuum tube circuits to compute trajectories at least ten times faster than contemporary computational equipment established its uniqueness as well as its significance.

The adaptation of existing technology in the ENIAC later became the source of some controversy, particularly in the 1971–1973 court case between the Honeywell and Sperry Rand companies. As previously noted, Honeywell sought to invalidate the ENIAC patent, which Eckert and Mauchly had assigned to Sperry Rand. Honeywell attempted to prove that the ENIAC was not a true invention, in the legal sense, because it was anticipated by prior technology. Many other important issues were raised in the trial, but this one has direct relevance to the concept of technological adaptation.

The Atanasoff-Berry Computer

The claim of prior invention was based on the pre-1943 invention of the RCA ring counter, the function table, a multiplying device developed by IBM, and the Bell Telephone Laboratories' relay computers. But the existence of a device called the Atanasoff-Berry Computer, or ABC, invented in the late 1930s by John Vincent Atanasoff with the assistance of Clifford Berry, became the focal point of this aspect of Honeywell's claim. The ABC stored binary numbers on capacitors, or condensers as they were then called, in rotating drums. Thus it employed the binary system and had a regenerative memory. Like the ENIAC, the ABC used vacuum-tube circuits to perform arithmetic, but its speed of operation—60 pulses per second—was quite low compared to that of the ENIAC. As Arthur Burks has pointed out, "The final ENIAC operated at 100,000 pulses/sec and thus became the first computer to exploit fully the vacuum-tube technology of the time."[21]

Moreover, Atanasoff had built only a small model of his device. Brian Randell reports that the "electronic part of the computer was operational but the binary card reader was still unreliable when in 1942 Atanasoff left Iowa State . . . so that the machine was abandoned, never having seen actual use."[22] Goldstine states that although Atanasoff apparently had a prototype of his machine working "early in 1940," the device "never saw the light of day as a serious tool for computation since it was somewhat premature in its engineering conception and limited in its logical one."[23]

The ABC was designed for one single purpose, the solution of systems of linear equations, and was never used to solve actual problems. The ENIAC, though designed with a particular application in view, was a general-purpose machine that solved actual and varied problems for many agencies during almost nine years of operation.

Finally, whereas Atanasoff had put his low-speed, special-purpose computer aside during the war, Mauchly had taken advantage of the urgency of wartime to spur development of the high-speed, general-purpose ENIAC.

Despite the critical differences between the two devices, the court in the end held that

> Eckert and Mauchly did not themselves first invent "the automatic electronic digital computer" . . . but instead derived that broad subject matter from Dr. John V. Atanasoff, and the ENIAC patent is thereby invalid . . . The utilization of ideas in a device prior to the time of the alleged invention, whether or not the device was subsequently abandoned, is evidence that when those ideas are incorporated in a later development along the same line, they do not amount to invention.[24]

The judge also stated that "the application for the ENIAC patent was filed by Mauchly and Eckert whom I find to be the inventors." He added, however, that in his view "the work on the ENIAC was a group or team effort and that inventive contributions were made by Sharpless, Burks, Shaw, and others."[25]

Mauchly's Role

Directly related to the issue of adaptation, indeed indistinguishable from it, is the role of John Mauchly in the development of the ENIAC. Since Mauchly had prior knowledge of Atanasoff's work, the findings of the court suggested that he was not a true inventor, but rather a transmitter of ideas ("pirate" was the intemperate term used by the Honeywell attorneys). Moreover, since Mauchly's role in the ENIAC project was as a consultant on existing computational techniques and technology rather than as an inventor or engineer per se, others have questioned the significance of his contribution.

In December 1940 Mauchly gave a lecture to the American Association for the Advancement of Science on the application of harmonic analyzers to weather forecasting. At that meeting, he met Atanasoff and discovered that he, like Mauchly himself, was influenced by Vannevar Bush's work on analog devices and had been working on an electronic digital computer which used vacuum tubes and solved linear equations. Mauchly immediately saw

The switches of Function Table A are being set by Pfc. Homer Spence and Cpl. Irwin Goldstein. Three manually set function tables served as read-only memory units. Courtesy Moore School of Electrical Engineering, University of Pennsylvania.

the potential significance of the ABC since he had previously considered the use of vacuum tubes in computational devices.[26] During the next few months, Mauchly wrote to Atanasoff seeking more information: "I am wondering how your plans with regard to computing devices are working out. Need I say again that I await with some suspense the time when you will be able to let me have more information."[27] Later in 1941 Mauchly visited Atanasoff and had the opportunity to see the machine first-hand. In that year, Mauchly brought his own ideas of a general-purpose computer, combined with his knowledge of Atanasoff's work on a small, special-purpose device, to the Moore School.

In 1976 Mauchly spoke at the Los Alamos conference on the history of computing and recalled:

My ideas about the feasibility of electronic calculation date back to the days in which I was teaching college physics at Ursinus, and reading the journals such as the *Review of Scientific Instruments*, in which circuits were published for "binary scalers" . . . At Ursinus College, some of the students remember my building small models of experimental digital circuits using some gas tubes as well as vacuum tubes. Some of these still exist and work. All of this predates a visit I made to Ames, Iowa, where I found it impossible to persuade Dr. Atanasoff that his projected machine did not realize the potential speeds of electronic calculation that I had in mind. He said he had not succeeded in making flip-flops reliable.[28]

In a similar vein, Mauchly wrote the present author in January 1979:

I strongly maintain that I took no ideas whatsoever from Atanasoff. I tried to give him some, such as using the "scaling circuits" with which I was already acquainted to make his proposed device much faster, but JVA said that he couldn't get flip-flops to work reliably.[29]

The claim that the initial concept for the ENIAC was not Mauchly's, but was derived by him from Atanasoff, appeared in Goldstine's *The Computer from Pascal to von Neumann*, even before the Honeywell trial was completed. Goldstine does not directly cite a source for the following account, but in a footnote implies that he drew on Atanasoff's testimony in the *Honeywell* v. *Sperry Rand* trial, then (1971–1972) in process:

During the period of Atanasoff's work on his linear equation solver, Mauchly was at Ursinus College . . . Somehow he became aware of Atanasoff's project and visited him for a week in 1941. During the visit the two men apparently went into Atanasoff's ideas in considerable detail. The discussion greatly influenced Mauchly and through him the entire history of electronic computers. Just about at the time Atanasoff confided his ideas to Mauchly, the latter left Ursinus to take a post at the Moore School of Electrical Engineering at the University of Pennsylvania. Atanasoff also apparently had ideas for a more general-purpose electronic digital computer and discussed his nascent ideas with Mauchly on this occasion.[30]

Goldstine's perspective supports the view that the *idea* is of critical import and the application or execution of that idea is of secondary significance.

Mauchly as Innovator

Mauchly's role in the ENIAC was that of an innovator, with "innovation" defined as the application or adaptation of an idea, even an existing one, in such a manner that the resulting technology is rendered practical and useful.

The following excerpt from the testimony in *Honeywell* v. *Sperry Rand* illustrates the point:

Question: Will you agree that the harmonic analyzer . . . was not entirely of your own design but was a modification of a design used by MIT some years prior to 1940?

Mauchly: This was not a flash from heaven, a full-blown device without any prior suggestion as to how anybody could do anything, but neither were the mechanical type calculators and harmonic analyzers as far as I know. I have always used prior art where it seemed proper, and useful and appropriate.[31]

Joseph Schumpeter uses the term "entrepreneur" to define this innovative component:

The defining characteristic is simply the doing of new things or the doing of things that are already being done in a new way . . . Many inventors have become entrepreneurs and the relative frequency of this case is no doubt an interesting subject to investigate, but there is no necessary connection between the two functions. The inventor produces ideas, the entrepreneur gets things done, which may but need not embody anything that is scientifically new . . . This definition that equates enterprise with innovation is a very abstract one.[32]

With Mauchly as the innovator and Eckert as the inventor, they formed a team utilizing a symbiotic approach to the technological process. Eckert's total attention was devoted to the development and construction of the ENIAC. Goldstine in his book states of Eckert:

From start to finish it was he who gave the project its integrity and ensured its success. This is of course not to say that the ENIAC development was a one-man show. It was most clearly not. But it was Eckert's omnipresence that drove everything forward at whatever cost to humans including himself.[33]

In this regard, Eckert's talents have been universally acclaimed, even by those who testified for Honeywell during the trial.[34] He devoted little time, however, to administrative matters or to the problems of his staff. Moreover, he was not specifically concerned with the application of his computer but rather with its overall design.

Mauchly, however, was the one who brought a more general, macrocosmic approach to the subject of electronic digital computers.[35] From his days at Ursinus, he sought to demonstrate that calculators and computers could be adapted for scientific work.[36] At the Moore School, he frequently presented his ideas on computers to governmental and scientific groups in an effort to promote the adaptability of these devices. In discussing the factors which led to the Army contract for the ENIAC in 1943, Mauchly stated that he was able to "adapt" one sales pitch for another in his proposals. During the two years preceding the contract, he recalled in 1975, "When I realized my only chance of building this machine was through the Army, I wasn't saying anything about weather prediction," his original concern; instead, he stated, "I developed a whole new sales talk about how the machine could solve problems a differential analyzer could, only more quickly and accurately."[37]

In general, Mauchly's efforts in the early development of the ENIAC were directed toward incorporating existing technology. His original memorandum, "The Use of High Speed Vacuum Tube Devices for Calculating," was an effort to indicate how an electronic digital computer could serve as an electronic analog to a desk calculator.[38] In addition, Mauchly was instrumental in adapting IBM equipment for input and output devices of the ENIAC. Moreover, he adapted existing computational methods for use in the ENIAC. In short, adaptation, a significant element in the design of the ENIAC, was also a major part of Mauchly's innovative contribution to the project.

Another facet of the innovator's orientation is the focus on the economic aspect of technological advance. Mauchly paid particular attention to economic factors, even before his ideas for an electronic computer were fully conceived. This focus can be discerned from his attitude toward Atanasoff's work, as noted during the trial:

Question: Did you inquire of him [Atanasoff] or did he tell you what kind of vacuum tube?

Answer: . . . Well, the particular kind of vacuum tube would be of very little interest to me. The cost might have.

Question: In any event, Dr. Mauchly, you knew . . . in December 1940 before you ever went to Ames, Iowa, that a computer which could use vacuum tube technology to solve 29 equations and 29 unknowns . . . would represent a considerable advance in the computing art?

Answer: Not necessarily.

Question: You didn't recognize that?

Answer: It depends on how efficient and how easy it is to use and how much it costs and so on. It's a matter of economics, too . . . Without some consideration of cost, utility, availability, whatever you want to call it, there is no advance really at all.

Question: And you are unable . . . to eliminate the question of cost in determining whether it would be an advance in the computing art in your own mind? Is that what you are telling us?

Answer: Yes.[39]

Mauchly's attention to application, adaptation, and economics is characteristic of innovators in general. It was this innovative component in the Eckert-Mauchly organization that enabled it to succeed where Atanasoff failed, that is, in producing fully operational computers. It was also this specific orientation of Mauchly's that led to serious conflicts at the Moore School. Since he did not provide tangible technological contributions to the ENIAC, his value to the project was questioned by some participants, particularly after the war.

The court's findings in *Honeywell* v. *Sperry Rand* form an assessment which suggests that an invention must be unique and that adaptation does not substantively contribute to the technological process. The development of the ENIAC during its first year and Mauchly's contribution to it are diminished by such a verdict. The history of technology is filled with cases in which innovative contributions were made by people who adapted technologies to suit specific needs or who incorporated existing technologies to produce a uniquely effective device.[40] The court's verdict fails to recognize this facet of the technological process. No matter what the circumstances of its development, however, the ENIAC remains a monumental contribution to the history of computing.

Who Invented the ENIAC?

In addition to raising questions of prior invention, the Honeywell–Sperry Rand trial sought to determine if Eckert and Mauchly were "sole inventors" of the ENIAC or if others had made contributions that would qualify them as inventors. Arthur Burks offered the following opinion in an affidavit:

Though Eckert and Mauchly were the chief inventors of the ENIAC, inventive contributions were also made by Shaw, Sharpless, and myself. Mauchly and Eckert gave us general plans, but these were mostly verbal and were not yet worked out, and hence constituted design problems. Sharpless, Shaw, and I solved these problems in nonobvious ways and formulated and solved other problems as the work progressed. We did logical and electronic designs to the point where draftsmen and technicians could draw up and construct the units under our direction. We tested the constructed units and decided on and supervised the modifications needed to make the equipment operate correctly . . . Eckert, Mauchly and I are clearly joint inventors of the ENIAC; Sharpless and Shaw are also joint inventors; but there are no other joint inventors of the ENIAC. The essential logical and electronic design of the ENIAC could not have been completed in the remarkably short time of 21 months without my joint inventive contributions and the joint inventive contributions of Sharpless and Shaw.[41]

On this issue, the court ruled:

Burks made significant contributions to the high-speed multiplier, the master programmer, the complement system for handling negative numbers and the divider square-rooter. Sharpless made similar contributions to the cycling unit and the multiplier. Shaw completed the function table, master programmer, and the constant transmitter . . . Arthur Burks made major contributions to the design of the accumulator and the multiplier of the ENIAC.[42]

This verdict gives appropriate credit to men who made very significant contributions to the design of specific features of the ENIAC. However, the overall design of the ENIAC as a system rests with Eckert and Mauchly.

The Moore School and the Private Sector

The previous discussion indicates that the government's direct involvement was the most important factor in initiating research and development of the first general-purpose electronic digital computer. In the private sector there is some evidence to suggest that major corporations had already investigated the feasibility of electronic calculators even before the ENIAC project began. J. W. Bryce, an IBM engineer, submitted an internal report in 1939 indicating confidence in the feasibility of such a device: "We have been carrying on an investigation in connection with the development of computing devices which do not employ the usual adding wheels, but instead use electronic effects and employ tubes similar to those used in radio work."[43]

In the early war years, National Cash Register and RCA were engaged in the development of electronic counters for computational equipment and for possible adaptation by NDRC for its fire-control devices.[44] In 1940, General Electric hired Irven Travis, a faculty member at the Moore School, to investigate the feasibility of electronic calculators.[45] These examples suggest that major corporations were aware of the possibility of applying electronics to computational equipment. That none of these firms actually committed itself to such development suggests the low priority given to the concept.

Nonetheless, those companies cooperating with the NDRC were worried that IBM might gain information and hence a competitive advantage. For example, George Harrison, a member of NDRC, wrote an employee of NCR: "Mr. Howard has just telephoned me in some trepidation, owing to the fact that you expressed worry to him regarding possible revelations of confidential developments made in your Laboratory to representatives of the IBM Company."[46]

The possible reasons for industry's lack of interest in developing computers are diverse. First, the war may well have inhibited major commercial research and development projects of this type. Second, the cost involved was relatively high. Third, with the absence of well-established industrial research laboratories at companies like IBM, such an undertaking may have been deemed too ambitious. Last, and most important, the necessary market demand had not been clearly established.

In any case, it would appear that in the early 1940s industrial organizations regarded research and development in electronic digital computer technology as economically unprofitable. The government's support served, in the end, to alter that economic view. Government funding not only fostered technology in this field but made technical information available to those companies which were later to construct their own computers.

In fact, the claim that wartime is a particularly fertile period for invention is based in part on the relatively free exchange of ideas and on the smooth

The ENIAC's cycling unit and accumulators. Courtesy Smithsonian Institution.

transfer of technology that usually takes place in periods of conflict and spurs industrial development. Some have claimed that restrictions placed on developments that were viewed as confidential made the transfer of technology during wartime particularly difficult. These constraints, however, probably applied only to smaller organizations lacking any connection with government-funded projects.

In the development of the ENIAC, the Moore School had a wartime interaction with several major corporations, among them RCA, Bell, and IBM. All three of these organizations even before 1943 had been informed by their own engineers of the feasibility of applying electronics to calculating equipment and they were themselves eventually to have a commercial interest in such technology.

The relationship that developed between the Moore School and these firms was at best cautiously cooperative. The Moore School participants were clearly aware of the dynamics of technological transfer and realized that as they were adapting technology in the development of the ENIAC, these organizations were learning something about developing electronic computers.

The Moore School and RCA

RCA was initially regarded as a major source of information on electronics largely as a result of its work on television and on wartime innovations. The very first reports sought by the ENIAC staff included one from RCA on its design of an electronic counter called the Computron. As previously mentioned, Eckert and Mauchly made several visits to the RCA laboratories to discuss megacycle counters and function tables. Also, the vacuum tubes used in the ENIAC were manufactured by RCA.[47]

RCA was clearly able to provide the Moore School with significant technical support. During the school's initial discussions with the Army, it had proposed that "one of the numerous units in the proposed new device be developed in the RCA Research Labs," leaving about "9/10ths of the work at the Moore School."[48] Despite RCA's willingness to cooperate with the Moore School, it was not interested in formally undertaking a part of the project. In May 1943, Brainerd reported to Colonel Gillon at Aberdeen:

The estimate of the cost of six months' developmental work on the electronic numerical integrator and computer has been delayed because of the previous inability of Dr. Zworykin of the RCA Research Laboratory to give a definite answer concerning RCA's proposed part of the work. Dr. Zworykin has now informed me that he will be glad to cooperate informally but RCA does not wish to undertake any definite part of the job.[49]

The reasons for RCA's decision to provide only informal assistance are difficult to determine, but oral records, in this case those amassed for legal rea-

Close-up of the ENIAC's accumulators. Courtesy Smithsonian Institution.

sons, shed some light on the matter. In a legal deposition taken in 1969, Jan Rajchman recalled his first contacts with the Moore School computer team as an RCA electronics engineer in 1943 and noted that "they impressed me as, excuse the word, but extraordinarily naive . . . In April of 1943, I had the impression that yes, they were enthusiastic and so forth and so on, but we were already much more sophisticated because we had already conceived of multipliers, adders, accumulators, shift registers, function generators, in fact, all the elements."[50]

Rajchman attributed RCA's decision not to participate in the ENIAC's development to Vladimir Zworykin, director of electronic research, and speculated that the refusal was related to the issue of technical feasibility: "The probability of a machine with so many tubes working was very small."[51] It is clear, however, that RCA's decision and attitude paralleled the sentiment of NDRC. Large, established organizations share the same sort of commitment to "normal science" and the same conservative attitude toward undertaking major, large-scale innovations, particularly in collaboration with a group of young, relatively inexperienced engineers.

It is reasonable to assume that RCA was also unwilling to commit itself to the ENIAC project for profit-related reasons, despite the war effort and the corporation's expressed desire to serve the country. Rajchman testified during the *Honeywell* v. *Sperry Rand* trial about wartime projects in general:

Question: Did RCA have an interest, and I am speaking not necessarily of you as a scientist, but RCA as a corporation, an interest in commercially exploiting the inventions of the time?

Rajchman: It is clear that RCA generally undertook projects during the war that might eventually have commercial need. I would say that particularly in the laboratory we use as a criterion for undertaking a project, possible use . . . We use the criterion of general application to the broad business of RCA which is extremely broad. It's only when the effort reaches a certain size that we really start to worry about its commercial implications. But I am sure that during the war some of these considerations were taken aside.[52]

Rajchman's testimony suggests that RCA's refusal to become directly involved with the Moore School on the ENIAC could well be attributed to that company's belief that the commercial value of such a device was negligible. Nevertheless, by providing informal technical assistance in the interest of "wartime cooperation," and without incurring any risk, RCA was able to keep abreast of developments in electronic computation.

The Moore School and Bell Telephone Laboratories

In general, Bell Telephone Laboratories also provided technical assistance in the early stages of the ENIAC's development. Relays similar to those used by Bell in switching circuits could be employed to achieve compatibility between the ENIAC's electronic circuitry and IBM punch-card equipment being used as input and output devices. Brainerd and Eckert visited the Bell Laboratories on December 9, 1943, and, at that time, Bell offered technical assistance on the relays.[53] In February 1944, however, Colonel Gillon expressed dissatisfaction with Bell's repeated delays:

I feel rather firmly convinced in my own mind that their reluctance stems directly from the fact that any delay which we are compelled to take as a result of development work necessary on input and output devices will be of considerable advantage to them in merchandising the Stibitz [relay computer] equipment. I am not at all certain that it would not be wise to completely sever any further negotiations with Bell.[54]

Gillon's convictions are corroborated to some extent by the fact that Bell sought to employ the technology developed at the Moore School for its own interest at an early date. On February 17, 1944, Vannevar Bush wrote Gillon stating Bell's interest in the decade ring counter for its own Signal Corps contract.[55]

Effect of World War II

World War II gave industrial organizations a chance to monitor some war-related research efforts, such as various computer projects, for possible future exploitation. Several organizations made specific contributions at the same time that they learned about innovations in the field, all without incurring normal economic risks. Hence, the attention of the industrial sector to potential commercial advantage during the war turned out to be a factor that helped speed the transfer of technology from the academic to the industrial setting in subsequent years.

The reluctance of industrial organizations to lend decisive support, uncomplicated by profit-oriented considerations, was not confined to the ENIAC project. Project Whirlwind originated during the war as a research and development project for a master flight trainer and experimental aircraft simulator. Its sponsor, the Navy's Special Devices Division, headed by Captain Luis de Florez, encountered similar problems:

De Florez initially had anticipated that the project would be undertaken jointly by Bell Telephone Laboratories and its manufacturing associate, the Western Electric Company, but ultimately the task was given to the Massachusetts Institute of Technology. All in all, some twenty-five commercial and industrial organizations were considered in the original canvass, but these either were eliminated or withdrew for various reasons. Apparently, both Bell and Western Electric were reluctant to undertake the program lest it interfere with Navy contracts of greater immediacy. Furthermore, by the fall of 1944, victory was visible over the horizon, and the two companies may have preferred not to commit their facilities to a long-term military responsibility rather remote from their prime peacetime mission of servicing the needs of their parent organization, the American Telephone and Telegraph Company.[56]

Accumulator and high-speed multiplier panels of the ENIAC. Courtesy Smithsonian Institution.

The Moore School and IBM

Finally, no discussion of industrial participation in early electronic digital computer technology would be meaningful without consideration of IBM. Here, again, the issue is complex. From the late 1930s on, IBM played an active role in computer technology even though it did not market any products. IBM funded the Watson Scientific Laboratory at Columbia University, where, under Wallace J. Eckert's direction, IBM punch-card equipment was adapted for scientific use. The corporation also supplied engineering assistance and funding to Howard Aiken's Automatic Sequence Controlled Calculator, the Mark I, an electromechanical relay computer developed at Harvard University. Hence, without incurring normal economic risks associated with developing and marketing a large-scale device, IBM was able to use these two university-related research projects to keep abreast of developments in computer technology.

During the war, Thomas J. Watson, president of IBM, expressed his intense desire for the corporation to make cooperation in the war effort its primary concern, and the activities of IBM during this period seem to bear this out.[57] In 1967 A. Halsey Dickinson, an engineer at IBM, recalled: "When World War II broke, Mr. Watson decreed that all engineers should devote themselves to the war effort and that development work on IBM machines should cease."[58] Correspondence between the Moore School and IBM during the first phase of ENIAC development indicated IBM's willingness to provide technical assistance,[59] but Eckert, in his testimony in *Honeywell* v. *Sperry Rand*, suggested a more self-serving reason for their interest:

Eckert: And in the final paragraph [of a contract for punch-card equipment], he [Watson] proposes that in consideration of no rental to be charged for those units that IBM receive a nonexclusive license under any patent issued for the specific calculating machine for which the IBM units were to serve as the input and output.

Question: Do you know whether that proposal was accepted or adopted?

Eckert: Dr. Goldstine told me that they did not wish to accept this.[60]

In summary, the first year of development work on the ENIAC was more than usually productive. The war assured the full support of the Army in funding the project and in providing assistance where necessary. The engineers at the Moore School were themselves highly motivated largely as a result of their desire to prove their abilities, particularly to their more eminent and skeptical colleagues. Moreover, they were eager to assist in the war effort. The war also constrained industrial organizations from taking a more competitive stance, a factor which also favored the development of the ENIAC. Thus, despite the existence of conservative forces within the government, industry, and the academic community that might have exerted an inhibiting influence, the ENIAC project in its first year realized remarkable progress. Later chapters will show how, after the war, more traditional institutional forces contributed to conflicts at the Moore School and slowed the project's completion.

3　ENIAC to EDVAC: From Confidence to Conflict

The ENIAC had been undertaken in 1943 to fill a specific military need. Mauchly, however, had originally conceived of a computer with far wider applicability. He even referred to the possible commercial value of such a machine in the memorandum he wrote in 1942 which eventually became the basis for the ENIAC proposal.[1] During the war the engineers and scientists working on the project had subordinated all other interests to wartime requirements, but by 1944, with the ENIAC's development well along and an eventual Allied victory almost assured, Mauchly and Eckert began to think about the commercial potential of computers. That fall, with the encouragement of the Army Ordnance Department, they set out to acquire the patent rights to the ENIAC. The Ordnance Department was anxious to have the patent issued because that would ensure the Army's license-free rights to the ENIAC.

The Patent Matter

The absence of a patent assignment on the ENIAC left the government in a precarious position, as Colonel Leslie E. Simon, director of the Ballistics Research Laboratory, pointed out to Colonel C. E. Herrstrom in the Patent Section of the Office of the Chief of Ordnance:

It is requested that this office take such steps as are deemed necessary to prevent the issuance of a patent to Samuel B. Williams and his assignee, Bell Telephone Laboratories, for an electronic calculating machine under patent application . . . Attention is also invited to the fact that the Electronic numerical integrator and computer, being developed for the Research and Development Service of this office under the contract cited in paragraph 1 above, was conceived prior to and independently of Mr. Williams. If the patent to Mr. Williams were granted, the Government and the University of Pennsylvania might be liable to the Bell Telephone Laboratories.[2]

On September 27, 1944, Eckert sent a letter to the Moore School engineers advising them that he and Mauchly intended to apply for a patent on

48

the ENIAC and asking them to state in writing any claims to which they thought they were entitled.[3] Only one of the participants, T. Kite Sharpless, responded:

Referring to your letter of 9-27-44 re patent claim the only device to which I feel I have claim is the mercury delay line and that claim by no means a complete one. My memory for details of who suggested what, when you and I were developing it, is none too clear but I have the feeling that I did make constructive suggestions. It seems to me that we should discuss this matter to clarify the issue.[4]

Despite Sharpless's initial response, he did not pursue any claim to the ENIAC.

Most of the engineers were either content to have Eckert and Mauchly designated as sole inventors of the ENIAC or they simply did not see the commercial potential of electronic computers. Herman Goldstine, looking back on the war years, remarked on his own lack of foresight regarding the possibility of marketing computers. "At that time," he stated, "I had no comprehension that the things that were involved would ever become anything of commercial interest or importance . . . I had never in my life been connected with patents and I therefore assumed that this whole business about inventorship assumed a very small importance."[5] Nonetheless, Eckert and Mauchly's patent claim caused considerable controversy at the Moore School.

While the university's administrators were content to have Eckert and Mauchly file as sole inventors, they wanted the rights to the patent assigned to the University of Pennsylvania. But since the university, like most academic institutions, lacked the kind of stringent patent agreement between employer and employee that is common in commercial organizations, it did not have a clear legal claim to the patent. The adminstration believed, however, that the following statement, printed in the college catalogue, sufficiently protected the university's rights:

Where researches in fields other than those affecting public health are carried out on grants or otherwise, patents may, with the approval of the President of the University, be applied for on inventions or discoveries, in which case the inventor shall assign his rights in the patent to the University upon payment to the patentee of his expense in securing the patent. The University will then exercise its own ownership of such patent with or without profit, with due regard for the interests of all persons concerned.[6]

George A. Smith, a patent attorney hired by Eckert and Mauchly, argued that the two men were not bound by this agreement, since they were operating under a government research and development contract and were in effect government employees. According to Smith, the university's position in the development of the ENIAC was

the rather passive one of merely supplying the facilities to the government for the development of the machine . . . Under this view the University cannot properly consider itself entitled, strictly speaking, to any benefit from the developments. The government is paying for the work and has chosen to ask merely for a non-exclusive license . . . Nominally, Messrs. Eckert and Mauchly were still employed by the University; actually, they were employed by the government.

Smith went on to suggest:

To leave settlement of [patent] questions solely to the University seems hardly fair. The University would be prosecutor, judge and jury in such a case. With due respect to the University, we believe it must be recognized that academicians frequently do not see eye to eye with businessmen . . . The University is a very large and diverse organization, many of the parts of which are perhaps very unsympathetic to the idea of private gain.[7]

In short, Eckert and Mauchly decided to file for the patent initially because the Army had requested it and because the University of Pennsylvania was not responding quickly enough to that request. Their decision not to assign the patent to the university suggests that they were motivated even in 1944 by commercial considerations. But they were also young men whom many established scientists and engineers regarded as naive and even pre-

---

ENIAC

Specifications from Martin Weik, BRL Report No. 971.

Manufacturer

Moore School of Electrical Engineering, University of Pennsylvania

Operating Agency

U.S. Army Ordnance Corps Ballistic Research Lab, APG

General System

Applications solution of ballistic equations, fire control problems, data reduction and related scientific problems.

Timing　　Synchronous
Operation　Sequential

Numerical System

Internal decimal in basic computer, binary coded decimal in magnetic storage
Decimal digits per word: 10 plus sign
Decimal digits per instruction: 2
Instructions per word: 5 or 6
Total no. of instructions decoded: 100
Total no. of instructions used: 97
Arithmetic system: Fixed-point
Instruction type: One-Address Code
Number range: $10^{-10} - 1$ to $1 - 10^{-10}$

Arithmetic Unit

Add time (excluding storage access): 200 microsec
Multiply time (excluding storage access): 2,800 microsec
Divide time (excluding storage access): 24,000 microsec
Construction: Vacuum-tubes
Number of rapid access word registers: 120
Basic pulse repetition rate: 60–125 kilocycles/sec variable.
Arithmetic Mode: Parallel
Information is transferred in parallel as a serial train of pulses.

Storage

Media	Words	Microsec Access
Vacuum tubes	20	200
Magnetic core	100	200
Function table	304	lines of 12 dec digits + sign on each constant set-switch
Plug board	96	lines of 12 dec digits + sign each (IBM)
Relays	8	buffer capable of storing contents of one card

Input

Media	Speed
IBM Cards	125 cards/min

Each card has 8 ten decimal digit words plus signs

tentious. Moreover, as men with no prior record of real accomplishment, they were sensitive to priority issues and claims. This sensitivity manifested itself in numerous ways then and in later years. It is likely that in addition to their desire to take advantage of the computer's commercial potential, they wanted to make certain that they received the credit they were due for this truly revolutionary device. Possessing the patent on the ENIAC would clearly accomplish this goal.

Harold Pender, dean of the Moore School, displayed some sympathy for Eckert and Mauchly's claims. Pender was a man with a unique background. He had received his Ph.D. in 1901 from Johns Hopkins University at a time when such degrees were exceedingly rare. Two years later he was invited by Henri Poincaré, one of the world's foremost mathematicians, to deliver a paper in Paris on the existence of a magnetic field around electrically charged bodies.[8] Later, Pender formed his own company, the International Resistance Company, which became a highly successful firm. Several Moore School associates believed that Pender's business experience made him sym-

---

Output

Media   Speed
IBM Cards   100 cards/min
200 millisec of card cycle are available for other computer operations. At 50 cards/min rate, 800 millisec are available for computer operations per card cycle.

Number of Circuit Elements

Tubes: 17,468
Tube types: 16
Crystal diodes: 7,200
Magnetic elements: 4,100

Physical Factors

Power consumption: Computer   174 kW
Space occupied: Computer   1800 sq. ft.
Air conditioning: Forced outside air.

Manufacturing Record

Number produced: 1
Number in current operation: 1

Cost

Additional equipment   Magnetic storage $29,706.50
Rental rates for additional equipment:
IBM card reader $82.50 per month
IBM card punch $77.00 per month
Approximate cost of basic system: $750,000

Personnel Requirements

Daily operation: 3 8-hr shifts. No. of Tech.: 6 7 days/week
A minimum requirement for operation and servicing on a 24-hour-day, 7-day-week basis. No engineers are assigned to operation of the machine, but they are used for design, development of improvements and consultation when total breakdowns occur.

Reliability and Operating Experience

Date unit passed acceptance test: 1946
Average error free running period: 5.6 hours
Operating ratio: 0.69. Good time: 113 hrs. (Figures for 1955) Attempted to run 164 hrs/wk
No. of different kinds of plug-in units: 44
No. of separate cabinets (excluding power and air cond.) 42
Operating ratio figures for 1954:
Operating ratio: 0.70. Good time: 116 hrs. Attempted to run: 166 hrs./wk.

Additional Features and Remarks

There are four modes of operation: Continuous, Pulse time, Add time, or Instruction time.
A manual pre-set stop box is available.
Count instructions and transfer instructions are used.

pathetic to Eckert and Mauchly's commercial objectives and to their patent problems.[9] In any case, in March 1945 Pender urged the university to acknowledge Eckert and Mauchly's patent claims and to drop its demand that the patent be assigned to the university. On March 15 the president of the University of Pennsylvania finally granted the two inventors permission to file for a patent without assigning the rights to the university.[10] Despite this resolution, the patent issue remained a controversial and divisive one as long as Eckert and Mauchly remained at the Moore School.

The reasons for the university's decision in favor of Eckert and Mauchly were twofold. First, its legal position was not only in doubt but was a potential source of embarrassment. With the university's right to the patent itself in question, its contractual obligation to grant a royalty-free license to the government could not be guaranteed—a matter of considerable concern, as mentioned previously, to the Army Ordnance Department. The Moore School feared that this problem would threaten future government contracts. Since Eckert and Mauchly were willing to grant the government the royalty-free license, their patent claim would enable the university to fulfill its contractual obligations and settle the matter before serious consequences could develop. As summed up in the findings of *Honeywell* v. *Sperry Rand*:

During March, 1945, Eckert and Mauchly pressed for recognition of their commercial interests by the University of Pennsylvania in return for assurances that they would help the University fulfill its obligations under the contract. Facing the fact that it would require the cooperation of Eckert and Mauchly to fulfill its contractual obligations to the U.S. government, the University yielded its commercial rights to any patent they might obtain based on the work on the contract.[11]

The second reason for the university's capitulation was that the controversy over the patent was interfering with progress on the ENIAC. With the patent matter resolved, the staff could devote full energy to the project.

Government-Funded R&D and Academic Ethics

The patent issue demonstrates that prewar patent agreements between academic institutions—with some notable exceptions such as at the Massachusetts Institute of Technology—and their employees were no longer adequate. Before the war, the formal patent arrangements usual in the business world were generally nonexistent at academic institutions. Industrial organizations required their employees as a matter of course to sign patent release forms relinquishing rights to any patentable invention or discovery. Universities, on the other hand, even those with engineering colleges, usually regarded releases as unnecesary. Engineers and scientists engaged in academic research were thought to be motivated by a professional ethic that focused on the advancement of knowledge and subordinated profit-oriented considerations. Furthermore, before the war major commercial breakthroughs at universities were far less likely, since most academic research projects were relatively small and not expected to result in economic advantage.[12]

During World War II the United States government began a program of support for numerous university research and development projects. While the objective of this work was to assist the war effort, both the government and the universities recognized that it would also enhance the United States' technological position and that postwar government support would ensure continued advances in high-technology fields.[13] The universities were, in general, eager to retain some measure of financial support through government-funded projects even after the war. They believed that their claim for such support would be bolstered by the fact that their research and development work would not be governed by the profit motive and hence was more tenable than that of industry. For the Moore School, Eckert and Mauchly's interests threatened that claim. This factor turned out to be the singlemost important reason for the ultimate split between the two inventors and the Moore School.

There were those at the Moore School, most notably John Brainerd, who considered Eckert and Mauchly's patent interests to be a flagrant violation of academic ethics. Many years later Brainerd testified about the matter in *Honeywell* v. *Sperry Rand:*

> Eckert asked that each man—and I should interpolate that there were separate letters to each man—waive his rights to any claim to invention with respect to the ENIAC. I knew nothing about this and when I learned about it, I called Eckert in and demanded to see the letter. He produced a copy and I then told him that the letter under any circumstances would have been interpreted as an action more or less of loyalty to the Moore School and that it would have been natural in a cooperative spirit to have waived this in a sense of formality . . . I did not believe that the inventions . . . were the work of any one or two people. It was a great cooperative effort . . . This very substantial disagreement led to a cleavage in our group . . . Sometime later, possibly March [1945] I sent a firm letter stating that I would have nothing whatever to do with any patent question and that he [Pender] would handle them all.[14]

In later years, Eckert said that he and Mauchly filed for the patent, not because of avaricious motives but because the university failed to do so:

> [Brainerd] was asked to do it [apply for the patent]. He failed to act. A date was arrived at which the patent lawyers said, "Look, we've got to know who to put on the patent." It is a factual matter of patent law that the patent must be taken out in the name of the inventors or inventor. Any deviation of this, either by adding people that weren't involved or substituting people who were involved invalidates the patent . . . It was a legal necessity to have these letters.[15]

This patent question, then, led to a conflict with Eckert and Mauchly on one side and others at the Moore School, including Brainerd, on the other.[16] As a result of this conflict Brainerd subsequently resigned as project supervisor of the EDVAC, although he retained his supervisory position on the ENIAC project.

In January 1945 Pender appointed S. Reid Warren, Jr., as supervisor of the EDVAC. Warren was not experienced in the field of electronic digital computers, but he was well respected and well liked. Pender hoped that Warren could eliminate, or at least minimize, the hostility and rancor that was threatening both the EDVAC and ENIAC projects.[17]

The relationship of Brainerd with Eckert and Mauchly was further strained by two additional incidents. On February 21, 1945, Warren Weaver, Chief of the Applied Mathematics Panel of the Office of Scientific Research and Development (OSRD), asked Brainerd, as project supervisor of the ENIAC, to provide a formal report on electronic digital computers.[18] Since OSRD was the government's chief research and development agency, such a request was of considerable importance. Brainerd did not immediately set to work on this report, however, since he first had to request and then await appropriate security clearance from the Army Ordnance Department.[19] As a result, preparation of the report was tabled for nine months until September 1945, when Brainerd finally received the authorization; the report was due November 30.

Eckert and Mauchly remained unaware of Weaver's request during the long delay caused by the need for clearance. Later, when Brainerd had almost completed the report, the two men were very upset that they had not been consulted. They wrote Reid Warren expressing their annoyance and suggested that they should be listed as coauthors of the report. They were primarily concerned about priority, since readers might assume that the author of such a report was the main inventor of the ENIAC:

Only a short time ago we learned indirectly that eight or nine months previously, the Applied Mathematics Panel had asked Grist [Brainerd] to write a report on the ENIAC. Up to that time and even afterwards, Grist had never mentioned this fact to us . . . Let us report that we fully believe that Grist would see to it that credit would in some way be given to those deserving it. It is nevertheless a fact that a great deal is implied by authorship. The reader of any report is more likely to remember the name of the author than any name mentioned in the text.[20]

Because the ENIAC was still classified, Eckert and Mauchly, even if they desired, could not establish their priority by publishing a report of their own on the machine. Thus, the Applied Mathematics Panel report, which would undoubtedly be widely distributed, represented a way to assert their claim as inventors. As a result of Warren's intervention, the report listed Brainerd, Eckert, Goldstine, and Mauchly as coauthors.[21]

It is interesting to note, however, that even after the security classification was lifted, Eckert and Mauchly failed to publish any report on the ENIAC. The two mathematicians on the project, Goldstine and Burks, did produce such reports—Goldstine in 1946 and Burks in 1947.[22]

In the 1971–1973 *Honeywell* v. *Sperry Rand* trial, Eckert was asked about the report for the Applied Mathematics Panel:

Question: Did Dr. Brainerd resist having your name and that of Dr. John Mauchly
             connected with the paper to be submitted to the Applied Mathematics
             Panel?
Eckert: Yes, he most certainly did.[23]

The incident points not only to the growing schism at the Moore School
but to Eckert's and Mauchly's heightened sensitivity to those at the school,
who, they believed, wished to deny them their rights as inventors.

The second major conflict resulting from the patent issue arose between
Brainerd and Mauchly and related to a conference on calculating machines
held at the Massachusetts Institute of Technology in Cambridge on October
29–31, 1945.[24] The conference was an important one within the computing
field. In fact, conferences of this type, which were held with increasing frequency after 1945, became the most effective method for disseminating information on inventions and their inventors. Since much of the work undertaken in computing was government-sponsored and still classified for
security purposes, the publication of important new results was, generally,
prohibited. In addition, the method of establishing priority and circulating
results through publication was clearly inadequate, since developments occurred so rapidly that they were frequently obsolete before the report describing them could be published.

For these reasons, the Moore School staff was eager to attend the MIT
meeting and present a detailed description of the ENIAC.[25] Of the major
participants, only John Mauchly failed to receive an invitation to the conference. He felt that Brainerd's antagonism was responsible for this omission.
Years later, Eckert stated that "John was a little disturbed that Dr. Brainerd
hadn't arranged for him to go and there was a little discussion about this
with Reid Warren and possibly others before the matter was straightened
out."[26] Because of Mauchly's concern, Warren wrote the following memorandum to Brainerd on October 9, 1945:

John Mauchly is highly incensed in his mild and polite way, that he has not been
asked to go to the MIT conference. My own feeling is that he and Eckert are on equal
footing. The Dean is noncommittal; he thinks you have strong feelings against John's
going. I think Caldwell can be persuaded to let four of us into the meeting.[27]

In the end Mauchly was asked to attend and even to participate in the preparation of the report that Brainerd and Eckert presented at MIT.[28]

In short, the problems of Eckert and Mauchly at the Moore School were
based, at least in part, on their commercial interest, which many in the academic sector regarded as inappropriate. Later, this factor became the basis
of the two men's difficulties with John von Neumann.

But there was an even more fundamental cause for conflict regarding
Mauchly's role. Several participants, particularly Brainerd, expressed a
growing impatience with Mauchly's claims because they were not convinced
of the significance of his contributions to the ENIAC project. This lack of

conviction became a basis for *Honeywell* v. *Sperry Rand* seventeen years later. Unlike Eckert, who was a consummate engineer, Mauchly made no actual engineering contribution to the project. To many at the Moore School this meant that his claim to priority was inappropriate.

Mauchly, however, was a key figure in initiating the ENIAC project. It was clearly his vision and sense of purpose that brought the project to fruition. "When I was at Ursinus College," he testified in *Honeywell* v. *Sperry Rand,* "I began thinking about electronic means of calculation. I wanted the rapidity and flexibility of electrical circuits to do more complex calculations with less error and greater speed than can be obtained by use of ordinary commercial mechanical computing machines."[29] In his memorandum on "The Use of High Speed Vacuum Tube Devices for Calculating," written in 1942, he pointed out:

There are many sorts of mathematical problems which require calculation by formulas which can readily be put in the form of iterative equations. Purely mechanical calculating devices can be devised to expedite the work. However, a great gain in the speed of the calculation can be obtained if the devices which are used employ electronic means for the performance of the calculation, because the speed of such devices can be made very much higher than that of any mechanical device.[30]

Mauchly, more than anyone else, was able to adapt techniques used in desk calculators and punch-card equipment for use in the ENIAC. He was also familiar with round-off problems and made contributions in this area as well. Later on his main responsibility was to prepare technical reports. Perhaps most importantly, throughout the project he served as a catalyst, constantly probing the ways in which the ENIAC could be refined; in this, he was a perfect partner for Eckert.

In short, while many disapproved of Eckert's commercial interests and of his rather acerbic method of communicating, which stood in sharp contrast to Mauchly's amicability, they were willing to acknowledge Eckert's engineering attainments and his critical importance to the project. Mauchly, on the other hand, was simply not regarded in the same way. As is often the case, people who bring together ideas and act as catalysts are not likely to be recognized for their contributions unless they can render them tangible. Goldstine summarizes his view of Mauchly and Eckert as follows:

At the beginning, at least, Mauchly was to continue to play a key role in the ENIAC project. He alone of the staff of the Moore School knew a lot about the design of the standard electromechanical IBM machines of the period and was able to suggest to the engineers how to handle various design problems by analogy to methods used by IBM. Then as time went on his involvement decreased until it became mainly one of writing up patent applications. Mauchly was at his absolute best during the early days because his was a quick and restless mind best suited to coping with problems of the moment. He was fundamentally a great sprinter whereas Eckert not only excelled in sprinting but was also a superb marathon runner.

. . . Eckert's contribution, taken over the duration of the project, exceeded all others. As chief engineer he was the mainspring of the entire mechanism. Mauchly's great contributions were the initial ideas together with his large knowledge of how in principle to implement many aspects of them.[31]

In his court testimony, Brainerd was even less enthusiastic about Mauchly's contribution:

Brainerd: I think there is no doubt I have the highest respect for Pres Eckert. I think he's a very brilliant fellow.
Question: And I take it that you also have a high respect for Dr. John Mauchly.
Brainerd: Well, speaking frankly, I felt that Eckert was an extremely good man and that John was not . . . he was much more of a sounding board.[32]

Mauchly's methods of operating added to the growing hostility directed toward him by members of the Moore School staff, particularly Brainerd. Mauchly was a quick thinker with ingenious and imaginative ideas, but he was not the type of individual to follow them through. This he left to Eckert and others, who developed some of his ideas and made them practical and workable. Moreover, he was habitually late in the preparation of reports. He was a popular teacher and a creative thinker but neither an engineer nor an administrator. In a real sense, he was the antithesis of a man like Brainerd who served best in an administrative role.[33]

In short, Mauchly's actual contributions to the ENIAC and EDVAC projects were a main source of controversy beginning in 1945. No one seemed to understand the rather special relationship between him and Eckert. Mauchly was more than a mere "sounding board" for Eckert; Eckert depended and relied upon him in an inexplicable way. Mauchly served as a catalyst for Eckert and provided a direction for the latter's genius. The strong points of each of the two men meshed in a way that made them, for about a decade, a unique and effective team.

Mauchly himself, in a diary entry from October 1945 entered as evidence in *Honeywell* v. *Sperry Rand,* contributed this explanation:

Eckert in recent conversations seems to indicate that he is a bit anxious about going into work on a new contract without me. He thinks one difficulty may be that his contributions are tangible, that mine are more intangible so that others (such as Brainerd and Pender) are not fully aware of what I contributed.[34]

Yet because Mauchly's strengths were intangible, many engineers tended to denigrate his contributions. In 1977 Eckert singled out perhaps his colleague's most valuable trait: "Mauchly inspired people."[35]

The conflicts that began to take shape at the Moore School in 1945 were to lead, within a year, to the resignation of Eckert and Mauchly and to a transition period in the history of electronic digital computers. Before these turning points were reached, however, three matters of first-order priority required the full attention of the Moore School staff: completing the ENIAC, beginning the EDVAC project, and final testing of the ENIAC. Completion of the ENIAC and design of the EDVAC became a dual effort for about a year. Before we look at the progress of this joint venture, we should consider how the EDVAC came into being.

The EDVAC Project

A significant omission in the ENIAC design was some form of internal program control. Instead, to save construction time, instructions for the ENIAC were to be set by a series of external switches. As time went on, the lack of internal program control was viewed as a serious shortcoming. In addition, the ENIAC's storage capacity was severely limited, and this would need to be adjusted in a future machine as well.

In August 1944 Goldstine suggested to Colonel Leslie Simon, Director of the Ballistics Research Laboratory, that "a new R & D contract be entered into with the Moore School to permit that institution to continue research and development with the objective of building ultimately a new ENIAC of improved design."[36] The new device was to be a stored-program computer to be called the EDVAC, an acronym for Electronic Discrete Variable Automatic Computer. In September, Brainerd wrote to Colonel Paul Gillon, assistant director of the Ballistics Research Laboratory, outlining the deficiencies in the ENIAC design which necessitated research on a new

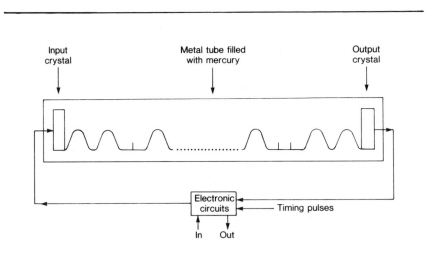

Mercury-delay-line memory. From Burks, "From ENIAC to the Stored-Program Computer," *A History of Computing in the Twentieth Century*, edited by Metropolis et al., p. 337.

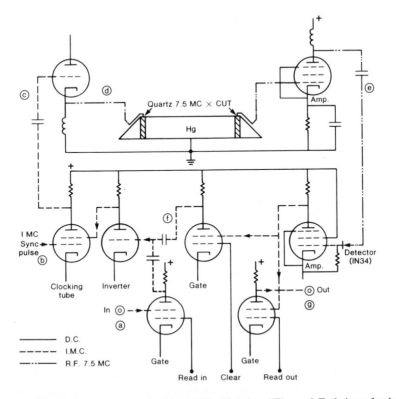

Mercury delay line as a memory unit. From T. Kite Sharpless, "Theory & Techniques for the Design of Electronic Digital Computers: Lectures Delivered at the Moore School of Electrical Engineering," 1946. Courtesy University of Pennsylvania Archives.

computer and emphasizing that John von Neumann had recently become involved in and enthusiastically supported this new project.[37]

The following month the Army Ordnance Department granted a supplement to the ENIAC contract, awarding $105,600 for research and development work at the University of Pennsylvania on the EDVAC for the ten-month period from January 1 through September 30, 1945.[38] Although some work on the EDVAC began during 1945, progress was very slow, since priority was placed on completing the ENIAC. Research on mercury delay lines for use as a computer memory device became a primary focus for Eckert and his staff. The mathematical-logical structure of the EDVAC was undertaken by von Neumann, Goldstine, and later Burks.[39]

Eckert had experimented with delay lines when he was working on a Moore School subcontract for MIT's Radiation Laboratory in 1942.[40] This device, invented by William Shockley at Bell Laboratories, was capable of transmitting a delayed electrical signal through a fluid. Electrical signals were transformed into acoustic signals and then transmitted through a mixture of water and ethyleneglycol. This process would delay a signal and, depending upon the fluid used, could regulate the length of delay as well.

Shockley's acoustic delay line was unsuitable for computers because it was incapable of reliably storing high frequency signals, but Eckert made some innovative changes to render the concept applicable. The use of mercury as the fluid and of piezoelectric crystals at either end of the tank would enable the unit to store high frequency signals. When the two ends of the tank were connected electrically, the device could store binary data indefinitely. The

Mercury-delay-line memory tank. Courtesy Sperry-Univac Archives.

binary digit "1" was represented by a pulse 0.5 microseconds wide and the binary digit "0" by no pulse. A tank 1.5 meters long could store approximately 1,000 binary digits. For each 1,000 binary digits stored in the EDVAC, 10 vacuum tubes, in contrast to the 1,000 needed in the ENIAC, were necessary to regulate the device. Hence, the number of such tubes was reduced by approximately 99 per cent, resulting in a considerably more efficient and effective device.[41] The ENIAC had a 20-word storage capacity; the EDVAC was designed to have a 2,000-word capacity.

As it happened, the subsequent development of the mercury delay line was not without its problems. Von Neumann, as well as Jan Rajchman at RCA, was convinced that one could use an iconoscope tube for a memory device. The EDVAC, as well as Eckert and Mauchly's later computers, incorporated the mercury delay line unit; von Neumann and his chief engineer, Julian Bigelow, incorporated the tube in the machine later developed at the Institute for Advanced Study. It took several years to perfect both designs.

ENIAC Delays

Despite the priority given to completion of the ENIAC during this period, numerous delays were encountered. In addition to completing construction of the individual units, the staff had to procure power supplies, input-output units, and a ventilating system. "Two accumulators are completed . . . ENIAC may be complete by Oct. 1," Herman Goldstine optimistically reported to Colonel Gillon on May 1, 1944. But in August, Goldstine had revised his prediction: "ENIAC should be ready by first of year." In December, as the new deadline approached, Goldstine again wrote Gillon: "At present we are in the throes of completing production of the ENIAC and preparing the space at Aberdeen for its installation. It seems now that within the next two months the machine should be completed."[42]

That prediction also required revision. In April 1945 Dean Pender of the Moore School wrote William DuBarry, the executive vice president of the university, that the ENIAC would probably be completed "sometime in May" and that by "June 15, 1945 we should have the machine thoroughly tested and ready for regular operation here in the Moore School." Pender followed this statement with another to DuBarry on May 12: "Transmitted herewith are three copies of a proposed contract between the Univ. Pa. and Eggley Engineers to provide consulting services in connection with ventilating equipment which will be required for attachment to the ENIAC when this machine is moved to Aberdeen."[43] Originally, the ENIAC was scheduled to be moved from the Moore School to the Ballistics Research Laboratory at Aberdeen in the fall of 1945, but the transfer was delayed a year primarily because the laboratory did not have a building to house the huge machine. The ENIAC was disassembled for the move on November 9, 1946, and was not in operation again until July 29, 1947.

The dual effort to complete the ENIAC and develop the EDVAC thus served to inhibit progress on both. Eckert was the chief engineer for both projects, and many of the engineers held dual responsibilities. Moreover, the growing tensions at the Moore School did not encourage the same spirit of cooperation that had existed the year before.

The ENIAC Test Run

Nonetheless, by the fall of 1945 the ENIAC was ready for testing. Interestingly enough, the initial test run of the computer in November 1945 was unrelated to ballistics. The urgent need for firing tables had dissipated when the war ended in late summer. War-related activities were, however, still being conducted at government laboratories.

At the Los Alamos Scientific Laboratory in New Mexico, research was being conducted on a new thermonuclear weapon called the Super, later known as the hydrogen bomb. John von Neumann was a consultant for the Los Alamos project and knew of its computational needs. Largely as a result of his suggestion, the initial test of the ENIAC was a large and complex problem designed to determine the feasibility of the Super.[44]

In the spring of 1945, when Nicholas Metropolis and Stanley Frankel, two physicists at Los Alamos, were developing a mathematical model that could be used in determining the possibility of a thermonuclear explosion, von Neumann informed them and Edward Teller, director of their division, of the existence of the ENIAC project and its ability to solve some of the problems necessary for establishing that model. Teller's testimony in *Honeywell v. Sperry Rand* indicates how and why Los Alamos became interested in the ENIAC:

It was he [von Neumann] who persuaded us in Los Alamos to use computing machines. First the IBM equipment, which at the time was mechanical and magnetic, rather than electronic . . . was, indeed, exceedingly clumsy . . . Johnny also made us aware . . . that this type of activity had a tremendous future. Particularly it had such a future because of the availability and increasing availability of electronic equipment which could and would speed up computing so as to surpass in the rapidity of execution what the human brain can do.[45]

After von Neumann suggested to Goldstine that the Los Alamos problem would be particularly suitable for the ENIAC's initial test, Goldstine actively sought support for this application. Von Neumann's efforts proved successful despite the objections of Dr. Louis Serle Dederick of the Ballistics Research Laboratory who thought that, even though the war was over, the first problem for the ENIAC should relate to ballistics.[46] In the summer of

1945 Metropolis came to Philadelphia to determine the capabilities of the ENIAC. For the next several months, he and Frankel worked on reducing the partial differential equations in their mathematical model to equations with finite differences that could be fed into a digital computer.[47] Because of the size of the problem and the complexity of the equations, one million IBM cards were needed as input to the computer. These cards indicated initial boundary conditions, each card containing a single mass point. The computations to be performed required the punching of intermediate output cards which were then resubmitted as input. The storage and input-output limitations of the ENIAC, made the process, at best, a cumbersome one.[48]

The Los Alamos problem was run on the ENIAC at the Moore School in November 1945 under the supervision of Frankel and Metropolis. Because the problem itself was classified though the equations were not, the Moore School staff could only supply peripheral support. Adele Goldstine, Herman Goldstine's wife, and several other women provided the needed programming assistance.*

The solutions to the calculations were obtained in December 1945. The Los Alamos group was satisfied with the results. In February, Frankel and Metropolis wrote Goldstine that "the Los Alamos Laboratory has good reason to be grateful to Aberdeen in connection with the problem on which we are now working."[49] The successful test run demonstrated the ENIAC's power and reliability. In March, the director of the Los Alamos laboratory wrote the Army officers in charge of the ENIAC project a note of congratulations:

The complexity of these problems is so great that it would have been impossible to arrive at any solution without the aid of the ENIAC . . . It is clear that physics as well as other sciences will profit greatly from the development of such machines . . .

I should like also to express my thanks for the direct cooperation and sustained interest of Captain Goldstine and of Eckert and Mauchly as well as the rest of the engineers and operators.[50]

The ENIAC had still wider implications for the scientists at Los Alamos. Frankel returned to Philadelphia in July 1946 to test a "Liquid Drop Fission Model," which was a more sophisticated mathematical model for the Super.[51] Frankel and Metropolis were later involved in developing a computer in the von Neumann tradition, called MANIAC, for use at Los Alamos. In short, just as the government's need dominated the design phase of the ENIAC, so, too, did it dominate the final testing phase.

---

*Many of the wives of the major participants of the ENIAC project became programmers—among them von Neumann's and Goldstine's wives. Mauchly's second wife had been a programmer even before they were married. Women dominated the programming field for several years. In addition, Eckert's first wife was a draftsman for the project.

TRANSMITTING CIRCUIT — CARRY-OVER CIRCUIT — PULSE STANDARDIZER — DECADE RING COUNTER

The court ruled in *Honeywell* v. *Sperry Rand* that the Los Alamos application was in fact an actual run and not, as Sperry had contended, a test of the ENIAC. Since this meant that the critical period of one year between first run and filing for the patent had been exceeded, the ENIAC patent was invalidated on this ground as well.

Dedication of the ENIAC

On February 16, 1946, the ENIAC was formally unveiled at a dedication ceremony at the Moore School. This ceremony demonstrated to the scientific and technological community the preeminence of the Moore School in the computational field, the foresight of the government in funding the project, the potential applications of such devices, and the need for scientists to develop improved mathematical methods which would enable electronic digital computers to have even wider applicability.[52] All of these factors were also to have a significant effect on the subsequent development of computers.

A comparison of components from, *top to bottom*, the BRLESC (Ballistics Research Laboratory, 1961), the ORDVAC (University of Illinois, 1952), the EDVAC, and the ENIAC. Courtesy Smithsonian Institution.

4   John von Neumann and the Moore School Computers

The influence of John von Neumann on the course of electronic digital computing has been substantial. Von Neumann's early computing work, during his interaction with the Moore School in the 1944–1946 period, had two different emphases. One was fundamentally intellectual, relating to his scientific and technical contributions. The other was fundamentally sociological, relating to his effort to legitimize the electronic digital computer as a scientific and mathematical instrument that could best be developed at academic institutions under the supervision of mathematicians rather than engineers. It was von Neumann's academic ideology that came into direct conflict with Eckert and Mauchly's growing commercial interests. This conflict, based on divergent institutional perspectives, eventually resulted in irreconcilable differences between the three men and contributed in part to the subsequent bifurcation of computer technology into an academically based sector and a commercially based one.

Background

John von Neumann was born in 1903 in Budapest, Hungary. He attended the University of Budapest, specializing first in chemical engineering and then in mathematics. He received a Ph.D. in mathematics from Budapest at the age of twenty-two, and in 1927, having already published several papers on algebra, set theory, and quantum mechanics, became a *Privatdozent* at the University of Berlin. In 1930 Princeton University invited him to be a visiting lecturer, an appointment he held for three years. In 1933, he received a permanent position at the newly created Institute for Advanced Study.[1]

By 1940 von Neumann's reputation as one of the world's most distinguished mathematicians was clearly established. A highly proficient and prolific scholar, he had already published important papers in such fields as ergodic theory, operator theory, and formal logic.[2] Moreover, like David Hilbert and Richard Courant before him, von Neumann was instrumental in promoting the discipline of mathematical physics as an appropriate subject for pure mathematicians.[3] He was well known for work on the logical and mathematical foundations of quantum theory and on problems in statistical mechanics. As Stanislaw Ulam, a close friend and a colleague of von Neumann at Los Alamos, stated: "He was not entirely what one might call a mathematician's mathematician. Purists objected to his interests outside of mathematics when very early he leaned toward applications of mathematics or when he wrote as a young man about problems in quantum theory."[4]

With the onset of World War II, von Neumann's knowledge of mathematical physics proved of great value to his adopted country. "Whether the war made him into an applied mathematician or his interest in applied mathematics made him invaluable to the war effort," P. R. Halmos, a fellow mathematician, has written, "in either case he was much in demand as a consultant and advisor to the armed forces and to the civilian agencies concerned with the problems of war."[5] His contributions to supersonic wind-tunnel development and solutions to nonlinear systems of equations and implosion were instrumental in advancing the Allied cause. During and after the war, his main professional interest shifted from pure to applied mathematics, a reorientation which lasted until his death in 1957. "The year 1940 was just about the half-way point of von Neumann's scientific life, and his publications show a discontinuous break then," Halmos has pointed out. "Till then he was a topflight pure mathematician who understood physics; after that he was an applied mathematician who remembered his pure work."[6] In all, his collected works, which include papers on both pure and applied mathematics, fill six volumes.

During the war, von Neumann was a consultant to various government agencies, including the Army's Ballistics Research Laboratory, the Navy Bureau of Ordnance, and the Los Alamos Scientific Laboratory. In addition to making significant scientific contributions to these organizations, von Neumann was instrumental in providing direction to the research undertaken.[7]

Such a dual role seemed particularly suited to his personality and was one he willingly accepted and actively sought after the war as well. His quick, intuitive mind enabled him to grasp specific technical and scientific problems easily and make invaluable recommendations for their solution. In addition, he was a man with entrepreneurial attributes, skilled in exercising an administrative or leadership role. In that capacity, he emphasized the need for written reports and papers to formalize and summarize fast-paced developments. He recognized the importance of delegating authority and responsibility and made every effort to solve major problems collaboratively by

John von Neumann. Courtesy Alan W. Richards, Princeton, New Jersey.

bringing together groups with differing interests. His own collaborative works during the war ranged in subject matter from economics to astrophysics. Such attributes are frequently used to describe the "innovator" who can turn new ideas and concepts into usable developments.

Von Neumann During World War II

Von Neumann's role during the war provided him with a status and influence achieved by very few mathematicians. Pure mathematics was at that time usually viewed as too abstract for most practical applications. Von Neumann—like such men as Vannevar Bush, James Conant, and Frank Jewett of the National Defense Research Committee and the Office of Scientific Research and Development—made every effort to establish the social utility of the sciences in general, and one specific concern was to legitimize the role of mathematics in particular as a practical and useful science. Ulam, in an obituary written for the American Mathematical Society, points to this aspect of von Neumann's interest:

. . . perhaps his main desire and one of his strongest motivations was to help re-establish the role of mathematics on a *conceptual level* in theoretical physics. The drifting apart of theoretical mathematical research and of the main stream of ideas in theoretical physics since the end of the First World War is undeniable. Von Neumann often expressed concern that mathematics might not keep abreast of the exponential increase of problems and ideas in physical sciences.[8]

In later years, when many scientists were expressing concern over the use of science for destructive purposes, von Neumann was extremely vocal in endorsing the application of mathematics and science for *any* social purpose, even military ones:

His political and administrative decisions were rarely on the side that is described nowadays by the catchall term "liberal." He appeared at times to advocate preventive war with Russia. As early as 1946 atomic bomb tests were already receiving adverse criticism, but von Neumann thought they were necessary and (in, for instance, a letter to the *New York Times*) defended them vigorously.[9]

By 1944, von Neumann had a reputation as a distinguished mathematician and as a scientific leader with vast influence in governmental and academic circles. His relationship with government agencies put him in a position to make policy recommendations, as well as technical and administrative ones, regarding the scientific resources of the nation. Moreover, he seemed to value this sense of power. Ulam remarked that "von Neumann seemed to admire generals and admirals and got along well with them"—a characteristic Ulam attributed to von Neumann's "admiration for people who had power."[10]

Interest in Computational Devices

It would be difficult to determine precisely when von Neumann *first* became interested in digital computers, but as a result of his war work on implosion he was cognizant of the critical need for advanced methods of digital computation. According to Goldstine, "von Neumann's main contribution to the Los Alamos project was to lie in his showing the theoretical people there how to model their phenomena mathematically and then to solve the resulting equations numerically. A punched card laboratory was set up to handle the implosion problem."[11]

But punch-card equipment was very slow and inefficient. Von Neumann became actively interested in more advanced computational equipment several months prior to his visits to the Moore School. His work on implosion at Los Alamos required solutions of systems of nonlinear equations in fluid dynamics.[12] Since existing manual methods for solving these problems were extremely time consuming, he sought an alternative. Von Neumann sensed that digital computers might prove useful in this regard.

Though von Neumann's interest in instruments for scientific calculations was shared by John Mauchly at the Moore School, Howard Aiken at Harvard University, John Atanasoff at Iowa State College, and others, it was decidedly uncharacteristic of pure mathematicians in general. Numerical methods give only approximate solutions of differential equations. Therefore, for pure mathematicians, who view theory as superior to empiricism, approximations were lacking in rigor and therefore totally unacceptable. Writing in the early 1940s, Thornton Fry of the Bell Telephone Laboratories and the National Defense Research Committee summed up the characteristic attitude of industrial engineers toward pure mathematicians: "Just now an attitude more commonly met . . . is one of amazed pride in pointing to some employee who isn't like most mathematicians; he gives you an answer you can use and isn't afraid of approximations."[13]

Von Neumann shared with applied mathematicians, particularly those engaged in war work, the realization that approximations serve a useful purpose in solving practical problems and can frequently facilitate the solution of theoretical problems as well. Von Neumann's unique and pragmatic attitude toward approximations is illustrated by a statement from his *Collected Works*: "I think that it is a relatively good approximation to truth—which is too complicated to allow anything but approximations—that mathematical ideas originate in empirics although the genealogy is sometimes long and obscure."[14]

Hence, his enthusiasm for computation went further than his effort to minimize the labor required for solving his own problems; he hoped to demonstrate its value to science. Again, von Neumann's pragmatism in this regard is more characteristic of innovators, who set out to produce tangible results, than of pure mathematicians who focus on the abstract in clear preference to the concrete. In fact, one of von Neumann's major contributions during and after the war was his legitimization of applied mathematics as a scholarly field and his attention to computers as scientific instruments.

Von Neumann's interest in calculating equipment dates back to a letter he wrote in January 1944 to Warren Weaver, chief of the Applied Mathematics Panel (AMP) of the Office of Scientific Research and Development, inquiring about existing facilities.[15] As previously noted, government agencies such as the AMP were created either to fund wartime projects or to provide liaison between them. Hence, they were the best source of information on existing areas of research and development. As its name implies, the AMP was specifically instituted to facilitate and coordinate efforts in the field of applied mathematics, indicating that by 1943, when this organization was established, applied mathematics had already become a major war-related discipline.[16] Many pure mathematicians turned their attention to applied mathematics during the war as a temporary effort to facilitate war-related research.

Von Neumann and the Moore School

Weaver directed von Neumann to Howard Aiken at Harvard University, George Stibitz at the Bell Telephone Laboratories, and Jan Schilt, an associate of Wallace J. Eckert at Columbia University's Thomas J. Watson Astronomical Computing Bureau.[17] Aiken was completing the Mark I, the first electromechanical relay computer, George Stibitz was also developing a relay computer, and Schilt was adapting IBM punch-card equipment for scientific applications.

Despite Weaver's desire to provide the information von Neumann requested, he did not inform von Neumann of the Moore School's ENIAC. Since the National Defense Research Committee, of which Weaver was a member, considered the ENIAC project naive, it is likely that Weaver was not impressed with its potential and hence failed to publicize its existence.

Von Neumann learned about the ENIAC in August 1944, after attending a Scientific Advisory Committee meeting at the Ballistics Research Laboratory in Aberdeen, Maryland. While he was waiting for a train, Herman Goldstine, the laboratory's liaison on the ENIAC project, ventured to introduce himself.

I was waiting for a train to Pennsylvania on the railroad platform in Aberdeen when along came von Neumann. Prior to that time I had never met this great mathematician, but I knew much about him of course and had heard him lecture on several occasions. It was therefore with considerable temerity that I approached this world-famous figure, introduced myself, and started talking. Fortunately for me von Neumann was a warm, friendly person who did his best to make people feel relaxed in his presence. The conversation soon turned to my work. When it became clear to von Neumann that I was concerned with the development of an electronic computer capable of 333 multiplications per second, the whole atmosphere of our conversation changed from one of relaxed good humor to one more like the oral examination of the doctor's degree in mathematics.[18]

Herman Goldstine, whose enormous respect for von Neumann characterizes much of his book on the history of the computer, states that "along with all his other attributes" von Neumann "had an almost insatiable interest in new ideas—sometimes! At other times—when, for instance, he was deeply committed to some intellectual pursuit—he was completely impervious to new ideas . . . But in general he was extremely receptive to new intellectual challenges."[19]

Beginning in September 1944 von Neumann took time from his Los Alamos work to make periodic visits to the Moore School to learn more about the ENIAC and to make technical recommendations on the EDVAC. From the outset, many of the Moore School participants were awed by von Neumann and, at least initially, reacted favorably to his presence.

Since the design of the ENIAC had been frozen in June 1944, von Neumann had little to do with the actual technological features of that machine. He did, however, suggest that the Los Alamos group working on the hydrogen bomb could use the ENIAC for its complex calculations. It was largely as a result of his influence that the first application, or test, of the ENIAC was for Los Alamos.

Von Neumann's interaction with the Moore School had three immediate effects. First, it legitimized and justified the project to other agencies such as the National Defense Research Committee. Despite the substantial technical accomplishments already achieved by the ENIAC, von Neumann's presence was an effective method for gaining added recognition.[20]

Second, it was soon after von Neumann became interested in the ENIAC that the Moore School requested and received a contract for the development of the new and more powerful EDVAC. This is not to say that von Neumann was responsible for this device, since the idea to build such a machine actually preceded his involvement; but it is nonetheless significant that contract negotiations were undertaken almost immediately after his interest had been sparked.[21] Presumably, von Neumann encouraged the ENIAC staff and bolstered their confidence. Moreover, although the Ordnance Department was satisfied with progress at the Moore School on the ENIAC and was eager to maintain its role in electronic digital computer technology, von Neumann's association with the group may well have provided an additional impetus for the EDVAC.

The Army's ENIAC can give you the answer in a fraction of a second!

Think that's a stumper? You should see *some* of the ENIAC's problems! Brain twisters that if put to paper would run off this page and feet beyond . . . addition, subtraction, multiplication, division — square root, cube root, any root. Solved by an incredibly complex system of circuits operating 18,000 electronic tubes and tipping the scales at 30 tons!

The ENIAC is symbolic of many amazing Army devices with a brilliant future for you! The new Regular Army needs men with aptitude for scientific work, and as one of the first trained in the post-war era, you stand to get in on the ground floor of important jobs

YOUR REGULAR ARMY SERVES THE NATION AND MANKIND IN WAR AND PEACE

which have never before existed. You'll find that an Army career pays off.

The most attractive fields are filling quickly. Get into the swim while the getting's good! 1½, 2 and 3 year enlistments are open in the Regular Army to ambitious young men 18 to 34 (17 with parents' consent) who are otherwise qualified. If you enlist for 3 years, you may choose your own branch of the service, of those still open. Get full details at your nearest Army Recruiting Station.

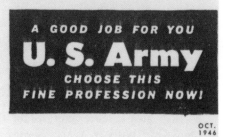

OCT. 1946

Advertisement from *Popular Science*, October 1946. Courtesy A. W. Rogers, GE Ordnance, Pittsfield, Massachusetts.

Third, his presence seemed to result in a more formal approach to technical issues. Prior to this period, technical direction was provided by Eckert and Mauchly and was based primarily on their informal discussions. Beginning in September, staff meetings with von Neumann were held with some regularity and minutes of these meetings were recorded and distributed. That these sessions were called "Meetings with von Neumann" suggests that his presence was of major significance. The minutes typically included such items as the following:

The possibility of being able to connect both the control unit and the computer to tanks was discussed. Dr. von Neumann suggested using manual switches so as to be able to put two or more tanks in series since, when this is done, switching takes place less often . . . Adder units were discussed. Dr. von Neumann suggested a couple of schemes in which tubes were both inhibited and energized . . . Dr. von Neumann also suggested a scheme in which the tubes would be used as inhibitors only.[22]

The main purpose of these meetings was to provide von Neumann with information on current technology in the field of electronic digital computation, but they served an additional function of providing a forum for the exchange and development of new ideas. Goldstine reported to Colonel Gillon of the Ballistics Research Laboratory: "As far as EDVAC is concerned, Johnny von Neumann has been working for us as a consultant and has been devoting enormous amounts of his prodigious energy to working out the logical controls of the machine. He has also been very much interested in helping design circuits for the machine."[23] Goldstine, himself a mathematician, was particularly pleased and encouraged by von Neumann's presence. Almost from the beginning, von Neumann became Goldstine's mentor and remained his idol.

The Stored-Program Concept

Von Neumann's perspective was not simply that of a potential user but of a scientific and technical contributor as well. In the remaining months of 1944 and throughout 1945, when he was not at Los Alamos, he took time to attend technical conferences on the EDVAC and to make contributions and suggestions on logical design. When at Los Alamos, he corresponded frequently with Goldstine, who informed him of new developments. Von Neumann transmitted his recommendations through Goldstine to the rest of the staff.[24]

After the war, von Neumann's relationship to the Moore School began to change. Earlier the mystique of the prestigious mathematician had dominated. Moreover, all of the individuals at the Moore School had subordinated their own specific interests for the sake of wartime cooperation. In the immediate postwar years, however, the differing perspectives and perceptions of the pure scientist, as opposed to the applied scientist or engineer, led to irreconcilable conflicts. Despite von Neumann's interest in applied mathematics and in administration, his perceptions remained those of the pure scientist in an academic setting. Despite Mauchly's background as a physicist, his perceptions were those of an applied scientist or engineer who began to look at the computer as a marketable product. He, with Eckert, then, focused on the commercial applicability of this device. These differing perspectives served to exacerbate tensions at the Moore School.

As previously noted, by 1945 the situation at the Moore School was already tense. Eckert and Mauchly had won their fight over the ENIAC patent, but the EDVAC patent was still unresolved. Still another priority problem arose in 1945, this time between von Neumann on the one hand and Eckert and Mauchly on the other, regarding the stored-program concept. This concept can be traced back to the initial ENIAC work in 1943, when the Moore School staff, bowing to wartime expediency, chose to develop the proposed machine with a manual setup procedure for entering instructions. The ENIAC progress report of December 31, 1943, emphatically stated that the project staff elected to omit any automatic programming capability:

No attempt has been made to make provision for setting up a problem automatically. This is for the sake of simplicity and because it is anticipated that the ENIAC will be used primarily for problems of a type in which one setup will be used many times before another problem is placed on the machine.[25]

In January of 1944, when the Moore School staff began to consider the development of a device more comprehensive than the ENIAC, Eckert wrote a three-page disclosure on a "magnetic calculating machine" broadly indicating a stored-program device:

. . . a great increase in the available facilities for allowing automatic programming of the facilities and processes involved may be made . . . This programming may be of the temporary type set up on alloy discs or of the permanent type of etched discs.[26]

Thus, months before von Neumann knew of the Moore School work, the stored-program concept had been conceived, if not developed. With von Neumann's assistance, however, this concept was carefully structured and developed in the 1944–1945 period.

Priority Issues

In June 1945 von Neumann prepared a report called "First Draft of a Report on the EDVAC," a paper on stored-program computers, which, as its title implies, was intended as a preliminary and informal document.* Gold-

---

*The report in its entirety is printed for the first time as the Appendix to this book.

stine distributed the 101-page report to members of the Moore School staff and also to interested scientists not associated with the EDVAC.[27]

The report was the first widely circulated document on electronic digital computers. The exact number of copies distributed at the time is not known; at least thirty-two people were on the original mailing list, but many others received copies later on. The report consists of a series of definitions of concepts relating to logical control and stored programming. It also includes a section on how computers, in principle, could be used to operate on data. The contents of these sections formed the basis for computer and stored programming design in the late 1940s. The draft report also includes a section emphasizing the similarity between computer processing and the activities of the human nervous system, a topic that was one of von Neumann's major interests.[28]

Since the draft report bore von Neumann's name as sole author, the stored-program concept was thought by computer professionals, as well as by many historians, to have originated with him.[29] As a result, most studies have credited him with the origin of this concept, to the exclusion of all other participants.

In *The Computer from Pascal to von Neumann*, Herman Goldstine has supported the claim that von Neumann was primarily if not exclusively responsible for this concept. Goldstine says that von Neumann's draft report "represents a masterful analysis and synthesis by him of all the thinking that had gone into the EDVAC from the fall of 1944 through the spring of 1945. Not everything in there is his, but the crucial parts are." Goldstine adds, "In a sense, the report is the most important document ever written on computing and computers."[30]

Arthur W. Burks, a mathematician who worked as an engineer on the ENIAC and EDVAC projects, supports the view that the ideas in the draft report were primarily von Neumann's:

Eckert and Mauchly designed circuits capable of operating at a pulse rate of 1 megacycle, 10 times the basic pulse rate of the ENIAC, and gave considerable thought to the design of a mercury delay line machine. Goldstine brought von Neumann in as a consultant, and we all participated in discussions of the logical design of such a machine . . . von Neumann then worked out in considerable detail the logical design of this computer. The result appeared in his "First Draft of a Report on the EDVAC" which was never published.[31]

In 1976, Nicholas Metropolis, the Los Alamos scientist who also had worked closely with von Neumann, collaborated with J. Worlton on an article that provides a different view of the derivation of the ideas explicated in the draft report:

Another point concerning the stored-program history which needs clarification is the unwarranted assumption that J. von Neumann alone deserves the credit for the stored-program concept . . . It is clear that the stored-program concept predates von

Neumann's participation in the EDVAC design. That von Neumann is often given credit for this fundamental concept is likely due to the fact that he wrote a preliminary report which summarized the earlier work on the EDVAC design, including the stored-program concept. Von Neumann contributed significantly to the development of this concept, but to credit him with its invention is an historical error.[32]

Harry Huskey, a Moore School engineer himself, provides a similar retrospective view:

After von Neumann's introduction to the ENIAC there were a number of meetings between him and the ENIAC staff discussing various ideas and proposals. As a joint effort, this group developed the concept of a stored program. The results of this activity were written up by von Neumann in a "draft" report which, not being in final publication form, did not give due credit to others for the development of the ideas. However, the report was reproduced in this draft form and circulated quite widely. As a result von Neumann has generally received credit for this idea.[33]

Responses by Eckert and Mauchly

Thus the dissemination of von Neumann's report caused some controversy in 1945 and even more controversy in later years. Almost immediately, it served to heighten the tensions that already existed at the Moore School over priority and patent claims. Mauchly was quick to point to the draft as simply the formalization of a collaborative work, but he and Eckert were concerned that von Neumann's document would jeopardize their own legal rights to a patent on EDVAC. The second progress report on the EDVAC tried to set the record straight:

As noted in Section 1 of *PY Summary Report No. 1* discussions have been held at regular intervals in the Moore School to develop a logical plan for the EDVAC. These discussions continue. Dr. John von Neumann, consultant for the Aberdeen Proving Ground, has proposed a preliminary draft in *which he has organized the subject matter of these discussions* [emphasis added].[34]

As it happened, the fears of Eckert and Mauchly were indeed warranted. Two years later, when they were attempting to file a patent on the EDVAC, the government attorneys indicated that because of its wide distribution the draft report in a legal sense constituted a formal publication. Since any document published more than a year prior to the filing of a patent places the ideas within the public domain, the concept of EDVAC-type stored-program computers was therefore unpatentable.

There has been some controversy over whether von Neumann actually intended to claim priority for this concept. Arthur Burks, a collaborator with von Neumann on later works, suggests in a paper prepared in 1976 that von Neumann was unaware of the credit he received. According to Burks, "In the spring of 1945, John von Neumann worked out the logical design of EDVAC in a draft report. Without his knowledge, this was issued as 'First Draft of a Report on the EDVAC' . . . Undoubtedly he would have given credit to others."[35] If Burks's version is right, one wonders why von Neumann did not attempt to correct the impression that he was sole author. He had ample opportunity to do so.

Eckert, testifying in *Honeywell* v. *Sperry Rand,* was more critical of von Neumann's actions: "There was a misunderstanding about this report which Dr. von Neumann never attempted to straighten out." Eckert further claimed that "Dr. von Neumann had translated some of the ideas of Dr. Mauchly and myself into a sort of semi-mathematical logical notation of his own."[36] Clearly, for Eckert the engineering features of a machine were far more important than any logical notation which von Neumann may have constructed.

In an article published just before his death in 1979, Mauchly provided his retrospective analysis of von Neumann's influence on the Moore School work:

Johnny learned instantly of course, as was his nature. But he chose to refer to the modules we had described as "organs" and to substitute hypothetical "neurons" for hypothetical vacuum tubes or other devices which could perform logical functions. It was clear that Johnny was rephrasing our logic, but it was still the same logic. Also, he was introducing different but equivalent symbols; nevertheless the devices still did the same things. Johnny did *not* alter the fundamental concepts which we had already formulated for the EDVAC.[37]

In 1945 von Neumann himself did not address the issue of priority, although the matter was later to generate a significant amount of hostility. Since he never disclaimed priority once the report was distributed, one can surmise that he was not entirely sympathetic to Eckert and Mauchly's point of view.

Differing Perspectives of Scientists and Engineers

The conflict between von Neumann and Eckert and Mauchly cannot be explained simply by stating that von Neumann, an academic, objected to the commercial interests of Eckert and Mauchly. Von Neumann, unlike many academic scientists and unlike pure mathematicians in particular, was *not* opposed to scientists with such interests so long as the interests were secondary to the advancement of knowledge. In 1945 he himself considered the possibility of serving as a consultant to IBM. Later in his career he actually assumed such a role for IBM and several other major industrial organizations. In the postwar years, therefore, his attitude toward the role of scholars in the marketplace seems to have shifted.[38]

However, von Neumann did expect scientists and engineers to subordinate their commercial interests when those interests conflicted with academic pursuits. Soon after the 1945 conflicts at the Moore School, he came to view Eckert and Mauchly as having abrogated their primary responsibility in this regard, even after the two inventors left the Moore School to form their own company. In a letter to his colleague Stanley Frankel in October 1946 von Neumann was adamant about the incompatibility of Eckert and Mauchly's commercial pursuits with the interest of academics:

I have the greatest respect for Eckert and Mauchly's ability, for their past achievements and for their future promise. It is no criticism on my part, just an observation of facts, that they are a commercial group with a commercial patent policy. On the basis of the information before me, I have to conclude that we cannot work with them directly or indirectly in the same manner in which we would work with an academic group which has no such interests . . . If you wish to maintain the same type of close contact with Eckert and Mauchly (as you have with us)—which is for you and you alone to decide—then you should not put yourself into an incompatible position by communicating with us too. I would appreciate your making your choice in this respect before we continue our discussions further.[39]

Another major conflict arose from the differing perspectives of scientists and engineers; although related to the commercial conflict, it is really separate from it. As early as 1941, Thornton Fry pointed to this dual perspective:

The typical mathematician feels great confidence in a conclusion reached by careful reasoning. He is not convinced to the same degree by experimental evidence. For the typical engineer these statements may be reversed . . . Because of this confidence in thought processes the mathematician turns naturally to paper and pencil in many situations in which the engineer or physicist would resort to the lab . . . For the mathematician an argument is either perfect in every detail, in form as well as in substance, or else it is wrong. There are not intermediate classes. He calls this rigorous thinking . . . The typical engineer calls it hair splitting . . . The mathematician also tends to idealize any situation with which he is confronted.[40]

Whereas Eckert and Mauchly were predominantly concerned with technical feasibility and with the actual construction of an operational product, von Neumann's primary interest was in providing a theoretical construct for electronic digital computers. While no categorization can ever be consistently applied to an individual, the dual perspectives of the pure scientist and the applied scientist or engineer are relevant to this discussion. Despite von Neumann's numerous applied interests, his ideology was that of a pure scientist, with objectives and goals dramatically different from those of the engineer or applied scientist.

The divergent orientation of engineers and scientists can be seen in their attitudes toward publication. Engineers are, in general, eager to read the works of others as part of their research, but they are less inclined to publish their own achievements, either as a result of legal considerations or of simple predilection. Scientists, on the other hand, often measure their achievement in terms of works published.[41]

This difference in attitude is borne out by the publication patterns at the Moore School. Prior to von Neumann's involvement, the main documents disseminated by the ENIAC staff were the semiannual progress reports required by the government. In the case of the EDVAC, these were short, general papers. There were also several one- or two-page informal "disclosures" written by Eckert. Von Neumann, on the other hand, in the early months of 1945 concentrated his efforts on formalizing concepts. Indeed, his draft report on the EDVAC served a very useful purpose: it became the formal document upon which subsequent computers were based.

The purpose of his paper was markedly different from the disclosures and progress reports describing specific engineering features that the Moore School engineers continued to publish even after the war. Its primary focus was on theoretical or conceptual features. Its objective as stated on its opening page was to consider the "logical control" of "a very high-speed automatic digital computer system." The generality implied by the latter phrase was clearly meant to suggest that the technical aspects of any specific high-speed computer were not of major significance. Rather, the logical structure to be developed was considered machine-independent and hence could be universally applied.

The report emphasized theory in several ways. It introduced the concept of five fundamental units or "organs"—von Neumann was fond of applying anthropomorphic terms to computing machines—which characterized all subsequent computers. These elements—the central arithmetic, central control, memory, input and output units—were described in structural and functional terms. Von Neumann discussed existing computational equipment as scientists discuss experimental results that verify their theory. Even later when the ENIAC was declassified and publication in journals no longer prohibited by security classification, Goldstine, Burks, and von Neumann published far more material than Eckert or Mauchly.

An anecdote by Arthur Burks illustrates how von Neumann's mathematical perspective focused his attention on logical structure, in the abstract, rather than on technical features:

We all knew that von Neumann's logical designs were realizable because he had worked out the building blocks with the group before he wrote the report. I remember well a meeting in the spring of 1945 at which we discussed serial adders. Pres [Eckert] and John [Mauchly] had designed several serial adders, the simplest of which took ten tubes. Not knowing of these results, von Neumann announced cheerily that he could build an adder with five tubes. We all looked amazed, and Pres said, "No, it takes at least ten tubes." Johnny said "I'll prove it to you," rushed to the board, and drew his adder. "No," we said, "your first tube can't drive its load in one microsecond, so an inverter is needed, then another tube to restore the polarity." And so the argument went. Johnny was finally convinced . . . "You are right," he said. "It takes ten tubes to add—five tubes for logic, and five tubes for electronics."[42]

Moreover, von Neumann's entire orientation toward computers tended to concentrate on the theoretical rather than the practical. In several later works, he drew further analogies between the computer and the structure of the human nervous system in an effort to emphasize that computer structure was part of a larger mechanical pattern that could be used to develop any theory: "It is easily seen that these simplified neuron functions can be imitated by telegraph relays or by vacuum tubes," von Neumann wrote. This analogy between the mind and a computer remained of considerable interest to him: "Although the nervous system is presumably asynchronous (for the synaptic delays), precise synaptic delays can be used by using synchronous setups."[43]

Von Neumann recognized that technological considerations might, in the end, impose constraints on his structure, but their import, in terms of the overall design, was minimal:

The point to which the application of this principle can be profitably pushed will, of course, depend on the actual physical characteristics of the available vacuum tube elements. It may be, that the optimum is not at a 100% application of this principle and that some compromise will be found to be optimal. However, this will always depend on the momentary state of the vacuum tube technique, clearly the faster the tubes are which will function reliably in this situation, the stronger the case is for uncompromising application of this principle.[44]

Impact of Von Neumann's Report

In short, von Neumann's report on the EDVAC was the first document to provide a logical framework for stored-program computers and for programming concepts. His attention to providing a written record and his development of automatic controls that had been conceived but not yet designed by the Moore School staff were factors leading others to credit him with priority. Whether he was indeed the inventor of the stored-program computer, however, is a matter of perspective. In an engineering sense, where ideas and their tangible realization are predominant factors in priority, Eckert and Mauchly built the first large-scale fully operational electronic digital computer and the first stored-program computer in the United States. Their attention was focused on producing an operational device, not on providing a mathematical theory formulating how such machines should operate.

In a scientific sense, however, where attention to theory and to logical design features are far more significant than any experimental results, von Neumann's preeminence is assured. His draft report itself, in addition to formalizing concepts and giving von Neumann recognition in the computing field, disseminated information on new developments, thereby facilitating the transfer of technology. Von Neumann's recognition of the importance of communicating recent ideas to a broad spectrum of scientists was clearly a motivating force.[45]

The differing perspective between von Neumann on the one hand and Eckert and Mauchly on the other manifested itself in other ways. Besides their divergent attitudes toward theory and publication, these men saw the ultimate purpose of the computer in different ways. Von Neumann focused on the mathematical use of the computer; Eckert and Mauchly focused on its labor-saving or commercial value. This divergence between scientific and commercial projects eventually resulted in a bifurcation in the computer field.

Von Neumann's interest in computers as tools for the mathematician led him, in the early part of 1945, to seek support for his own computer project. The manner in which he sought and achieved his objective sheds light on his entrepreneurial and innovative abilities. Although the project itself lies beyond the limits of our discussion, the circumstances surrounding its beginnings are relevant.

The IAS Computer

During the war, von Neumann was still a member of the Institute for Advanced Study (IAS), an institution noted for its pure research and its "ivory tower" attitude toward applied work. Even in physics, a major subject field at IAS, the emphasis was theoretical rather than experimental. IAS had limited laboratory facilities, prompting von Neumann's friend and colleague, Norbert Wiener, to write him, "You are going to run into a situation where you will need a lab at your fingertips and labs don't grow in ivory towers . . . Harrison wants to find out if you would come to MIT."[46]

Yet von Neumann set out to establish his computer project at IAS, a task of considerable magnitude, even for a man of his stature.[47] He began by actively seeking a commitment for his project from other major universities and from IBM as well. MIT, Harvard, the University of Chicago, and IBM were all eager to support his work.[48] By the summer of 1945, it was clear to Frank Aydelotte, director of IAS, that von Neumann would resign if his project were not approved.[49] As a result, in a radical departure from its traditional role, IAS agreed to undertake a computer project. Von Neumann's skill in achieving this objective is clearly analogous to the innovator's ability to "sell" his product.

In addition to whatever interest von Neumann might have had in establishing priority, he had two primary motives for undertaking such a project. First, he was firmly committed to demonstrating the utility of a computer "as a research tool" and not, he repeatedly emphasized, "as a production facility."[50] Second, despite his pure science ideology, he was committed to establishing the social utility of mathematics in general. Since computers were socially useful machines and von Neumann had already demonstrated their mathematical-logical structure, the computing field represented an ideal discipline in which mathematicians could firmly establish their social value. Mathematicians who engaged in computer design would stand to benefit from the government-funded research that was to become a postwar norm; at the same time, they could formalize their role in applied science.

Funding for the IAS project was obtained from a variety of sources. The institute itself and the Army and Navy ordnance departments each provided $100,000. In addition, von Neumann entered into a joint research and development contract with RCA, which was to build the memory unit for his machine. RCA had extensive experience with electronic counters and other electronic devices and had recently established its research laboratories at Princeton to facilitate a free interchange with Princeton University. Unlike its earlier hesitation to provide formal support to the Moore School, RCA expressed an immediate interest in the joint venture.

Von Neumann's willingness to participate in an academic-commercial undertaking suggests again that he had no objections to interest groups deriving profit from computer development.[51] He was a pragmatic man who understood that in a capitalist society industrial organizations regard the profit motive as primary.

Still Another Conflict

Von Neumann's direct involvement with the RCA engineers, however, precipitated another conflict at the Moore School. On November 12, 1945, he attended a technical meeting at RCA with Jan Rajchman and Vladimir Zworykin, two distinguished electronics experts, to discuss the development of an electrostatic memory device called the "selectron," to be incorporated in the IAS computer.[52] Within several weeks, Francis Reichelderfer, Chief of the United States Weather Bureau, learned of Zworykin's work on computers and of its possible applicability to meteorology. Reichelderfer asked Zworykin to meet with Weather Bureau representatives to discuss the matter.[53] Zworykin agreed and suggested that von Neumann might be interested in such an application. Von Neumann also was asked to attend.[54]

The meeting, held on January 9, 1946, demonstrates the increasing interaction of institutional organizations in technical and scientific matters: the government's weather agency, the IAS, and RCA, each with its own distinct motivations, hoped to apply computer technology to a specific scientific problem. The following day, January 10, the *New York Times* printed an article entitled "Electronics to Aid Weather Forecasting," which summarized the meeting and focused on von Neumann and RCA's pioneering efforts in electronic computing.[55]

The published article caused an immediate furor at the Moore School. Publicity had not yet been released on the ENIAC, which had just been completed and was not to be dedicated for another month. The *New York Times'* disclosure implied that von Neumann and RCA were the major pioneers in the computing field. Von Neumann's failure to acknowledge the priority of the ENIAC appeared to many to be improper. Eckert and Mauchly, who were already sensitive to priority claims, were very distressed; in addition, the Army, which had funded the ENIAC, considered von Neumann's actions unethical. Mauchly's diary entry of January 14, 1946, sheds additional light on the matter: "No explicit reference to Army Ordnance work was made but Major Wexler [of the Weather Bureau] remembering information I had given him last April realized that what was discussed at the conference was probably based on our work and assumed that John von Neumann spoke for us."[56]

Von Neumann subsequently apologized, but in this case at least, his enthusiasm for establishing a new IAS-RCA computer and his eagerness to run meteorological problems on a computer, seemed to surpass the bounds of academic propriety. On January 24 Reichelderfer wrote in a Weather Bureau memorandum that Colonel Gillon of the Army Ordnance unit at Aberdeen, Maryland, "also stated that it has caused them considerable embarrassment because their office and a number of collaborating scientists and research laboratories had been responsible for the development of the machine about which Dr. Zworykin and Prof. von Neumann had spoken and that the premature release without credit to the scientists really responsible for the development had caused considerable resentment."[57] Here again, despite his perceptions of himself as conforming to an academic ideology, von Neumann was not always consistent.

Eckert and the IAS Project

This last incident served further to exacerbate tensions between von Neumann and Eckert and Mauchly. At one time, von Neumann had hoped to employ Eckert on the IAS project; the previous November he had written to offer him "on behalf of the Institute for Advanced Study a position as a member of the electronic computing project at a salary of $6000 a year." But by the beginning of 1946, the conflicting interests between the two men were irreconcilable. By March, von Neumann rescinded his offer:

On November 27, 1945 I offered you on behalf of the Institute for Advanced Study a position as a member of the electronic computing project . . . During the last months it also became clear, however, that your further commercial interests in the automatic computing field on the one hand, and the requirements and the stability of the Institute research project, particularly in its basis of cooperation with our other partners, may not be easily reconciled . . . Under these conditions I can no longer assume the responsibility to the Institute or to the project and our partners for delaying the organization any further, or by limiting it in any way which might have been justifiable if you had accepted our original offer. I must therefore, much to my regret, consider our past discussions with you and our offer made to you as null.[58]

Eckert charged that the real reason for von Neumann's withdrawal of his offer was somewhat different:

The real reason was that the original plan was to have Princeton University, IAS and the University of Pennsylvania work on a cooperative three-way organization to build computing equipment in which all would share in this project together. When von Neumann pulled RCA into this otherwise educational group, this was deeply resented by Dr. Pender [Dean of the Moore School] who told me that my ability to stay at the University of Pennsylvania would not be possible if I were to become involved in such a group containing RCA.[59]

Von Neumann in Retrospect

In a 1977 interview, Eckert pointed to the dichotomy described above:

In the first place, you have to realize that most mathematicians compared to engineers are intellectual snobs . . . I think John [Mauchly] and I wanted to get the computer out there and being used by people . . . We didn't care whether you called us scientific or engineering or mathematical or non-mathematical. We wanted to get this job done . . . [von Neumann and Goldstine] attempted to make it look as if all we were looking for was money, that we didn't really care about whether people got good computers or not, or did mathematics . . . We knew the only way this was going to fly was to get a lot of commercial money behind it.[60]

Note that while Eckert acknowledges a dichotomy, he believes that the distinctions sometimes characterizing a scientific versus engineering or pure versus applied science ideology were based more on von Neumann's *perceptions* than on real or valid distinctions.

Von Neumann was a complex man who despite his focus on academic values and his disapproval of Eckert and Mauchly's commercial interests was himself less single-minded than might have appeared on the surface. His efforts to undertake a major computing project at the Institute for Advanced Study, an institution committed to pure research, was enterprising, innovative, and applications oriented. His interest in applied mathematics and computers themselves was considered by many of his colleagues as inappropriate for a pure scientist. Thus his conflicts with Eckert and Mauchly arose less out of actual ideological differences than perceived ideological differences. That is, von Neumann perceived Eckert and Mauchly as pursuing interests that were ideologically irreconcilable with his own.

In summary, von Neumann helped to formalize the logical design features of the EDVAC, the world's first electronic digital computer designed to incorporate stored-program capability. He also undertook a computer project at the Institute for Advanced Study, which, when completed, served as a model for numerous other academic and research institutions.

But there was another dimension to von Neumann's influence, one that is at least as important as the previously mentioned elements. His ability to bring together various groups, those which were capable of contributing to computer development and those which could benefit from it, was of singular importance. Moreover, his efforts to disseminate information on computer development contributed to the transfer of technology to other spheres, as well as to the widespread applicability of these devices.

Despite these and later numerous contributions, there are areas in which his work depended, in varying degrees, on other people. The stored-program concept, as a major example, was one such contribution.

5 Transition to the Private Sector

A preliminary press conference and a formal dedication ceremony in February of 1946 unveiled the ENIAC, made public the plans for the EDVAC, and clearly established the Moore School as the leading institution in the development of electronic digital computers. The press releases from the War Department and the University of Pennsylvania which announced the dedication were the first official publications to describe the ENIAC and its unique features.

"The formal dedication ceremony itself was a considerable success," according to Herman Goldstine, who helped plan it. The University of Pennsylvania held a dinner for "scientific celebrities" at which its president, George W. McCelland, presided.

The principal speaker for the occasion was Dr. Frank B. Jewett . . . then president of the National Academy of Science . . . General [Gladeon M.] Barnes carried out the actual dedication; after giving a short speech, he pressed a button that turned on the ENIAC. The guests then proceeded to the Moore School to see the actual demonstration.[1]

Arthur Burks was in charge of demonstrating the ENIAC at both the press conference and the formal ceremony. Looking back after nearly three decades, he recalled:

I explained what was to be done and pushed the button for it to be done. One of the first things I did was to add 5,000 numbers together. Seems a bit silly today, but I told the press, "I am now going to add 5,000 numbers together" and pushed the button. The ENIAC added the 5,000 numbers in one second. The problem was finished before most of the reporters had looked up!

The main part of the demonstration was the trajectory. For this we chose a trajectory of a shell that took 30 seconds to go from the gun to its target. Remember that humans using desk calculators could compute this in three days, and the differential analyzer could do it in 30 minutes. The ENIAC calculated this 30-second trajectory in just 20 seconds, faster than the shell itself could fly![2]

The dedication and the publicity promoted the Moore School's work not only nationally but internationally as well.[3] Almost immediately government organizations both in the United States and abroad expressed interest in electronic digital computers. Within the next several months Alan Turing, John Womersley, Douglas Hartree, and Maurice Wilkes, all of Great Britain, came to the Moore School.[4] Even the government purchasing commission of the Soviet Union inquired whether the Moore School could accept its "order for manufacturing the Robot Calculator"—a request the Army advised the school to deny.[5]

Despite the Moore School's growing international and national reputation, however, it began at this time to lose its position of leadership. Policy changes instituted at the school during the months following the dedication of the ENIAC were largely responsible for this loss of preeminence. Some of the changes resulted from the school's effort to establish a fixed policy to deal with anticipated postwar government support of academic projects. Others were instituted to prevent individual inventors from deriving personal financial gain from work conducted for the University of Pennsylvania. Many people within the school believed that such personal gain could embarrass the university and jeopardize future support.

Because they were unable to accept the new conditions of employment resulting from these policies, Eckert, Mauchly, and several others left the Moore School. Eckert and Mauchly subsequently formed their own company to build commercial computers. Most of the others who left went to work for either Eckert and Mauchly or John von Neumann at the Institute for Advanced Study in Princeton. The departures served to disperse the school's expertise in the computing field, thereby facilitating the transfer of technology to other academic institutions and to the private sector as well.

The Moore School and Government Funding

One major outcome of wartime research and development was the government's willingness to continue funding basic research at academic institutions. This meant, of course, a major expansion in the scope of research at universities. Despite the obvious benefits to be derived, however, many universities were somewhat ambivalent about the prospect. They were skeptical about the effect of government funding on academic freedom and feared that the type of research undertaken would be greatly influenced by the government's military needs. Many scholars and university administrators expressed concern that academic institutions might be compromised if they were permitted to function as "industrial shops" with a government-funded scientist or engineer supervising the staffing and acquisitions of a new laboratory.

This ambivalence regarding government funding was clearly evident at the Moore School. George McClelland, president of the University of Pennsylvania and formerly a professor of English, was not entirely convinced that such funding would be beneficial to the university. He was specifically disturbed by the controversies that had ensued over patent rights for the ENIAC; further, he feared a similar furor was almost certain to be raised over the EDVAC patents. He regarded these conflicts as inappropriate to the conduct of academic affairs, a violation of academic norms, and a direct and unavoidable result of government funding.[6]

Harold Pender, the Moore School's dean, was anxious to maintain government support of research, but he recognized that major problems had to be overcome. The conflicts over patents within the computer group certainly highlighted the need for a consistent and rigorous patent policy.[7]

Moreover, the way in which the computer projects were administered created serious financial difficulties. Because the EDVAC was funded as a supplement to the ENIAC, the exact expenditure for each computer was difficult to assess and control. In addition, the project's supervision and the staff's working relations were seriously strained by von Neumann's disclosures. The dissemination of his June 1945 draft report on the EDVAC and the *New York Times'* report on computers that failed to acknowledge the Moore School's central role in the ENIAC project were considered to be the result of ineffectual leadership and control.[8]

In an effort to inject new leadership into the existing projects and to resolve some of the immediate administrative problems, Dean Pender appointed Irven Travis as supervisor of research in January 1946. Prior to the war, Travis had been assistant professor of electrical engineering at the university and was directly involved in the construction of the Moore School's differential analyzer. He had also participated in a prewar project for General Electric, the purpose of which was to determine the feasibility of using devices that incorporated digital methods of computation for solving differential equations. Hence, he had experience in the field of computation that Pender hoped would prove useful to a supervisor of research.

A naval reserve officer before the war, Travis was called to active duty in 1941. He served as a contracts administrator in the Naval Ordnance Department, assessing the feasibility of war-related technological research and recommending support for projects he deemed worthwhile. When he was discharged at the end of the war, he had attained the rank of commander and had acquired substantial knowledge of how various institutions administered and conducted government-supported research. Pender was very impressed with this aspect of Travis's administrative experience. When Travis returned to the university in 1946, the dean offered him a full professorship and the position of supervisor of research.[9]

The Departure of Eckert and Mauchly

When Travis took charge in January 1946, the direction of research and development at the Moore School changed dramatically. Since he had not been involved in the ENIAC or EDVAC projects, he was less influenced by the success and prestige that they afforded the Moore School. His primary concern was to establish an effective research organization, one that would ensure continued government support for the school. The school's pre-eminence in computing was, for him, of secondary importance.

Almost immediately, Travis set out to establish a patent policy similar to those followed by most industrial organizations and a few prominent universities. In his testimony in *Honeywell* v. *Sperry Rand,* he looked back and described his perception of the situation in 1946:

When I returned to the Moore School, I looked into several aspects of the research program there. One was the technical content and the capability of the personnel and the general technical complexion of the accounting, management, organizational structure. The former I found in fair shape. The latter I was a little unhappy about because as a contracting officer in the Navy, I was familiar with the operations of research labs associated with educational institutions such as the Applied Physics Lab at Johns Hopkins and the Department of Industrial Cooperation at MIT and I greatly admired the way these two were operating . . . After discussions with Dean Pender, I set about to put the house in order, as it were, to get an organization and a structure which would allow the soliciting of sponsored contract work for both governmental and industrial sponsors and to build a strong research organization.[10]

The policy Travis advocated included the assignment of patents to the university so that individual researchers would not be permitted to derive financial benefits from inventions developed while they were university employees. Travis also sought to limit the consulting work of researchers and professors.

It is important to note that not all administrators at universities believed there was a need for a policy that denied financial gain to inventors. Even John von Neumann—whose attitude toward academics with commercial interests was discussed in the previous chapter—believed that to some extent inventors at academic institutions were entitled to derive financial benefit from their work. He wrote a colleague in the spring of 1946:

The time has come when the Institute [for Advanced Study] has to adopt a patent policy with respect to its employees on the computing project. I think that the policy I suggest strikes a reasonable middle position between leaving everything to the employee or taking everything for the Institute. I am not in favor of the former procedure since it may lead to commercially minded control of the inventions developed with our money. On the other hand, if the Institute has complete control over policies, I see no reason to withhold royalties from the inventors.[11]

Even within the Moore School, there were those who disagreed with the policy Travis advocated. Carl Chambers, who was supervisor of other research projects at the school, for example, was critical of Travis's patent policy.[12]

Travis announced his research objectives and his patent policy to the Moore School staff at a meeting on March 15, 1946.[13] In addition, each member of the staff was asked to sign a patent release form. When Eckert, Mauchly, and several of their colleagues, including Robert Shaw, C. Bradford Sheppard, and John Davis, refused to sign, they were given additional time to consider the consequences of their actions.

Thus, by mid-March of 1946, less than two months after the ENIAC dedication ceremony, Eckert and Mauchly began to realize that their affiliation with the Moore School was about to come to an end. Unwilling to sign the patent release form, they had no choice but to resign. On March 22 they received an official letter from Dean Pender outlining the conditions for continuance of employment at the Moore School and giving them until 5:00 p.m. the same day to accept or reject the following conditions:

    (a) that you execute the University's standard patent release
    (b) that you agree to remain as full-time employees of the University for at least one year
    (c) that you certify you will devote your efforts first to the interests of the University of Pennsylvania and will during the interval of your employment here subjugate your personal commercial interests to the interests of the University.[14]

Mauchly and Eckert still refused to sign a patent release and therefore submitted their resignations effective March 31, 1946. This sequence of events suggested to the two men that they were, in fact, fired. To others, such as Travis and Brainerd, Eckert and Mauchly had a viable alternative; hence their resignations were purely voluntary. In either case, Travis's policy persevered; the Moore School, regardless of the consequences, would require its employees to fully subordinate their own commercial interests to those of the university. Whether consciously or unconsciously, Travis and Pender chose to jeopardize the Moore School's preeminence in computer technology rather than abandon this policy.[15]

As noted in an earlier chapter, Pender, at least, was somewhat sympathetic to Eckert and Mauchly's business interests. He himself had strong commercial ties; in addition to being dean of the Moore School, he had served as president of the International Resistance Company. Thus, he did not view commercial interests as antithetical to academic ones. Indeed, he seemed unsure of how to resolve the conflicting goals of engineers at an academic institution who were also considering commercial ventures. His ambivalence, which became evident during the ENIAC patent controversy, permeated his handling of the ultimatum on patent assignments as well. In the end, however, he chose to support his newly appointed supervisor of research and suffer the consequences to the EDVAC project.[16]

At this juncture, the opportunities available to Eckert and Mauchly were diverse. The previous December, Eckert had been offered a position as chief engineer for the Institute for Advanced Study's computer project. Despite the fact that von Neumann had rescinded the offer several weeks earlier, claiming that Eckert was too commercially oriented, the latter probably could have taken a conciliatory stance and requested that the offer be reactivated.[17] There were, after all, numerous advantages to working at IAS. Clearly there was enormous prestige associated with a von Neumann project; moreover, one could be relatively assured of continued funding and few, if any, bureaucratic problems.

In addition, both Eckert and Mauchly had received an offer from Thomas J. Watson, Sr., of IBM to establish their own computing laboratory. Eckert was very interested in this offer because it would have given him the opportunity to work independently, unencumbered by institutional constraints. Mauchly, however, did not trust IBM; he was convinced that he and Eckert could produce and market their own computers at substantial profits. Eckert's wife and father agreed with Mauchly. In the end, Eckert was persuaded to attempt an independent commercial venture.[18]

The departure of Eckert and Mauchly from the Moore School was followed by the resignation of several other important engineers. Arthur Burks left to join von Neumann at the Institute for Advanced Study. Robert Shaw and C. Bradford Sheppard, who also refused to sign the patent release forms, eventually joined Eckert and Mauchly. Although many first-rate engineers, such as T. Kite Sharpless and F. Robert Michaels, chose to remain at the school, its new patent policy resulted in a serious depletion of competent people in the computing field. Consequently, the EDVAC project suffered many delays. The central processor was not accepted by Army Ordnance until 1949, and the input-output system was never fully operational. Ironically, only a year after he instituted his research policy, Travis left the Moore School to be vice president of Burroughs Corporation. There his primary responsibility was to establish an electronic digital computer division.[19]

Although the university may have steered Eckert and Mauchly onto a commercial course, the two innovators might well have taken that path anyway. In any case, the Moore School's effort to place academic principles above the individual motivations and interests of its staff members served not only to accelerate the loss of its preeminence in this field but to facilitate the transfer of technology to the private sector, where the technology received its biggest boost, and also to other academic institutions.

Course on Computers

As an academic institution, the Moore School was consciously committed to fostering this transfer of technology to other spheres. As a prime example, in the summer of 1946 Carl Chambers organized a six-week course entitled

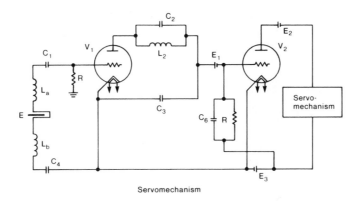

Servomechanism

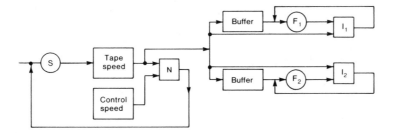

Four Servo System

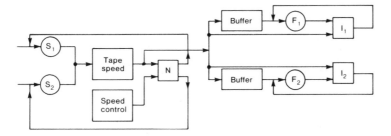

Three Servo System

Diagrams from the Moore School's "Progress Report on the EDVAC," June 30, 1946. Courtesy University of Pennsylvania Archives.

"Theory and Techniques for Design of Electronic Digital Computers," which had, as its main objective, the dissemination of information on electronic digital computers to participants from 20 institutions including the Army, the Navy, the National Bureau of Standards, MIT, Columbia, Harvard, the Institute for Advanced Study, Cambridge University in England, and such companies as the Bell Telephone Laboratories, IBM, Eastman-Kodak, National Cash Register, and General Electric.[20] The course, jointly sponsored by the Office of Naval Research and the Army Ordnance Department, focused on mathematical methods for computation, engineering features of new computers, and the potential for government-supported research. Lectures were offered by many pioneers, including Eckert and Mauchly, who had resigned four months before, Herman Goldstine, John von Neumann, and others.[21]

EDVAC

Specifications from Martin Weik, BRL Report No. 971.

Manufacturer

Moore School of Electrical Engineering
  University of Pennsylvania

Operating Agency

U.S. Army Ordnance Corps Ballistic
  Research Lab, APG

General System

Applications solution of ballistic equations,
  bombing and firing tables, fire control, data
  reductions, related scientific problems.
Timing   Synchronous
Operation   Sequential
A general purpose computer which may be
  used for solving many varieties of
  mathematical problems.

Numerical System

Internal number system: Binary
Binary digits per word: 44
Binary digits per instruction: 4
  bits/command, 10 bits each address
Instruction per word: 1
Total no. of instructions decoded: 16
Total no. of instructions used: 12
Arithmetic system: Fixed-point
Instruction type: Four-address code
Number range: $-(1-2^{-43}) \le x \le (1-2^{-43})$

Arithmetic Unit

Add time (including storage access): 864
  microsec (min 192 max 1536)

Multiply time (including storage access):
  2880 microsec (min 2208 max 3552)
Divide time (including storage access): 2930
  microsec (min 2256 max 3600)
Construction: Vacuum tubes and Diode gates
Number of rapid access word registers: 4
Basic pulse repetition rate: 1.0 megacycle/sec
Arithmetic mode: Serial

Storage

Media	Words	Microsec Access
Mercury Acoustic Delay Line	1024	48-384
Magnetic Drum	4608	17,000

Includes relay hunting and closure. The
  information tranfer to and from the drum is
  at one megacycle per second. The block
  length is optional from 1 to 384 words per
  transfer instructions.

Input

Media		Speed
Photoelectric Tape Reader	942	sexadec char/sec
	78	words/sec
Card Reader (IBM)	15	rows/sec
	100	cards/min

Output

Media		Speed
Paper Tape Perf.	6	sexadecimal char/sec
	30	words/min
Teletypewriter	6	sexadecimal char/sec
	30	words/min
Card Punch (IBM)	100	cards/min
	800	words/min

The Moore School course provided a forum for those who hoped to initiate their own computer projects. Indeed, this course was of singular importance in providing critical information to many academic, commercial, and governmental organizations in the United States and Great Britain. Influenced by lectures given during the course, Maurice Wilkes of Cambridge University built the EDSAC, the first fully operational stored-program computer and the National Bureau of Standards later developed its own computers.[22]

The Moore School's willingness to foster development in this area was particularly significant in light of a serious lack of communication among institutions with regard to computing devices.[23] During the war, security classifications were primarily responsible for this communication gap. After the war, however, the problem remained, perhaps the result of the predilection of engineers to protect their patents by not publicizing their work. Another

---

Number of Circuit Elements

Tubes:	3563
Tubes types:	19
Crystal diodes:	8000
Magnetic elements:	1325 (relays, coils and trans)
Capacitors:	5500 approx.
Resistors:	12000 approx.
Neons:	320 approx.

Checking Features

Fixed Comparison—Two arithmetic units perform computation simultaneously. Discrepancies halt machine.
Paper tape reader error detection.

Physical Factors

Power consumption: Computer,	50 kW
Space occupied: Computer,	490 sq. ft.
Total weight: Computer,	17,300 lbs.
Power consumption: Air Cond.,	25 kW
Space occupied: Air. Cond.,	6 sq. ft.
Total weight: Air Cond.,	4345 lbs.
Capacity: Air Cond.,	20 tons

Manufacturing Record

Number produced: 1
Number in current operation: 1

Cost

Rental rates for additional equipment:
IBM card reader $82.50
IBM card punch $77.00
Approximate cost of basic system: $467,000

Personnel Requirements

Daily Operation: 3 8-hr shifts. No. of Tech: 8.
7 days/week
No engineers are assigned to operation of the computer, but are used for design and development of improvements for the computer. The technicians consult with engineers when a total breakdown occurs.

Reliability and Operating Experience

Average error free running period: 8 hours
Operation ratio: 0.79. Good time: 130.5 hrs.
(Figures for '55) Attempted to run: 166 hrs./wk.
No. of different kinds of plug-in units: 3
No. of separate cabinets (excluding power and air cond.): 12
Operating ratio figures for 1954:
Operating ratio: 0.79. Good time: 129 hrs.
Attempted to run: 163 hrs./wk.

Additional Features and Remarks

Oscilloscope and neon indicator for viewing contents of any storage location at any time.
Exceed capacity options: halt, ignore, transfer control, or go to selected location.
Unused instruction (command) halt
Storage of previously executed instruction and which storage location it came from, for viewing during code checking.
Storage of current instruction and storage location from which it originated.
Address halt when prescribed address appears in any of 4 addresses of instruction to be executed by computer.
Tape reader error detection.

reason for this problem was a scarcity of appropriate communication vehicles, such as journals specializing in the field of computing, for disseminating information. The Moore School lectures in 1946 provided such a vehicle and established a tradition of computer conferences that continued for several decades and is indeed still the prevailing method for publicizing developments in technology.

Eckert and Mauchly's conflict with the academic community did not end with their departure from the Moore School. They remained competitors of the University of Pennsylvania and the Institute for Advanced Study for several years, vying for recognition, priority, and governmental support. Although the patent issue that gave rise to the initial Moore School conflict was settled for the ENIAC in 1945, the question of who was to hold the patent on the EDVAC or its components was still unresolved when the two men left the Moore School. It remained a major concern of all parties for over a year, until it was finally resolved on April 8, 1947.

Von Neumann submitted his controversial "First Draft of a Report on the EDVAC" to the Legal Branch of the Army Ordnance Department as a patent disclosure in April 1946.[24] An assistant of Irven Travis, Jules Warshaw, documented this fact in 1947:

In building up historical background, I found that the first attempt by von Neumann to claim any patents on the EDVAC was on 22 March, 1946 when Drs. von Neumann and Goldstine had a spur of the moment meeting with Mr. Woodward and Mr. Stevens of the Legal Branch in the Pentagon Building. Dr. von Neumann inquired as to the patent situation and mentioned that he thought he had some patent rights. He was asked to file an Army War Patent Form and to submit any disclosures he might have. He returned the form and submitted as his patent disclosure his report entitled "First Draft of a Report on the EDVAC" dated 30 June 1945.[25]

This disclosure incensed Eckert and Mauchly, who believed that they were sole inventors of the EDVAC and were therefore entitled to the patent.

In addition, this patent controversy over the EDVAC once again jeopardized the Moore School's ability to fulfill its contractual obligations. As in the case of the ENIAC, the Moore School had agreed to grant the government a license-free right to use the EDVAC; until the patent matter was resolved, the Moore School could not legally grant this license-free right. In his Moore School report, Warshaw pointed out that he had informed the Patent Office "that Dr. Pender had become concerned as to our contract obligations concerning the patent situation and was therefore anxious to get acquainted with the facts to date and see what could be done to straighten the matter out."[26]

It remained for the Legal Branch of the Army Ordnance Department to decide on the validity of the von Neumann and Eckert-Mauchly patent claims. The situation became acute in the spring of 1947. First, Goldstine, and presumably von Neumann as well, came to regard the Legal Branch as partial to Eckert and Mauchly—an opinion that was shared by the University of Pennsylvania. Warshaw reported that "Dr. Goldstine had recently accused the Patent Branch of favoring Eckert and Mauchly . . . While the Patent people denied this accusation, it became apparent that they were indeed very strongly on the side of Eckert and Mauchly."[27]

In a communication from the Office of the Chief of Ordnance (OCO) to Herman Goldstine the government responded to these allegations: "The attitude of the Ordnance Department in this matter is not so much that of arbiter as it is one of desiring to assist in the resolution of any differences which may exist between the parties concerned over right and title to the various patents involved."[28]

To settle the question of priority and patent rights, the OCO arranged a meeting for April 3, 1947, at the University of Pennsylvania, where Eckert and Mauchly, von Neumann, and the Moore School would be represented. It was hoped that an equitable agreement among the parties might be reached at this meeting: "Since the government has a right to the use of the patents, it is naturally concerned that the patents be filed at an early date in order to reduce to a minimum the possibility of being put to the expense of establishing its right in connection with the patents should some party other than those presently involved file patents which would infringe on those with which we are now concerned."[29]

At the meeting, representatives of the Legal Department of OCO pointed out that one may apply for a patent on an innovation only if that innovation has been operational for one year or less. Moreover, the attorneys for OCO held that because von Neumann's draft report of June 1945 was widely distributed, it constituted, in the legal sense, a formal document. Its status as a formal publication, written almost two years prior to the April 1947 meeting, meant that the critical date for filing a patent had long since passed. The OCO's patent attorney told von Neumann at the meeting that "it is our firm belief from the facts that we have now that this report of yours dated 30 June 1945 is a publication and will prohibit you or anyone else from obtaining a patent on anything that it discloses because it has been published more than a year ago and a statute provides that if you don't file disclosures within a year it constitutes a bar to patenting that device."[30] Hence all ideas relating to EDVAC-type machines contained in the report were placed in the public domain.

Had von Neumann's draft report been considered an informal memorandum, patenting of the EDVAC would have been feasible and a bitter patent fight would have ensued. The OCO's legal department thus was instrumental in resolving some of the issues relating to the patenting of the EDVAC concepts. But all the EDVAC concepts were not included in the draft report. Those concepts not published in the report were still patentable.

The meeting continued with some acrimonious exchanges between von Neumann and Eckert and Mauchly. Then, in an effort to sort out any claims not relating to ideas presented in the draft report, the two parties were asked to share their disclosures with each other. Von Neumann indicated that he

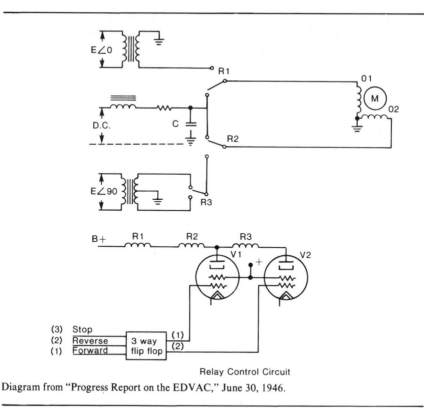

Relay Control Circuit

Diagram from "Progress Report on the EDVAC," June 30, 1946.

would not be filing any further disclosures. Eckert and Mauchly finally agreed to *consider* showing their disclosures to von Neumann, although they never did, and the meeting was adjourned with the agreement that no patents would be filed.[31]

The bitter controversy over the EDVAC points to the conflicting standards that affect engineers and scientists working at academic institutions. A noted sociologist of science, Jerome Ravetz, suggests that this situation is not confined to the specific projects under consideration here but is a direct outgrowth of the new research and development industry itself:

Although this new industry of "R. and D." employs many scientists (indeed, the bulk of graduates in science and technology go there rather than into teaching or university research), its working ethics are descended from industry, private and state-supported, rather than from academic science. In America, the enormous defense and aerospace industries carry on in the time-honored tradition of "boondoggling" on Government funds; the most effective path to super profits being to keep the relevant Government agencies for cost-accounting and quality-control either remote, weak or complaisant.[32]

Von Neumann's role in this entire matter is particularly interesting. His stated commitment to traditional academic values apparently did not stand in the way of his application for a patent. Many of his associates, especially Goldstine, have since claimed that his real motive was to patent the ideas so that they could be placed in the public domain. In his history of the computer, Goldstine indicated that "the placing of the EDVAC report in the public domain was very satisfactory to both von Neumann and me."[33]

But von Neumann's previous efforts to establish priority in the computing field seem to suggest that recognition and priority were very important to him. Indeed, in a later passage in his book, Goldstine expresses doubt about the wisdom of placing computer concepts in the public domain:

In looking back I am convinced that neither the University of Pennsylvania nor the Institute for Advanced Study received the credits which were their due . . . it was probably unwise from the Institute's point of view for us to put our basic ideas into the public domain instead of obtaining patents covering them. What is free is perhaps only very nominally valued by the world.[34]

The EDVAC patent controversy demonstrates that academic institutions and academics themselves were subject to the same sorts of patent fights and priority claims as were prevalent in industrial organizations. Although the Moore School staff and John von Neumann were not entirely influenced by the profit motive, in the commercial sense, their desire for recognition and government support resulted in the same sorts of conflicts that characterize business organizations.

Quest for Contracts

The immediate concern of Eckert and Mauchly in 1946 was to obtain sufficient support to form a company. They looked to the government for that support. In time, the National Bureau of Standards (NBS) became their main source of funding and a prime mover in facilitating the transfer of computer technology from the Moore School to other organizations.

Actually there were two governmental agencies that had a great impact on electronic digital computer development during this period. In addition to the National Bureau of Standards, the Office of Naval Research (ONR) was a major funding agency. Staffed with many scientists and engineers, ONR was the first to commit itself to the support of a wide range of basic research efforts, including several computer projects. Later, it served as a model for the National Science Foundation.[35]

The Whirlwind project at MIT and Howard Aiken's Mark III at Harvard were both funded primarily with ONR resources. The lectures given at the Moore School in the summer of 1946 were funded in part by ONR, which was interested in facilitating the transfer of technology as well as in supporting basic research.[36]

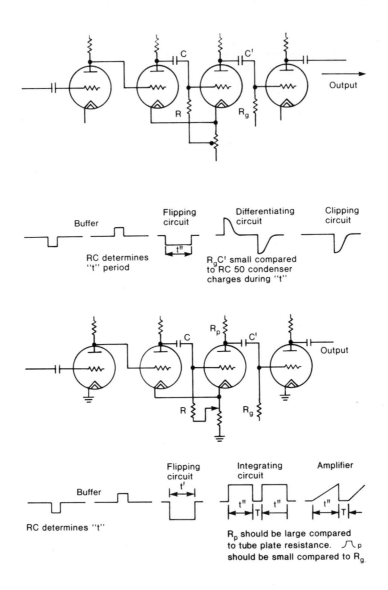

Diagrams from "Progress Report on the EDVAC," June 30, 1946.

The National Bureau of Standards

The National Bureau of Standards had an even more direct and substantive influence on electronic digital computers generally and on the Eckert-Mauchly organization specifically. It functioned not only as a funding agency but also as an institution that provided directives, guidelines, and a computer research and development program of its own. This support was singularly effective in sustaining the growth of computer technology during the postwar period.

The NBS was established in 1901 as an agency of the Commerce Department to give aid to "manufacturing, commerce, the makers of scientific apparatus, the scientific work of the government, of schools, colleges and universities."[37] Its primary functions were directly analogous to those of the National Physical Laboratory in England.

From the outset, the bureau's influence as a regulatory, advisory, and even research agency was significant, but its influence declined substantially during the Depression, when its funds were drastically cut.[38] In the 1940s the bureau's advisory role was again expanded. During the war years the bureau served as a central agency for research and development, despite the opposition of Vannevar Bush, director of the Office of Scientific Research and Development, to expansion of its activities. When "legislation to strengthen basic research at the Bureau" won Secretary of Commerce Henry Wallace's approval, Bush "demurred . . . He wanted no fundamental research for science or industry carried out at the bureau except in the field of metrology."[39] Bush's attitude here once again points to the tendency of his organization to favor large, well established academic and industrial organizations as opposed to smaller institutions or government agencies.

In 1945 Edward Uhler Condon, a distinguished theoretical physicist with strong ties to both the academic and industrial sectors, was named director of NBS. He "was the first director of the National Bureau of Standards to be appointed from outside the Bureau's ranks, the first director to be recruited from industry, the first theoretical physicist to head the Bureau."[40] Condon's appointment, then, signaled a new era for the bureau, one in which basic research was to be strongly emphasized.

At the bureau, "Dr. Condon brought to an organization largely staffed with experimental physicists the new broom outlook of the theoretical physicist . . . As one who had made important contributions to pure science and at Westinghouse brought it to bear on industrial work, he was determined to advance pure science at the Bureau and to move the Bureau rapidly into the post-war period."[41] Moreover, Condon was eager to support new research projects and to encourage the work of young scientists. He was praised after his death for having concentrated his attention on good science at NBS and having "hired the next generation of scientific leadership."[42]

Although Condon was enthusiastic about supporting many different research projects and enhancing the relationship between science and government, he believed strongly that such support should be provided primarily for nonmilitary applications of science. In fact, Condon "described himself as unable to serve at Los Alamos because he felt so strongly that scientific research should not be conducted under military jurisdiction."[43]

Condon did, however, recognize the need for greater interaction among government, industry, and the universities. Like Henry Wallace, the secretary of commerce who had appointed him, he was particularly interested in providing support to small businesses.[44] In an interview in 1968, Condon contrasted his own attitude toward governmental support of science with those of "conservative businessmen types . . . like Vannevar Bush and Karl Compton . . . who looked down their nose at Henry Wallace, an extreme left wing New Dealer."[45]

From the very beginning of his tenure, then, Condon sought to provide a direction to the peacetime application of science, one which would be unrelated to atomic research and sympathetic to the interests of small businesses. Since funding for the bureau was problematic, Condon succeeded in drawing funds from other agencies:

With these, he strengthened sound, on-going activities and initiated new ones in mass spectroscopy and betatron studies, for example, and through the creation of new divisions, as in applied mathematics and electronics.[46]

In short, the research objectives of NBS made it an ideal organization for fostering the growth of electronic digital computers. Moreover, the concern for small businessmen and struggling young scientists expressed by Condon and his associates made the bureau an ideal agency for support of Eckert and Mauchly's organization.

NBS, the Census Bureau, and Eckert-Mauchly

The National Bureau of Standards became the major force behind Eckert and Mauchly's organization through another government agency, the Census Bureau. While still at the Moore School, Mauchly had approached the Census Bureau to see if it would be interested in funding the development of an electronic computer.[47] Since this agency was clearly in need of high-speed tabulating equipment, Mauchly thought that it might be an appropriate source of funds. Moreover, the Census Bureau had a long history of providing support for the development of computational equipment. In the late nineteenth century, Herman Hollerith and James Powers had been funded by the Census Bureau to build electromechanical tabulating devices. Mauchly, for his part, had a special interest in statistical applications of computers and was particularly eager to build machines for such purposes.[48]

Eckert and Mauchly's initial discussions with the Census Bureau were conducted on behalf of the Moore School. But after March 1946, negotiations were conducted on their own behalf, since they were no longer formally affiliated with the University of Pennsylvania.[49]

The Census Bureau, in a report to the General Accounting Office in 1957, provided the following account of its early interest in computers:

Shortly before the end of World War II we at Census were visited by Dr. John Mauchly and Mr. J. Presper Eckert who at that time were on the faculty of the University of Pennsylvania. They told us about the electronic computer—the ENIAC—they were building for the Army and suggested that similar but still more advanced equipment might prove valuable to us . . . From time to time, until the war was over, we met with Mauchly and Eckert to discuss Census problems. Once relieved of their war responsibilities, these men devoted much of their time to the research and design aspects of a general purpose data processor for our use. Also our attitude at Census changed from one of casual curiosity to serious interest.[50]

By the spring of 1946 the Census Bureau was definitely interested in Mauchly's proposal, but it could not directly fund such a project. For one thing, the bureau was not permitted to contract for products that were in the development stage; it could award contracts only for finished products. In addition, the bureau lacked a scientific or engineering staff capable of judging the technical feasibility of the proposed computer. Thus, on March 28, 1946, the Census Bureau met with the National Bureau of Standards and formally requested "two types of assistance from NBS: (a) an appraisal by experts in electronics of the practicality of the equipment Drs. Mauchly and Eckert indicated they can build, (b) assistance in writing specifications to be included in a contract for building such equipment if it is deemed advantageous to negotiate such a contract."[51]

Thus, despite Eckert and Mauchly's great achievement with the ENIAC, it became clear that they would encounter some difficulties with their commercial venture. As Mauchly indicated in an interview many years later:

Well I'm saying that we tried to get something with which we were comfortable, and we were uncomfortable, you might say, in the trying because it took time to do that even, and here we had to live a few more months you might say before we actually got all these things arranged. First of all, we thought in March that we could get the Census Bureau to make a contract directly with us, and we thought that we'd get business as a partnership. Wouldn't have to incorporate and rush into things, you might say, to get the contract. Then we found out that the Census Bureau couldn't give a contract for things that weren't already developed and that we got a promise that the mechanism would be to transfer the money to the Bureau of Standards that could enter into development contracts. That was just one little operation you know, somehow to transfer that money—in order to transfer it and at the same time not have the money expire at the end of the year; that is fiscal year June 30th, and have that money continue to be available for a contract that lasted more than a year. They had to do something which turned out to have a rider on some bill that went through Congress.[52]

Fortunately for Eckert and Mauchly, NBS was able to contract for research and development projects. Moreover, bolstered by its desire to serve as a national research center, it had both the technical expertise and the interest to provide such support. Since both NBS and the Census Bureau were under the jurisdiction of the Department of Commerce and had representatives on the department's science committee, a formal arrangement between the two agencies posed no organizational problems.[53]

During the next few months, several meetings were held in Washington and Philadelphia to consider a formal contract proposal with Eckert and Mauchly. John H. Curtiss, a mathematician and assistant director of NBS, was assigned the task of negotiating with Eckert and Mauchly on behalf of the Census Bureau.[54]

During this period, the Census Bureau's interest in the Eckert-Mauchly computer proposal was specifically related to its own tabulating needs. NBS's concerns, however, were of a more scientific and general nature. Administrators at NBS were eager to promote their organization's role in technological research. This meant funding engineering projects and developing its own laboratories for high-technology research. Moreover, Curtiss, like Mina Rees at ONR, was anxious to stimulate an interest in applied mathematics. He recognized that mathematicians would be needed to develop numerical methods to be used with the new computers and that the nascent computing field would promote an interest in applied mathematics.[55]

In short, NBS's willingness to engage in negotiations with Eckert and Mauchly on behalf of the Census Bureau was part of a wider program. Since large-scale industrial organizations were apparently unprepared to expend the funds necessary for further research and development in this area, the interest of these government agencies was critical in sustaining the growth of computers. Moreover, their willingness to support independent inventors who were not affiliated with major organizations served to foster and broaden development in this field. In one of the lectures given at the Moore School's course on "Theory and Techniques for Design of Electronic Digital Computers" in the summer of 1946, Curtiss himself emphasized the importance of the government's role in the transfer of computer technology:

In their current state of development, general purpose automatic digital machines of reasonably large capacity cost between $300,000 and $500,000 a piece. Few private organizations have the resources to invest in such an expensive gadget and indeed very few private organizations have computing requirements which would justify the investment. On the other hand numerical federal agencies have very extensive urgent requirements in mathematical computation and in related fields of applied mathematics and some of these agencies quite properly have substantial funds for developing machines to assist in meeting computational requirements.[56]

The UNIVAC Contract

In April 1946, $300,000 was transferred to the Census Bureau from the Army Ordnance Department for the development of a computer.[57] NBS proceeded cautiously, however, strictly adhering to bureaucratic formalities. But despite this caution, Eckert and Mauchly were optimistic that they would be awarded a contract.[58]

As was customary, before it would agree to let a contract, NBS employed a consultant to provide recommendations. George Stibitz was asked to report on the feasibility of the computer proposed by Eckert and Mauchly.[59] Stibitz—a mathematician, the inventor of the Bell Telephone Laboratories' relay computer, and a past member of the National Defense Research Committee—was certainly well qualified to judge the technical feasibility of Eckert and Mauchly's proposed computer and to suggest guidelines for contract negotiations. But in 1943 he had not been very impressed with the ENIAC project, which he had regarded as naive; in 1946 he was no more enthusiastic about Eckert and Mauchly's new venture. "I find it difficult to say much about the Mauchly-Eckert proposal," he wrote Curtiss in May. "There are so many things still undecided that I do not think a contract should be let for the whole job." He added, however, that "their suggestion seems promising enough to let a contract to study the problem, leading to a solid proposal and schematic."[60]

Although the tenor of Stibitz's report was conservative, if not entirely negative, NBS made a decision, as had the Army Ordnance Department regarding the ENIAC venture, to proceed. Here, again, a traditionally conservative government agency was willing, indeed eager, to support the young inventors, despite the caution expressed by a member of the scientific elite.

Stibitz suggested that the procurement of a computing machine should be divided into three stages. Curtiss, however, decided to negotiate in two stages, first for a research and study contract, and second for a development contract. Stibitz also suggested that bids be solicited from industrial organizations, as was the typical procedure for government contracts. J. C. Capt, director of the Census Bureau, feared that this procedure would favor large, well-established concerns that could bid more effectively than Eckert and Mauchly.[61]

Mindful of Capt's concern, Curtiss agreed to solicit bids from some major manufacturers, but few were forthcoming. Only the Hughes Tool Corporation and Raytheon Manufacturing Corporation expressed even an initial interest. Hughes and Raytheon had expertise in electronics as a result of their radar work during the war. In the end, only Raytheon submitted a bid, and it was significantly higher than the Eckert-Mauchly proposal.[62]

By June 1946 Curtiss had decided to award a study contract to Eckert and Mauchly. The two inventors then formed a partnership, called the Electronic Control Company. They leased the second and third floors of a building at 1215 Walnut Street in downtown Philadelphia and set out to acquire equipment and personnel. Within several months, the Electronic Control Company was staffed by a handful of professional people, including Al Auerbach, Isaac Auerbach (no relation), Herman Lukoff, Brad Sheppard, Gerry Smoliar, Frazier Welsh, John Sims, Bob Shaw, and Betty Snyder.[63]

NBS and the Electronic Control Company signed a contract on September 25, 1946, which was to become effective on October 7.[64] The contract called for a research and study project which would provide specifications and scale models of two mercury delay tubes for storage "complete with associated pulse shaping and regenerative circuits" and for one complete tape transport mechanism "with necessary drive motors" at a fixed fee of $75,000.[65] The original name for the device was "EDVAC-type machine"; this was formally changed on May 24, 1947, to UNIVAC, an acronym for Universal Automatic Computer.[66]

It was originally anticipated that the research and study phase would take six months, and after it received a speedy approval, the design phase would be completed in the following six months.[67] This schedule proved to be overly optimistic. The research and study phase itself took one year to complete. Moreover, it was not until June 25, 1948, that the actual design contract was executed at a fixed fee of $169,600.[68]

The Census Bureau, as noted, was prepared to spend $300,000 on the Eckert-Mauchly computer. This figure included $75,000 for the original study contract, $169,600 for the design contract, and a 15 percent overhead fee to be paid to NBS. Based on Eckert and Mauchly's own calculations in June 1946, the development cost was estimated to be $400,000. Despite their limited assets, the two men were willing to absorb the anticipated loss, because they believed that if they were successful, additional machines could be sold to both government and industry at substantial profits.[69]

In light of the state of the art in 1946 and their financial position, Eckert and Mauchly were more than optimistic, they were naive. Despite their technical expertise, their economic prospects were very limited. They had no real way of knowing how much time and money would be needed to construct a suitable memory or the magnetic-tape storage devices they were developing, since neither of these components had thus far been successfully completed. Moreover, despite the potential commercial market for such computers, industrial organizations had not yet expressed more than a passing interest in acquiring them. Eckert and Mauchly's willingness to make this attempt, despite the odds, and NBS's willingness to fund a company in such a precarious financial position, paved the way for further development in this area.

NBS and the National Research Council

The National Bureau of Standards' relationship with Eckert and Mauchly was only part of its burgeoning role in electronic digital computer development. In 1946 NBS provided technical support to the Office of Naval Research for the design and construction of another electronic digital computer. As it did for the Census machine, NBS sought bids from prominent electronics firms. After many months of negotiations, Raytheon, a large well-established firm, was granted the ONR contract on a cost-plus-fixed-fee basis, enabling it to make a profit or fixed fee above whatever the project costs came to be.[70] Eckert and Mauchly, with no experience in government contracting, settled for a fixed-fee arrangement that provided them with a set amount, which by their own estimates was well below cost. The advantage to a fixed-fee arrangement is that the company unquestionably retains the patents; but even with a cost-plus-fixed-fee contract, most companies are usually able to file for patents on their inventions as well. By 1950, Eckert and Mauchly realized their mistake: "We freely admit at this time that the contract should have been on a cost-plus-fixed-fee basis."[71]

In addition to its liaison role with ONR and Raytheon, NBS also began to establish its own computing facilities. In 1947 the National Applied Mathematics Laboratories of the National Bureau of Standards were established. They were to consist of four main operating branches: "The Institute for Numerical Analysis, to be located in California near a major university; and the Computation Laboratory, the Machine Development Laboratory and the Statistical Engineering Laboratory, all in Washington, D.C."[72]

In addition to undertaking the liaison role with ONR and Raytheon, the Bureau also began to establish computing facilities of its own. In 1947 the National Applied Mathematics Laboratories of the National Bureau of Standards were established. They were to consist of four main operating branches: "The Institute for Numerical Analysis, to be located in California near a major university; and the Computation Laboratory, the Machine Development Laboratory and the Statistical Engineering Laboratory, all in Washington, D.C."[72]

NBS sought to serve as contracting agent for other government-supported projects and to provide technical support as needed. Curtiss wrote Eckert and Mauchly in November 1946 about the bureau's plans "to ensure free exchange of technical and progress reports between itself and all its contractors in the machine computing field." In this connection, he stated, "the Scientific Officer has already taken steps to have the advantages of such interchanging of information brought to the attention of Army Ordnance and it is hoped that the Institute [for Advanced Study] and Moore School projects will be included in the information 'pool.'"[73]

gineers is necessary for the successful accomplishment of this task."[74] These efforts were directed at promoting NBS as the nation's leading computational center.

In the spring of 1947, NBS made still another effort designed, at least in part, to integrate major developments in this field and to further its own position as the nation's central computing agency. On April 24, 1947, at a meeting of the National Research Council (NRC), itself a subdivision of the prestigious National Academy of Sciences, Curtiss requested that a subcommittee be appointed to conduct an evaluation of the projects undertaken or being considered by NBS, namely, the UNIVAC, the Raytheon computer and the Moore School's EDVAC.[75] On August 11, 1947, the National Research Council agreed to appoint a subcommittee to conduct such an evaluation: "Since the Committee is an organ of the NRC and of the National Academy, and the Bureau of Standards is an organ of the U.S. government, it is an obligation of the committee to undertake such a task directly or indirectly if requested."[76]

A major reason for Curtiss's request was that many members of NRC were themselves key figures in the development of computers. These included Howard Aiken of Harvard; Samuel Caldwell of MIT; George Stibitz, formerly of Bell Labs; and John von Neumann at the Institute for Advanced Study, all of whom agreed to serve on the subcommittee, called Subcommittee Z on High-Speed Computing.[77] An evaluation of the bureau's study projects by men who were themselves actively engaged in building computers would ensure that the development work at NBS would be broadly based and would receive appropriate attention and publicity.[78]

In fact, the bureau hoped that the evaluation by this NRC subcommittee would contain valuable information on the technical features of Aiken's computers at Harvard, von Neumann's IAS computer, MIT's Whirlwind, and activities at the Bell Laboratories. Curtiss reported to the Electronic Control Company in October 1947:

It appears advisable to let you know exactly what arrangements have been made by the Bureau to secure the technical assessment of the NRC Committee on High Speed Computing on the evaluation of designs for electronic digital computing machines . . . Since the design evaluations will probably include the EDVAC, the IAS machine and the computer designed by the Servomechanism Lab at MIT, in addition to the UNIVAC and the Raytheon machine, it is obvious that the designs compared will have been aimed at different applications.[79]

To allay any fears regarding competition, Curtiss's letter added: "For this reason, it seems necessary, to be fair to the participants, to avoid carefully any advertisement of the evaluation of computer designs as a 'competition.'"

The National Research Council's subcommittee, however, interpreted its role rather narrowly. It focused on the evaluation of NBS projects only and chose *not* to supply any information on its own members' academic activities in this field, all of which were unclassified.[80] Unlike NBS, members of the NRC subcommittee were less sensitive to, or concerned with, the need for a free and open exchange of ideas. The evaluation, which was completed on March 9, 1948, and submitted to the bureau in a March 16 memorandum, included no mention whatever of the IAS, Harvard, or MIT projects. Years later, an NBS spokesman wrote:

In many regards, the NRC Committee evaluation of computer designs was unsatisfactory to the Bureau. For example, the NRC Committee considered only three designs, namely those of Eckert-Mauchly (the UNIVAC), the Raytheon Manufacturing Company and the Moore School of Electrical Engineering (EDVAC). The IAS computer, a project under the direction of Dr. von Neumann, Chairman of the Committee, was not mentioned. Neither was the Harvard machine compared with any of the designs studied by the Committee. The work on computer design under the Whirlwind Project, an immense and costly undertaking, was disregarded also.[81]

The failure of the subcommittee members to provide a formal comparison of the bureau's projects with their own ventures is particularly significant in view of their backgrounds. These men, as gatekeepers and scientists of enormous prestige, would be expected to adhere to the professional norm in science which encourages the free exchange of information and ideas. The absence of any comparative analysis in their study suggests not only a possible effort on their part to inhibit the exchange of ideas but also a belief that academic ventures were simply not comparable to commercial ones, despite the seeming similarity of the design efforts.

The NRC evaluation was a disappointment for other reasons as well. It failed to provide even an adequate analysis of the technical features of the machines under evaluation. After studying the descriptions of the three proposed machines provided by Eckert and Mauchly's Electronic Control Company, the Moore School, and Raytheon, the subcommittee decided that:

a detailed technical discussion of these reports at this place is not what is primarily called for . . . since the mathematical and logical bases for machines in the speed and capacity range involved have already been extensively discussed in technical meetings and in the generally accessible literature . . . a considerable body of reasonably homogeneous scientific and technical "public opinion" on many of the major questions that are involved is already in existence.[82]

The underlying message of the NRC report was that the three machines did not merit an extensive technical analysis since the design principles were part of the standard literature. Considering the wide range of discussions and disagreements that prevailed in the postwar period over such topics as parallel versus serial operation, binary versus decimal arithmetic, and electrostatic versus mercury-delay-line memory, the consensus implied by the report was rather surprising. Moreover, the focus of Eckert and Mauchly on high-speed input-output equipment such as magnetic-tape devices, was completely ignored by the group. The members of the subcommittee either failed to see the significance of this equipment for commercial users or regarded it as technically unimportant.

The NRC report denied, in a sense, the value of the three projects by claiming that they were all essentially the same:

The three machine plans differ from each other in many details, in particular regarding certain important characteristics of the codes used, the arithmetic system and operational procedures used, the methods of checking, etc. It seems nevertheless that in the basic principles that control these arrangements they have a great deal in common. The members of the subcommittee are unanimous in their opinion that these divergences are not of primary importance . . . It would therefore seem that these three proposals do not represent three really different and independent intellectual risks but that all are predicated on essentially the same estimation of what the most promising engineering approach is . . . In view of these facts it appears to the subcommittee that a choice between the three proposal reports on a primarily technical basis is hardly possible.[83]

Reactions to the NRC Report

The bureau was highly disappointed with the tenor and the contents of the overall evaluation. The suggestion that the projects were fundamentally the same was publicly refuted a year later in a report prepared by Curtiss's assistant, Edward Cannon. "From the standpoint of the machine designs," Cannon stated, "the Raytheon is a 'mathematician's' machine and the UNIVAC is a 'businessman's' machine."[84] His comment implied that the Raytheon machine focused on improving high-speed processing components whereas the UNIVAC focused on high-speed input-output for business operations.

A historical report written by NBS years later sums up the general dissatisfaction with the NRC evaluation:

Again the Committee disregarded the very things concerning which the Bureau had hoped to obtain advice, for example, arithmetic systems, operational procedures, methods of checking, etc. The committee report was confined to a phase of the Bureau's program, namely, engineering features and soundness of designs which the Bureau had believed that its electronics engineers and those of the companies preparing the design were competent to evaluate without assistance . . . Thus it is seen that the NRC committee evaluation was not relevant to the question of the mathematical sufficiency of design proposals.[85]

Furthermore, the NRC subcommittee took more than eight months to prepare its report. This seriously delayed the progress of the projects under consideration since Eckert and Mauchly, as well as Raytheon, awaited the assessment of von Neumann, Stibitz, and Aiken in the hope of receiving some valuable design recommendations.

The reaction of the NRC members to Eckert and Mauchly's work points once again to an attitude on the part of the scientific and technological elite toward the two men; this attitude pervades the subcommittee's entire study. Many of the NRC subcommittee members were biased against commercial ventures, believing that they made less of an intellectual contribution and therefore were of less significance than academic projects. Moreover, there seemed to be a specific hostility directed at Eckert and Mauchly that began really in 1943 when the National Defense Research Committee evaluated the initial ENIAC proposal. As previously indicated, this negativism seemed to be initiated by members of the scientific elite who regarded the Moore School group headed by Eckert and Mauchly as naive and unsophisticated. Whether consciously or unconsciously, these men were evaluating Eckert and Mauchly on the basis of their own work or that of their associates.

Caldwell, for example, even while serving on NDRC, was highly critical of the ENIAC venture, regarding it as a poor investment compared to the MIT computer projects. Undoubtedly, he compared the UNIVAC project three years later to Whirlwind, which was being developed during that time at MIT. Stibitz was similarly critical of the ENIAC when he served on the NDRC. His relay computers, built for Bell Telephone Laboratories during the war, were direct competitors of the Moore School computers, both vying for Army Ordnance and Ballistics Research Laboratories' support. Von Neumann, chairman of the NRC subcommittee, was particularly unsympathetic to Eckert and Mauchly. He had previously acknowledged to many of his associates that he regarded the commercial interests of these two men as unprofessional and their inventions as directly competitive with his own. Moreover, the bitter patent fight that ensued in 1947 heightened the intensity of von Neumann's reaction to the two men.

Aiken never seemed to be unsympathetic to Eckert and Mauchly specifically, despite his own work in the computing field. Rather, his concern was more with the government agencies that funded this "foolishness with Eckert and Mauchly" than with the inventors themselves.[86] According to Cannon, Aiken had told Curtiss and himself

that we were . . . misleading not only the Govt agencies which had made money available for development of such equipment, but the general public in pursuing this course of trying to develop such equipment, giving the impression that this program could be justified . . . because he said there will never be enough problems, enough work for more than one or two of these computers . . . you two fellows ought to go back and change your program entirely, stop this . . . foolishness with Eckert and Mauchly.[87]

In summary, then, the National Research Council subcommittee consisted of notable academic scientists who were regarded as having a basic commitment to objectivity, academic freedom, and the dissemination of knowledge. These men, responsible for advising the government on research and development policy matters, were at best conservative and perhaps even somewhat biased in their overall approach. Their attitudes stood in sharp contrast to those of the traditionally conservative government agencies, such as NBS and ONR. Despite the stereotype image of these agencies' adherence to standardized and bureaucratic procedures, they were eager to explore new and broader areas of computer development and utilization. Thus, despite the NRC subcommittee report, NBS awarded a design contract to Eckert and Mauchly and to Raytheon as well.[88] In this way, the bureau was successful in effecting a transfer of technology to spheres other than the academic and brought about a rapid and more dramatic development process.

NBS's Relationship with Eckert and Mauchly

The National Bureau of Standards was farsighted and even courageous in its decision to support Eckert and Mauchly, but its staff remained cautious as well. Curtiss was particularly concerned about committing funds to a small company that could quite possibly become insolvent. According to Mauchly in 1948:

John Curtiss has stated that our financial position is what worries him the most. If he was sure that we were well financed, he would be disposed to give us more machine contracts. He is apparently afraid that we will go broke and the more orders he gives us, the worse it is for him if we fail.[89]

NBS was so concerned that it arranged a meeting with prospective commercial customers regarding the computer corporation's financial position; Eckert and Mauchly were expressly barred from this meeting.[90]

Because of the Electronic Control Company's precarious financial position and because of the delays encountered in obtaining reports, NBS also instituted a series of checkpoints with prescribed deadlines, so that rigid standards and appropriate controls could be maintained. The idea was a sensible one that in subsequent months helped to structure and organize the Eckert-Mauchly venture; it demonstrated the technical expertise of the bureau's staff as well.[91]

The method of payment for the design contract also created a problem. Eckert and Mauchly needed a major commitment of funds upon the signing of the contract in order to finance the development of the computer. Government agencies, however, usually pay only for a finished product. The bureau investigated the possibility of committing the entire amount immediately, but discovered that this was legally not feasible. Instead, NBS found it could, at best, make payments in stages. One of its representatives, Harry Huskey of the National Applied Mathematics Laboratories, wrote Mauchly in April 1948: "Our lawyers have come up with the answer that with our funds there is no way to make even an initial 20% down payment. In other words, our contract will have to be written in terms of payment after certain steps have been completed."[92]

Thus, after each checkpoint was completed and approved, Eckert and Mauchly would receive partial payment. The bureau's inability to provide a large sum of working capital, combined with the delays encountered in obtaining contracts and payments, remained serious problems for the Electronic Control Company. Thus, despite its good intentions, NBS had to adhere to bureaucratic regulations that in some ways inhibited the progress Eckert and Mauchly were able to make.

To help alleviate the financial burdens of the Electronic Control Company, NBS encouraged other government agencies to consider purchasing a UNIVAC. Here, again, the bureau was eager to assist Eckert and Mauchly but was also hoping to expand its role as a national computing center. The Air Comptroller's Office at Wright Field agreed to release $400,000 to the bureau for computational equipment. In addition, the Army Map Service, which performs extensive computational work in converting survey information to standard map coordinates, asked NBS to serve as liaison in negotiations with Eckert and Mauchly for purchase of a UNIVAC. Other government agencies were also beginning to express an interest in the computer.[93]

Although the NRC subcommittee report had no apparent effect on the bureau's plans to purchase a UNIVAC for the Census Bureau except perhaps to delay them, the report did adversely affect these other orders. After March 1948 the Air Comptroller's Office, the Army Map Service, and several other agencies decided to proceed very cautiously. "There will be some delay involved in committing our National Defense funds," Huskey wrote Mauchly in April, "so we propose to write a contract for one UNIVAC [Census Bureau] with options for two more."[94]

When Mauchly asked for an explanation of this shift in policy, he was told that the NRC report was in part responsible. He dictated a memorandum in May 1948 summarizing events pertaining to a meeting with NBS representatives that spring:

In conversation immediately following this meeting, Huskey and Cannon inquired if we were not disturbed by the fact that they were now intending to order only one machine rather than three. I said that I was much interested in knowing what had happened to cause this change. They did not explain fully but merely said that Curtiss had been somewhat hasty in informing us that they would contract for three machines . . . We tried to discover what was back of the switch from three machines to one, and were told that so far as the Bureau was concerned, they would still like to place an order for three machines, but that they had instructions from Wright Field which prevented them from doing this . . . Col. Maier (at Wright Field) said that they had been affected by the report of von Neumann and the advice of von Neumann and Bartky that these machines were still in an experimental stage.

But Mauchly was not convinced that this was the main reason for the policy change. His memorandum further noted that "Col. Maier also said that there were other elements affecting their policy which he would not care to discuss over the telephone."[95]

As if the financial burdens of the Electronic Control Company and the hostility of important technical advisors to the government were not enough, Eckert and Mauchly had to face a security clearance problem as well. The minutes of a meeting on April 7, 1948, of the Department of Commerce's Committee on Use of Mechanical Equipment recorded:

On April 6 Dr. Curtiss of the National Bureau of Standards conveyed the following to us by telephone: A unit of the Navy recently considered contracting with the Eckert-Mauchly Company for some electronic equipment other than a UNIVAC. This unit required a security investigation and report on the Eckert-Mauchly Computer Corporation [formerly, Electronic Control Company]. On the basis of the report it was decided not to contract with Eckert-Mauchly for the equipment.[96]

At a time when the politics of scientists were under close scrutiny and any questionable prior associations created suspicion, several employees, including Mauchly himself, were found to have had some political connections that were deemed a threat to national security. Mauchly had attended a prewar meeting of an organization that, unknown to him, had a Communist affiliation. In addition, several members of the Electronic Control Company were accused of Communist leanings or alleged associations with Communists. Mauchly was asked, for example, whether he knew that one employee's college roommate was "a card-carrying Communist."[97]

The Eckert-Mauchly security matter was eventually resolved and their security clearance reinstated, but not without a loss of valuable time and potential sales. Several government agencies initially interested in a UNIVAC, for example the NEPA (Nuclear Energy Powered Aircraft) group at Oak Ridge, decided to support other projects instead.[98]

Thus, during the entire period between the signing of the NBS study contract in 1946 and the awarding of the design contract in 1948, the two entrepreneurs received only $75,000 from the government. Mauchly commented at the end of March 1948, "our largest problems are at present not technical ones but rather the securing of adequate capital so as to assure the government as well as others that we can carry out the contracts which we make."[99] The $75,000 was far short of the $400,000 he and Eckert had estimated for UNIVAC development costs, and it forced them to seek additional contracts in the private sector.

To overcome their lack of working capital, they had signed a contract with the Northrop Aircraft Company in October 1947 for the design and construction of a small mathematical computer called BINAC, an acronym for Binary Automatic Computer, which will be discussed in more detail in the following chapter.

In December 1948, in an effort to attract investors, Eckert and Mauchly incorporated, forming the Eckert-Mauchly Computer Corporation. Mauchly became president and served as the entrepreneur, seeking additional contracts and funding. He acted as liaison with other organizations. Although he took part in discussions on technical matters, he frequently subordinated his opinion to those staff members whom he deemed technically more competent. Eckert became vice president. He served as chief engineer and remained essentially behind the scenes.[100]

Eckert and Mauchly, but Mauchly particularly, showed considerable foresight in recognizing and promoting the commercial potential of these devices in the immediate postwar years. It was this vision, combined with Mauchly's enterprising attributes, which served to broaden the scope of computers from devices with scientific applicability to devices with far greater utility.[101]

6 The BINAC: A Controversial Milestone

By 1947 numerous computer projects had been undertaken in the United States.[1] At the Harvard Computation Laboratory, the electromechanical Mark II, the second Sequence Controlled Calculator, was being tested under the direction of Howard Aiken. The Harvard group was also beginning work on the Mark III, an electronic device. Bell Telephone Laboratories, which had built several models of computers under government contracts, remained in the forefront of relay computer development. IBM was preparing to announce its Selective Sequence Electronic Calculator, which was really a combined electromechanical-electronic device. It was not a stored-program machine, but one for which instructions were entered on paper tape.

In addition to the electromechanical work, several electronic digital computer projects were underway by 1947. The Moore School's EDVAC project was still in its early developmental stages, as was John von Neumann's Institute for Advanced Study computer. The former, funded by the Army Ordnance Department, was to be a serial-transmission machine with delay-line storage. The latter, funded jointly by RCA and the United States Army and Navy, was to be a parallel-transmission machine. It was initially designed to use a Selectron tube storage device invented by RCA, but eventually was redesigned to use the Williams electrostatic storage tube.

Project Whirlwind, undertaken at MIT, was another academic electronic computing project. Whirlwind was originally intended to be an analog device, but in 1945 its designers recognized the decided advantages of digital computation and shifted their approach. This project was supported by funding from the Special Devices Center of the Office of Naval Research.[2]

In addition to Eckert and Mauchly's company, two other commercial organizations had begun computer projects. The Raytheon Manufacturing Company was developing a mercury-delay-line electronic digital computer with a magnetic tape recorder also for the Special Devices Center of the Office of Naval Research. Engineering Research Associates of St. Paul, Min-

116

nesota, an organization formed in 1946, was designing a computer with magnetic drum memory for cryptological purposes. This project was also funded by the Navy.[3]

In England, Colossus had been built and was in operation deciphering codes during the war. By 1947 several additional projects like those at Manchester University, Cambridge University, and the National Physical Laboratory in Teddington centered on computers.[4]

The BINAC

One of the most difficult periods for Eckert and Mauchly's company was the transition from the signing of the NBS study contract in 1946 to the awarding of the actual design contract in 1948. During this period, the funds received from the government totaled $75,000, which was simply not enough to enable Eckert and Mauchly to develop a computer. During this transitional period, therefore, the two men signed a contract with the Northrop Aircraft Company of Hawthorne, California, for a small-scale computer called the BINAC, an acronym for Binary Automatic Computer. This machine subsequently became the first stored-program electronic digital computer completed in the United States.* It also provided Eckert and Mauchly with some of the funding necessary to sustain their company.

In 1947 Northrop was working on a classified project for the Air Force at Wright Field. The project called for development of the "Snark," a long-range guided missile.[5] To meet its contractual obligations, Northrop needed a machine to provide in-flight navigational control of the missile. On April 8, Northrop hired Mauchly as a consultant to determine whether electronic digital equipment could be adapted to satisfy its needs.[6] By June 25, Northrop was sufficiently convinced of the feasibility and desirability of such equipment (based on Mauchly's recommendations) to enter into negotiations with the Electronic Control Company for the design and construction of a scientific computer. Although the BINAC was a general-purpose machine that could be used for a wide variety of problems, Northrop had a very specific application in mind:

The experimental computer is needed in order to prove the feasibility of a particular method of navigation. It should be less than 20 cubic feet, in volume, and weigh 700 lbs. or less, and be capable of operating from 117 volts, 60 or 400 cycles. Ultimately,

---

*The first practical stored-program electronic digital computer, the EDSAC, built at Cambridge University under the direction of Maurice Wilkes, was completed in the spring of 1949, several months before the BINAC. Another English computer, the Manchester Mark I, a small experimental machine with electrostatic storage, also began operating in the spring of 1949. See Randell, ed., *The Origins of Digital Computers,* p. 353, and Lavington, *Early British Computers,* chapters 6 and 7.

The BINAC in "operating position"; one of the two mercury memory units is at the far left.
Courtesy Sperry-Univac Archives, Blue Bell, Pennsylvania.

a compact, airborne computer will be wanted. Please submit a quotation or quotations on the cost of developing an experimental computer which will accomplish the aims outlined in this letter.[7]

Although a "compact, airborne computer" was desired, this phrase was not included in the final contract.[8] It was Eckert and Mauchly's intention to build the BINAC according to the precise specifications outlined by Northrop but at the same time to have the machine serve as a prototype for the larger, general-purpose UNIVAC.

The contract for the BINAC was let on October 9, 1947. The machine was to be completed by May 15, 1948, for a total cost of $100,000, of which $80,000 was to be paid immediately and $20,000 upon completion.[9] The immediate payment provided Eckert and Mauchly with the working capital necessary to sustain their organization. Unlike government agencies required by law to adhere to rigid financial arrangements, Northrop as a private company was at liberty to make whatever contractual arrangements it deemed appropriate.

Technical Features

The BINAC, as designed, had a capacity of 512 words, each consisting of 31 binary digits. Like the proposed EDVAC, it utilized mercury delay lines for storage and used a series of separate delay lines, or channels, in the same tank of mercury. The BINAC had two processing units, each with 700 vacuum tubes—a significant improvement over the 18,000 tubes used in the ENIAC. The BINAC was capable of performing 3,500 additions or subtractions or 1,000 multiplications or divisions per second. All operations were performed in the binary number system and displayed in octal notation. There was no provision, as in the UNIVAC, for representation of alphabetic characters. This made the computer more suitable for scientific applications than commerical ones.

The BINAC was designed to be small enough to fit into an airplane. The final dimensions of each of the two arithmetic and control units was five feet by four feet by one foot.[10] The other units included:[11]

2 mercury tank memories, each	2'6" × 3' × 3'6"
2 power supplies, each	1'6" × 1'6" × 4'
1 input converter unit	2'6" × 2'6" × 3'6"
1 input console	3' × 2' × 3'

In addition to its small size, the BINAC had two distinctive operational features. It was a stored-program computer, the first to be completed in the United States, and although it was designed for a special use, it was capable of solving numerous types of mathematical problems. It had arithmetic, data

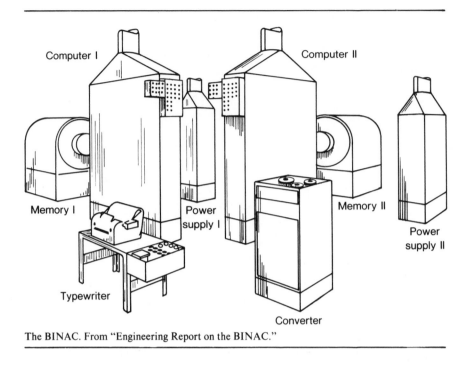

The BINAC. From "Engineering Report on the BINAC."

transfer, and logical control commands similar to other computers being built at that time.[12] Second, it was specifically designed to minimize the occurrence of computer errors. It incorporated two processing units, each capable of checking the other: "Actually twin computers, BINAC has duplicate arithmetic channels so that it can check itself at every step, and two mercury tube memories."[13] Thus, the BINAC was a pair of machines: it had dual storage, each with a 512-word capacity; two computing elements; and two control units. Each machine would perform a given calculation and then check the results against the other. If the results matched, the computer would continue executing; if they did not match, the computer would halt. Since the probability of both machines producing identically erroneous results was very small, the built-in duplication represented a relatively foolproof method of ensuring that the results were accurate.[14]

The input to the BINAC came from either a typewriter keyboard or an encoded magnetic tape. Similarly, output was produced either on a modified electric typewriter or on tape. The tape, similar to that used in tape recorders, was not very reliable and was later replaced on the UNIVAC with metallic tape plated with nickel. Even though the BINAC's tapes were somewhat unreliable, they represented a revolutionary first step in the use of magnetic tape as a high-speed input-output medium.

BINAC mercury memory unit. Courtesy Joseph Chapline.

As its name implies, the BINAC operated in the binary rather than the decimal system. Numbers were entered decimally but were converted to binary for processing. The output was displayed in the octal system, since conversion from binary to octal was considerably easier and faster than conversion from binary to decimal. The clock rate—the rate at which the simplest events in the computer happen—was originally to be 4.0 million pulses per second. This speed was found to be impractical, however, and the clock rate was reduced to 2.5 million pulses per second.[15]

Eckert and Mauchly had difficulty in meeting construction deadlines in this undertaking, as they did in their development of the UNIVAC. Although May 15, 1948, was the contracted date for completion, the BINAC was not operational until August 1949. It was formally accepted by Northrop on August 22, after a demonstration in Philadelphia during which the computer solved Poisson equations. In a little more than three hours, including some downtime, the BINAC obtained 26 solutions. For each solution, the computer performed in a period of approximately five minutes 500,000 additions, 200,000 multiplications, and 300,000 transfers of control.[16]

This demonstration also satisfied a requirement of NBS with respect to its

BINAC converter. Courtesy Joseph Chapline.

UNIVAC contract. Eckert and Mauchly had convinced NBS that since the BINAC contained many of the features to be included in the more comprehensive UNIVAC system, the former could be regarded as a prototype of the latter. The completion of the BINAC, then, satisfied a UNIVAC checkpoint and permitted Eckert and Mauchly to receive additional funds from NBS.

In the acceptance test, the BINAC was operational for seven hours and ten minutes, of which forty minutes was downtime for replacing or repairing components.[17] This performance was deemed adequate by both Northrop and NBS. The following month the computer was disassembled and shipped to Northrop's headquarters in Hawthorne, California.

Eckert and Mauchly flatly underestimated the cost of constructing the BINAC. As with the UNIVAC, the two men were unable to provide good cost estimates. Their business acumen failed to match their considerable technological know-how. Building computers with development costs far in excess of the actual purchase price was a major factor leading to the eventual insolvency of the Eckert-Mauchly Computer Corporation in 1950.[18]

The final construction costs of the BINAC were $278,000; the contracted price was $100,000.[19] Whereas large, well-established corporations can afford to absorb such losses during the first few years of a major research and development project, small companies cannot. Efforts to renegotiate the contract with Northrop, both before and after the BINAC was completed, proved fruitless. Although the government representatives at Wright Field were "duly sympathetic, they protested that procurement regulations prevented the granting of relief in this matter and that they would advise carrying this sum as unreimbursable development to be written off against future contracts."[20] As in the case with the UNIVAC contract, the government's regulations inhibited its ability to assist the nascent company, now called the Eckert-Mauchly Computer Corporation (EMCC).

That larger, well-established companies were capable of absorbing such losses can be seen from Northrop's own situation relative to the government. Mauchly, in an interoffice memorandum dated December 7, 1949, observed that this "attempt to secure price adjustment appears to be further complicated by Northrop's own predicament." Under another contract, Northrop apparently "engaged to build 23 aircraft of an experimental nature" and took "a loss of several million dollars on the fixed price of this contract."[21]

Both the EDSAC, or Electronic Delay Storage Automatic Calculator, and the BINAC belong to the class of "EDVAC-type" machines. Both were serial computers that utilized mercury-delay-line memories of 512 words, with data represented in binary form. Both machines were begun in 1947, the EDSAC under the direction of Maurice V. Wilkes at the Cambridge University Mathematical Laboratory. The EDSAC executed its first program in May 1949, three months before the BINAC, and was demonstrated to the public the following month. Unlike the BINAC, which was shipped from Philadelphia to California, the EDSAC was never moved. It was used for computing services at Cambridge University until July 1958.[22]

Assessing the BINAC

Controversy still surrounds the BINAC. Was it ever a fully operational computer? How did it affect the development of the UNIVAC, undertaken during the same period? Since the BINAC was the first stored-program computer completed in the United States, these questions are not insignificant ones.[23]

The work of Eckert and Mauchly and their associates on the BINAC is difficult to assess. They contracted to build the machine in eight months; it required, in fact, fifteen additional months to complete. In December 1948 Richard Baker of the Northrop Company came to Philadelphia to learn about and report on the progress being made. He stayed eight months and sent periodic letters to Frank Bell, project engineer at Northrop, citing major technical problems. The following composite, from reports written during May and June 1949, is characteristic of the Baker-Bell correspondence:

The computers require many small changes to be complete. Both memory units are unreliable . . . Memories [are] working very unsatisfactorily . . . BINAC operated as completed machine about one hour during week but very poorly. Cheaper crystal diodes substituted by Eckert-Mauchly (for economy apparently). Economizing and poor workmanship indicated.[24]

In the end, Northrop accepted the computer and acknowledged that the work performed by EMCC was satisfactory: "Eckert and Mauchly are sadly in default in the matter of their BINAC contract with us having run past their contract date for delivery by more than a year now," Frank Bell reported to Edward Cannon of the National Applied Mathematics Laboratories in July 1949. "Nevertheless," Bell added, "their work has been satisfactory to us, though the calendar schedule has not."[25]

The device was delivered in September 1949, and the following month Northrop paid EMCC the remaining $20,000 of the $100,000 contract. Bell even stated that "the BINAC actually does *exceed* [emphasis added] the specified requirements of the contract in a very considerable measure."[26] But official documents from Northrop indicate that the company's top management was extremely dissatisfied with the workmanship of the computer. Based on first-hand experience with the device after it was delivered to California and reassembled, Northrop claimed that the BINAC's operational difficulties were "not simply a result of the deplorable condition of the BINAC as received" but were "also inherent in the unreliability and insensitivity of the machine in operation."[27] A report Northrop prepared five months after the BINAC's delivery in California noted twenty-eight serious deficiencies:

The following items refer specifically to redesign, replacements or work never completed in which the reliability of the BINAC was involved . . . New circuit never completed—old one operative but unreliable . . . Original circuit unsatisfactory. New circuit partly wired in but not finished or checked.[28]

The reasons for such dissatisfaction are diverse. On the one hand, the device was not constructed to sustain the effects of dismantling, crating, shipping, and reassembling. Byron Phelps, an IBM representative at the BINAC demonstration, stated that although "the covers were removed for our observation during demonstration, it was obvious from the haywire and components hung on the outside that much of it was not ready to be covered up. It did not present the appearance of a machine ready for delivery."[29]

BINAC input typewriter. Courtesy Joseph Chapline.

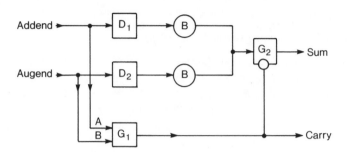

BINAC: half adder and complementer. From the Eckert-Mauchly Computer Corporation's "Engineering Report on the BINAC," 1949. Courtesy Joseph Chapline.

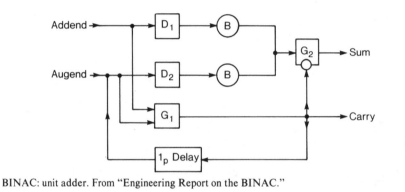

BINAC: unit adder. From "Engineering Report on the BINAC."

On the other hand, Northrop agreed to accept the BINAC in Philadelphia and to assume full responsibility for its crating and shipping. It is possible that Northrop's management did not realize the delicate nature of such a machine, particularly one with mercury-delay-line storage. Moreover, Northrop appeared to underestimate the time and technical expertise necessary to reassemble and restore the computer.[30]

As a result of the BINAC's difficulties, Northrop became increasingly dissatisfied with the device and made numerous requests of EMCC to reconstruct several parts.[31] Eckert and Mauchly, who had already received the balance of the $100,000, were facing insolvency and were focusing all of their technical attention and energies on completing the UNIVAC. They failed to meet many of Northrop's demands, not because of technical incompetence but because of a critical lack of funds. The BINAC, therefore, had a short and somewhat disappointing history in California. It never worked to the satisfaction of Northrop.

Northrop Engineers and the BINAC

Despite Northrop's initial acceptance of the BINAC, many of the company's engineers later claimed that after it was shipped, it never functioned at all. Richard Sprague, a Northrop engineer, recalled in 1972:

The BINAC was completed and tested in 1949 in Philadelphia. A demonstration and press conference was held during which the machine did perform the calculations. Dick Baker from MX775 computer group was nominated to take charge of BINAC when it was delivered to Northrop. It never did operate in California. The mercury had apparently deteriorated as had some other parts of the system. There are those who say it could not have been working properly in Philadelphia.[32]

Other Northrop engineers have been less critical of the BINAC, but the implication of technical deficiency has persisted.[33]

Some of the company's engineers, however, had personal reasons for their decided lack of enthusiasm for the BINAC. From the outset of the Northrop missile project, many of them had hoped to build their own computer and were disgruntled when the BINAC contract was announced. Don Eckdahl, one of the engineers, explained in 1972: "While we were doing this work of trying to develop the special-purpose computer as we saw it then for this guidance system, this other side of Northrop ended up contracting for the BINAC."[34]

In recent years, several Northrop engineers have attempted to set the record straight on BINAC's actual performance. Though the perspective of a participant may change over a period of thirty years, the retrospective view is certainly worthy of note. Jerry Mendelson, a Northrop engineer, responded to a 1979 article[35] that addressed this issue; he directly contradicted Sprague's statement quoted above:

First, I can state categorically that, contrary to what Dick Sprague stated . . . the BINAC did run successfully after it was installed in Hawthorne, California. I know this to be a fact because a colleague of mine named Bob Douthitt and I made two absolutely successful uninterrupted runs, each in excess of 25 minute duration, on one of the machines after it was finally brought into successful operation. These runs involved the exact bit-for-bit simulation of the Quadratic Arc Computer, a special-purpose computer Don Walter and I designed for the Snark Guidance System computations . . . We made two independent runs to ensure the validity of our results.[36]

Mendelson went on to describe the severe problems encountered when the BINAC was first delivered and the efforts required to make it operational:

What was not foreseen (this is my opinion, not absolute fact) was the miserable state of the equipment and its drawings when it was shipped. The two machines, which were supposed to be identical to each other and run in exact synchronism, had major differences in their components and wiring. Neither machine corresponded to the drawing package that accompanied it . . . Dick Baker, Jim Sprong and Rudy Ru-

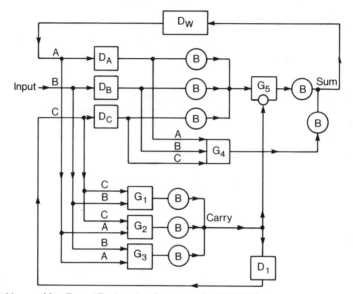

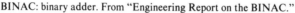

BINAC: binary adder. From "Engineering Report on the BINAC."

tishauser proceeded systematically to reevaluate each circuit, bring it up to performance level or redesign it, make it identical in each machine and document it correctly. Painstakingly and systematically they reconstructed the mess they had received into a working unit with proper documentation. Despite that effort, they never did (to my knowledge) bring the two machines into a working unit with proper documentation.[37]

Another response to the BINAC article mentioned above is by Florence R. Anderson, who also worked with the BINAC at Northrop. She states that the BINAC was indeed operational in California, for a time:

Routines were written and checked out on the BINAC. These routines included the solution of a system of n linear equations (n ≤ 16), solution of a system of ordinary differential equations, and various mathematical functions. A random deicing problem was solved on the BINAC for the thermodynamics group with a compute time of 15 minutes.[38]

But Anderson also attests to the problems in the BINAC's original design:

Problems were encountered with the vacuum tubes, which were just standard radio tubes purchased from the factory without any quality control. After an emission tester was designed and built by Sprong to check the tubes before their use, it was found that only about 25% of the purchased tubes were suitable for computer operation . . . BINAC seemed to operate well on sunny days, but poorly on rainy days; the windows were normally open in the BINAC room.[39]

In brief, Eckert and Mauchly completed the first United States stored-program electronic digital computer, which was sold to Northrop for $100,000. The computer worked logically and reliably at EMCC's Philadelphia headquarters and was used in California as well, but only after it was reworked and never to the satisfaction of Northrop. This accomplishment, by these two men and their associates, was a major technological achievement, particularly in light of their serious financial difficulties. But because of constraints on Eckert's time and the company's monetary problems, not enough care was given to finishing the device; it remained in an experimental state.

BINAC as an Airborne Device

Another issue which has cast the BINAC in an unfavorable light relates to whether it was Eckert and Mauchly's responsibility to build an airborne device. Since the BINAC was never operational as an airborne computer, did EMCC fail to meet its contractual obligations? The original letter of intent stated that "ultimately, a compact, airborne computer will be wanted."[40] This statement does not clarify whether EMCC was to develop such a device or whether the Northrop engineers would make the necessary adaptations. Furthermore, the contract itself left the matter ambiguous: "The scope of the license shall be restricted to the use of the inventions in connection with the control of aircraft and missiles and to the use of inventions for all navigational purposes."[41]

Nine months before delivery, Dick Baker wrote: "While BINAC will probably be adequate for laboratory operations, it is not suited for reliable airborne use."[42] At no time did Northrop suggest that EMCC focus on this feature, nor did Eckert and Mauchly, in interoffice memoranda, indicate that they viewed it as part of their responsibility. However, Jerry Mendelson, as well as other engineers at Northrop, has claimed that Eckert and Mauchly failed to meet their obligations in this regard:

The original BINAC was to have actually been an airborne computer at least by contract, although I don't think that Eckert and Mauchly ever had any intention of making it so. Clearly the machine they built never had any potential for flying at all.[43]

Mauchly, on the other hand, claimed in 1977 that this airborne feature was never EMCC's responsibility.[44] Moreover, the management of Northrop was convinced that its company's engineers would be able to adapt the device for its intended purpose.[45]

Thus, although there is no verbal or written data concerning this matter, it seems reasonable to assume that the construction of an operating electronic digital computer for a purchase price of $100,000 was a bargain; the requirement that it operate as an airborne device would have been unrealistic.

The BINAC as Second-Order Priority

Independent of the airborne issue, Eckert and Mauchly fulfilled their contractual obligations in ways that contributed to delays in BINAC production. The difficulties that developed between EMCC and Northrop were largely a result of Eckert and Mauchly's conscious policy to subordinate the development of the BINAC to the development of the UNIVAC. Moreover, EMCC's precarious financial position meant that the company was often involved in efforts to ease its monetary problems, efforts which detracted from development work.

Initially BINAC was viewed by EMCC as a prototype of the more comprehensive and potentially more lucrative UNIVAC, that is, a machine that would serve as a fully operational model. The development of this device before completion of the UNIVAC would serve three important purposes. First, Eckert and Mauchly could publicize the fact that they had constructed a working computer and thus attract more customers. Second, such a device would satisfy actual and potential UNIVAC customers that EMCC was well on its way to constructing large-scale commercial computers. Third, EMCC could begin to build a service-bureau organization that would charge customers a fee for work performed on a computer owned and operated by Eckert and Mauchly:

Production of at least one BINAC is essential to provide this company with an operating computer which may be demonstrated to prospective purchasers . . . We need an operating computer for both demonstrations and service work as quickly as we can build one.[46]

Although Northrop was sympathetic to Eckert and Mauchly's financial problems, it did not want the BINAC used as a vehicle for future contracts because of the potential of such efforts to further delay completion of the device.[47] For the same reason, Northrop objected to EMCC's intention to use the BINAC for service-bureau work. In June 1948 Kellett Aircraft offered EMCC a fee to solve some of its navigational problems with the use of the BINAC. Since the computer was technically Northrop's property, that company's approval was necessary. Mauchly noted in an EMCC memorandum: "I brought up the question as to whether we could run the Kellett flutter problem on the computer during the test period." Frank Bell, the engineer at Northrop to whom he addressed the question, "did not respond favorably."[48]

As noted, Eckert and Mauchly's contract with NBS for the UNIVAC required the completion of a series of checkpoints to ensure adequate progress and to release funds at periodic intervals. Bell at Northrop was displeased that the completion and acceptance test of the BINAC was to be checkpoint 5A for the UNIVAC. In a letter to Edward Cannon of NBS Bell complained

Upper left, Eckert and a BINAC memory unit. *Upper right*, the Eckert-Mauchly Division of Remington-Rand, Inc. *Lower left*, BINAC components. *Lower right*, detail of a processor. All from Herman Lukoff, *From Dits to Bits*, © dilithium Press, Beaverton, Oregon, 1979. All rights reserved.

that such a checkpoint served the interest of NBS but would only delay delivery of the BINAC to Northrop:

The contract between Eckert-Mauchly and Northrop is certainly independent of the provision for a BINAC checkpoint in your contract with them . . . It is clear that you [NBS] gain a considerable advantage from this situation by your proposed checkpoints at no particular cost to you, but it appears at considerable cost to us.[49]

Bell eventually allowed the acceptance test, having been persuaded by NBS that it was in the national interest.

Thus, Eckert and Mauchly developed the BINAC as a model for the UNIVAC, a fact of which Northrop was not initially aware and which later served to antagonize its management. In a 1972 interview, Jerry Mendelson summed up the situation from Northrop's point of view:

It became clear that there were going to be severe problems with Eckert and Mauchly because at that time they were building or trying to build the UNIVAC I. Their key people were assigned to that machine and they were in my opinion and in the opinion of others, delaying, holding the BINAC in a partially completed state because it was the only piece of hardware they had to show any potential customer.[50]

In the end, NBS was also dissatisfied, arguing that the design of the BINAC took valuable time away from the UNIVAC project:

Unfortunately the BINAC design proved to be one that required a great deal of adjustment in order to achieve suitable levels of operation . . . Because of the intended close relationship between the BINAC and the UNIVAC systems, the company considered it essential to delay most of the UNIVAC work until all of the problems of the BINAC were solved. This led to a considerable delay in the work on the UNIVAC system.[51]

The Effect on EMCC

Eckert and Mauchly's simultaneous research and development efforts on both the BINAC and the UNIVAC in 1948–1949 may have been too great an undertaking for a small, financially unstable corporation. On the one hand, they were forced into this overcommitment as a result of the delays encountered in getting the original UNIVAC contract. On the other hand, they actively sought additional contracts.[52]

Partly because of EMCC's decision to concentrate its efforts on both the Northrop-BINAC and the NBS-Census UNIVAC at the same time, and partly because of Eckert and Mauchly's financial difficulties, NBS decided in 1948 to design and construct its own interim computer. This device, which incorporated features from many different machines, was later called the Standards Eastern Automatic Computer (SEAC). It was a small electronic digital computer constructed with funds provided by the Air Comptroller's Office.[53] NBS's decision to build such a computer was only in part motivated

A Comparison of Architecture, Performance, and Physical Characteristics of the Eckert-Mauchly Computers

	ENIAC	EDVAC	BINAC	UNIVAC
Architecture				
Programming	Manual wire panels	Stored program	Stored program	Stored program
Data transmission	Parallel	Serial	Serial	Serial
Number representation	Decimal	Binary	Binary	Decimal
Word length	10 digits	44 bits	31 bits	11 digits + sign
Other data types	—	—	—	12 characters/word
Instruction length	2 digits	44 bits	14 bits	6 characters
Instruction format	1-address	4-address	1-address	1-address
Instruction set size *	97 (100)	12 (16)	25 (32)	45 (63)
Accumulators / programmable registers	20	4	2	4
Main memory size	—	1,024 words	512 words	1,000 words
Main memory type	—	Delay line	Delay line	Delay line
Secondary memory	Function tables	Magnetic drum	Magnetic tape	Magnetic tape
Other I/O devices	Card reader & punch	Cards, paper tape	Typewriter	Typewriter, cards, printer
Error detection	—	Redundant CPUs	Redundant CPUs	Redundancy, parity
Performance				
Clock rate	60–125 KHz	1 MHz	4 MHz‡	2.25 MHz
Add time	0.2 ms	0.864 ms†	0.285 ms†	0.525 ms†
Multiply time	2.8 ms	2.9 ms†	0.654 ms†	2.15 ms†
Divide time	24.0 ms	2.9 ms†	0.633 ms†	3.89 ms†
Physical Characteristics				
Approximate measurements:				
Vacuum tube count	18,000	3,600	1,400	5,400
Diode count	7,200	12,000	n/a	18,000
Power consumption	174 kW	50 kW	13 kW	81 kW
Floor space of computer only	1,800 sq. ft.	490 sq.ft.	n/a	352 sq. ft.

n/a: Data not available.

 * Number of instructions used (number encoded).

 † Includes memory access time for instructions and operands.

 ‡ Later reduced to 2.5 MHz (interview with Eckert by Stern, January 23, 1980).

Sources: C. G. Bell and A. Newell, *Computer Structures: Readings and Examples* (New York, 1971); E. C. Berkeley and Lawrence Wainwright, *Computers: Their Operation and Applications* (New York, 1956); Eckert-Mauchly Computer Corporation, "Engineering Report on the BINAC" (Philadelphia, 1949); Simon Lavington, *Early British Computers* (Bedford, Mass., 1980), p. 125; Martin H. Weik, *A Survey of Domestic Electronic Digital Computing Systems*, BRL Report 971 (Aberdeen, Md., 1955), and *A Third Survey of Domestic Electronic Digital Computing Systems* (Aberdeen, Md., 1961).

by EMCC's lack of business expertise. It also grew out of NBS's interest in establishing itself as a prime center for computer development.[54] The construction of a computer in its own laboratories was a useful method for achieving that goal.

During this period, Eckert and Mauchly began to realize that they would need to decide how best to use their limited resources. Should they build small, reliable computers similar to the BINAC and primarily suited to engineering or scientific work? Or should they concentrate on constructing large, commercial computers like the UNIVAC?

In 1948 Mauchly was eager to manufacture additional BINACs. He found that many industrial organizations and universities were interested in acquiring small computers—among them General Motors, the University of Illinois, the NBS Institute for Numerical Analysis at Los Angeles, and the Arthur D. Little company in Cambridge, Massachusetts. Mauchly therefore concluded:

From the business point of view it seems to me that we should be much more interested in selling BINACs than in selling UNIVACs at this time. If we can assume that the modifications necessary to make the BINAC suitable for many engineering and mathematical uses are not incompatible with our obligations regarding UNIVACs and that we can offer BINACs for delivery in something like 6 to 8 months, then we have in the BINAC a product which can bring us income approximately one year earlier than any income and profit derivable from UNIVACs. Moreover, the sale of a BINAC will in most cases not compete with the sale of a UNIVAC, that is, the customer who buys a BINAC either is not in the market for a UNIVAC at all, or if he is in the market for a UNIVAC, will probably buy one anyway when they are available.[55]

However, the engineers at EMCC, especially Eckert, were more interested in building large-scale, comprehensive computers. They argued that a major effort to adapt the BINAC for more general use would require too much time, time which would be better spent on the UNIVAC. Eckert made the engineering judgment that since the latter's development was well along, it would be easier to complete it and produce other UNIVACs than to make the BINAC more reliable and produce additional small computers.

Mauchly chose to accept Eckert's opinion on this matter, despite the fact that he was the company's main liaison with customers and potential users and therefore in a better position to judge marketability. He reversed the position he had taken ten days before:

As I see it, the decision to go ahead or not go ahead with BINAC modification must rest with the facts and opinions supplied by the engineering department. The statements made by Eckert and the sentiments expressed by other members of the Executive Committee last Tuesday pointed definitely to the abandonment of BINAC modification and construction.[56]

The staff of the Eckert-Mauchly Computer Corporation in 1948 included, *back row, left to right*, Albert Auerbach, Jean Bartik, Marvin Jacoby, John Sims, Louis Wilson, Robert Shaw, Gerald Smoliar; *front row*, Presper Eckert, Frazier Welsh, James Weiner, Bradford Sheppard, and John Mauchly. Courtesy Louis D. Wilson.

This perspective regarding the UNIVAC was in large part responsible for many of the technical problems which later beset the BINAC. The fact that BINAC was delivered while still in an experimental state was a result of the decision to make the BINAC an item of second-order priority.

Mauchly, in short, subordinated his own marketing instincts to those of the engineers. This decision was critical in plotting the future course of EMCC. Engineers are typically motivated by their desire to invent and frequently are less attuned to commercial factors than are entrepreneurs, who face commercial prospects on a day-to-day basis. Hence some decisions, particularly those related to business policies, are best relegated to individuals who are able to subordinate engineering judgments to entrepreneurial, economic, and administrative ones. EMCC, however, was primarily an engineering organization that chose to follow the advice of its engineers. Had the corporation decided instead to set its goals more conservatively and to focus on small-scale mathematical devices like the BINAC, the financial difficulties which it later faced might well have been minimized or even avoided.

The divergence of opinion between Eckert and Mauchly regarding the priority to be placed on BINAC design was the first major problem of its kind that the two men faced. Eckert's clear-cut dominance on technical matters, both at the Moore School and in the company, was generally viewed as an asset. On business matters, however, he generally seemed content to leave the details and the decisions to Mauchly. Eckert initially wanted Mauchly to be president of their company so that the latter would be in the best possible position to negotiate with other organizations on such matters. Eckert's uncompromising stand on BINAC design priorities, however, made it appear as though he felt that engineering decisions should take priority over business concerns. In some ways, his dominance (as well as Mauchly's submission to it), while a distinct asset technologically, was a barrier to the success of their business.[57]

Ironically, once the BINAC was delivered to Northrop, it no longer played a significant role in the computing field. Northrop never really used the computer for the purpose originally intended. After August 1949 Eckert and Mauchly focused all of their technical attention on completion of the six UNIVACs that were on order: three for the government, one for the Prudential Insurance Company, and two for the A. C. Nielsen Company.

7

The UNIVAC
and
Beyond

Despite their success in obtaining contracts through the National Bureau of Standards and with the Northrop Corporation, the Eckert and Mauchly firm remained in serious financial straits in 1947 and 1948. The signing of the three government contracts had been subject to numerous delays, and bureaucratic regulations later prevented the two men from receiving any funds until portions of the UNIVAC were complete. The series of checkpoints instituted by the Bureau of Standards to monitor progress and permit the release of funds actually created additional constraints on Eckert and Mauchly's research and development efforts.

More importantly, the BINAC contract meant that Eckert and Mauchly had agreed to build not one but two computers, and to complete the BINAC in May 1948. They hoped that an operational computer in 1948 would attract potential customers for a UNIVAC and were confident that if they could remain solvent until the first UNIVAC was operational, additional contracts would be forthcoming and would enable them to prosper. But in the spring of 1948 it was clear that the BINAC would not be completed on time, thus delaying the UNIVAC's checkpoints as well and reducing the capital on hand.

To attract potential investors, the two men had incorporated in December 1947 as the Eckert-Mauchly Computer Corporation. While Eckert and his engineers focused on research and development for the BINAC and UNIVAC, Mauchly set out to find more customers in the private sector. Within a year, he succeeded in obtaining contracts with the Prudential Insurance Company and the A. C. Nielsen Company.

The Prudential Insurance Company

The Prudential Insurance Company had been a major user of IBM tabulating equipment for several decades. It was one of a handful of organizations, like the Census Bureau, that actively sought more efficient equipment for statistical tabulation. One of its actuaries, Edmund C. Berkeley, had been researching alternatives to IBM punch-card equipment as far back as 1939.[1] Berkeley's naval service from August 1945 to April 1946 further sparked his interest in computational devices. He was assigned as liaison to Howard Aiken's Computation Laboratory at Harvard University, where the Mark II and III were being developed, in part with Navy funds. During his brief tenure there Berkeley worked closely with Aiken and learned a great deal about the potential of digital computers for a variety of applications.[2]

When he returned to Prudential, Berkeley found that a new insurance law was creating an immediate and critical need for high-speed computational devices. The Geurtin Act, which was to go into effect on January 1, 1948, called for the use of a more complex experience table for the preparation of insurance rates. For Prudential, as well as other insurance companies, this meant that extensive calculations would be required to recompute rates.[3]

Prudential appointed Berkeley chief research consultant and asked him to determine whether the new digital computers could be profitably applied to meet the needs of insurance companies. Berkeley investigated the possibility of using Aiken's Mark I and inquired about IBM's new semielectronic selective sequence controlled calculator, the SSEC.[4] He also wrote John Mauchly toward the end of January 1947 to ask about the UNIVAC.[5]

Berkeley recognized that the fully electronic UNIVAC was vastly superior in processing speed to both the Mark I, which was an electromechanical device, and the SSEC, which was in part electromechanical. But what Prudential really wanted was high-speed input-output equipment, not necessarily high-speed processors. Mauchly had some difficulty convincing Prudential's management that the processing speed of an electronic computer would be of value:

> Your specifications for a Prudential machine do not call for arithmetic speeds such as we will provide in an EDVAC [later called UNIVAC], and it may be that you are not yet convinced that this speed is essential for the type of work which you expect the machine to do. However, in our study of operations in other companies as well as in the Census Bureau, we have always found that high internal speed of operation can be translated into reduced cost of operation by proper use of the machine.[6]

Since Prudential was really in the market for high-speed punch-card devices, it viewed the UNIVAC's use of magnetic tape for input and output with some trepidation. Although the concept seemed attractive, there were as yet no working models to prove its feasibility. More importantly, Prudential relied heavily on IBM punch cards for storing data. The use of tapes in place of cards would mean that the entire data processing operation would need to be revamped.[7]

Although a card-oriented system with optional magnetic-tape drives might have appealed to more organizations, Eckert and Mauchly's system, as originally conceived, focused exclusively on tape as an input-output medium. They reasoned that because tape processing was faster and more efficient, it could effectively compete with the standard punch-card systems for which IBM had most of the patents.[8]

Mauchly and Berkeley were able to convince Prudential's management that the UNIVAC system was not only feasible but that it had great potential as an alternative to IBM punch-card systems. But convincing Prudential of the advantages of a UNIVAC system and actually obtaining a contract for such a system proved to be two very different things. Prudential was concerned that a deal with Eckert and Mauchly would jeopardize its relations with IBM.[9] This fear was later expressed by many other potential UNIVAC customers as well.

In addition, Eckert and Mauchly's precarious financial position was a major obstacle. A large organization like Prudential was unwilling to sign a contract with a small company that had serious financial problems, particularly when a sizable investment would be required. Prudential also realized that the cost of a UNIVAC in 1947 would include research and development as well as production expenses.

While it was not willing to contract for a machine in 1947, Prudential was prepared to assist Eckert and Mauchly in developing the UNIVAC in return for an option to buy one later. If the option were exercised, the money provided for development would be applied to the purchase. This initial agreement, signed August 4, 1947, required Eckert and Mauchly to hold demonstrations of the tape and tape devices as they were completed.[10] Mauchly also was to serve as a consultant to Prudential and provide details on how a UNIVAC could be applied to insurance problems.   Prudential paid the Electronic Control Company $20,000 for Mauchly's services and for the demonstrations, which were to be completed by January 1, 1948, or half the money would have to be returned. In addition, the Electronic Control Company was to submit monthly progress reports to Prudential.[11]

Here again Eckert and Mauchly were overly optimistic in their time estimates. By January 1948 the demonstrations were not ready. Prudential could have insisted that half its funds be returned but agreed instead to amend the contract several times to allow Eckert and Mauchly's company more time to fulfill its obligations. In short, Prudential was sufficiently impressed with the progress being made to permit extensions to the deadlines.[12]

Despite the delays and the financial problems that continued to plague Eckert and Mauchly, Prudential signed a contract on December 8, 1948, for construction of a UNIVAC system at a cost of $150,000. This system was to be delivered by September 15, 1950.[13]

The contract called for one card-to-tape converter and two tape-to-card converters, devices which would allow Prudential to retain its punch-card data processing systems. In a rather cumbersome and inefficient operation,

Employees of the Eckert-Mauchly Computer Corporation in 1948. *Back row, left to right,*
George Gingrich, Marvin Gotlieb, Louis Wilson, Douglas Wendell, Charles Michaels, Maurice
Stad. *Middle row,* John Sims, Marvin Jacoby, Paul Winsor, Gerald Smoliar, Arthur Gehring,
Lillian Jay, Edwin Blumenthal, Robert Mock, Jean Bartik, Herman Lukoff, Seamond Leavitt,
Bernard Gordon, Edmund Schreiner, Lawrence Jones. *Front row,* Frances Morello, Robert
Shaw, Presper Eckert, Bradford Sheppard, Frazier Welsh, John Mauchly, James Weiner,
Albert Auerbach, Frances Snyder. Courtesy Louis D. Wilson.

cards would be converted to tape, which would be processed by the UNI-VAC, and the output tape converted back to cards.[14]

It is ironic that Eckert and Mauchly had to agree to develop these converters in order to obtain the Prudential contract since their intention from the beginning was to provide a viable and vastly more efficient alternative to punch-card processing. Instead, they were burdened with the development of two additional devices that would enable an organization to continue functioning in a punch-card environment.

The Prudential contract called for other UNIVAC devices as part of the overall system design: a central computing element, a supervisory control unit, two alphanumeric UNITYPERS that were key-to-tape encoders, five UNIPRINTERS or line printers, and twelve UNISERVOS or tape drives.[15] Even by 1948 standards, $150,000 was a paltry sum for such an array of revolutionary equipment.

Eckert and Mauchly began to realize that their initial cost estimates, like their time estimates, were vastly underestimated. They attempted to renegotiate with Prudential for a higher, more realistic price.[16] These efforts in September 1948 so disturbed Prudential that the insurance company threatened to cancel the contract altogether. EMCC immediately withdrew its request for a higher price and accepted the contract on its original terms.[17]

The A. C. Nielsen Company

The relationship of the A. C. Nielsen Company with the Electronic Control Company and the Eckert-Mauchly Computer Corporation was similar to that of Prudential. Both Nielsen and Prudential had been trying to acquire more efficient tabulating equipment even before they knew of Eckert and Mauchly's enterprise. As major users of IBM equipment, both had expressed an interest in acquiring more sophisticated machines from IBM but were disappointed by the latter's unresponsiveness. Nielsen, like Prudential, was interested in investing in new developments, even those undertaken by small companies, despite the obvious risks.

In October 1946 Arthur Nielsen, Jr., wrote to his friend John Curtiss, then scientific officer of the National Bureau of Standards, inquiring about recent advances in calculating equipment. He explained that his firm was "running into a rather serious problem" in connection with its tabulating operations, because of the growing volume of business and the inability to secure a permit "to build additional office space to house additional equipment." Nielsen concluded, "It would be very helpful to us if you would put us on the right track either with people in your organization or elsewhere."[18]

Curtiss replied a few days later that it was "premature to try to get any ideas" about computers "from present projects, Government or otherwise," and explained:

Nobody really has any exact concept of what the new machines will look like. In two years, or even in one year, the whole situation will be quite different . . . You could send your men directly to two concerns whom I consider now the best ones to bet on among the small electronics outfits with brains (and I think such outfits may win the race). The Electronic Control Corp. and Engineering Research Associates, Inc., St. Paul, Minn.[19]

Despite Curtiss's caveats, Nielsen and his staff conferred with both Engineering Research Associates and Eckert and Mauchly's Electronic Control Company. As a result, they determined that Eckert and Mauchly "may be at least a year ahead of the people in St. Paul by virtue simply of prior practical experience and intensive specialization."[20] Moreover, Nielsen noted in a memorandum:

I cannot help being impressed with the specific fact that Mr. Eckert is the man who developed ENIAC for the Army, and that Mauchly and Eckert seem to have the inside track with the Bureau of the Census and with the Bureau of Standards, at this writing . . . The least that can be said is that some others in high and responsible places evidently have a great deal of confidence in these two men.[21]

As a result of Nielsen's enthusiasm, his company began negotiations with the Electronic Control Company in December 1946, a month before Mauchly was approached by Berkeley of Prudential.[22]

On January 4, 1947, Eckert and Mauchly offered to sell the Nielsen Company a UNIVAC system equipped with a key-to-tape recorder and a printer for $100,000, all units to be completed within a year.[23] But Nielsen, like Prudential, was reluctant to sign a purchase agreement with the Electronic Control Company because of its precarious financial position. The rapidly changing state of the art in computing added to this reluctance. Unlike Prudential, however, the Nielsen Company was willing to contemplate giving up the punch-card concept.

On February 13, 1947, the Nielsen and Electronic Control companies signed an agreement for a "free exchange of ideas." Nielsen received an option to purchase a UNIVAC and Eckert and Mauchly were given the opportunity to earn consulting fees and expenses.[24] The contract was originally to run until July 1, 1947, but it was extended several times. Before signing a purchase order, Nielsen wanted Eckert and Mauchly to develop their equipment, gain more business expertise, and acquire more working capital.[25]

In December 1947 Arthur Nielsen, Jr., set out to acquire controlling interest in the newly formed Eckert-Mauchly Computer Corporation, which had just incorporated December 8.[26] He was still uncertain about the business acumen of the two men, recognizing that they had seriously underestimated UNIVAC development costs. In May 1947 he complained to a colleague about the agreements that Eckert and Mauchly had made with Northrop and Prudential:

These agreements will, they [Eckert and Mauchly] feel, provide adequate financing with the exception of the patent work required. They seem to feel that they could not charge these customers for the patent investigations because neither of these customers had the slightest interest in their getting patent protection. My own view is that they did a bum job of planning and negotiation in this respect because if patents are important to Electronic Control, they should put them in the price even if, like the proverbial salesman's overcoat, they did not actually show up in the expense account. However, they don't seem to feel that they are in a position to change any of their terms with either of these prospective customers.[27]

Eckert and Mauchly had a great deal to learn about business and were still floundering financially, but convinced of their ultimate success, they rejected Nielsen's offer to buy a controlling interest.

Despite Arthur Nielsen's reservations, on April 23, 1948, the market research firm signed a contract for a UNIVAC system with several peripheral devices at a cost of $151,400. The system included one UNIVAC, six UNITAPES, six UNITYPERS and one UNIPRINTER. The sum of $30,280 was to be paid on signature of the contract and installments of $7,570 were to be paid monthly.[28] The following year, Nielsen contracted for a second UNIVAC with similar specifications.

But before the initial contract could be executed, Nielsen required the Eckert-Mauchly Computer Corporation to have $240,000 in working capital. Moreover, Nielsen wanted assurances that EMCC had at least two other customers.[29] By September 30, 1948, Mauchly was able to write Nielsen:

We have signed UNIVAC contracts (in addition to the Nielsen contract) with the following customers: 1. Bureau of Standards—Census, Total Price: $169,600, Delivery Date: Feb. 1, 1950; 2. Watson Labs/Teleregister contract for $100,000 is broken down into a $75,000 contract with Teleregister and a $25,000 contract with Watson Labs. Both contracts contain the standard government partial payment method, namely receiving 75% of actual costs each month up to 80% of the actual contract price, with the balance being paid on delivery.[30]

The Culmination of EMCC's Financial Problems

Despite the fact that by the summer of 1948 EMCC had several substantial contracts, its financial problems did not diminish; in fact, they became more severe. Although assets as of June 30 totaled $206,000, development costs of UNIVAC systems were already in excess of $100,000. Moreover, the company grew from seven people in October 1946 to forty people, including twenty engineers, by 1948. It outgrew its original quarters on Walnut Street and moved to a larger facility at Spring Garden and Broad streets, also in central Philadelphia.[31] At that point EMCC by its own estimates required an additional $500,000 in working capital in order to remain in business.[32]

The financial support that was so essential came from the American Total-isator Company of Baltimore, Maryland, in 1948–1949. This company supplied racetracks with the pari-mutuel machines or totalisators used for posting odds and recording race results. In 1948 the company had a monopoly on this equipment, but in March of that year a Delaware racetrack owner had approached Eckert and Mauchly about developing electronic devices that could replace relay-operated totalisators.[33] Although Eckert and Mauchly were not interested in undertaking such a venture at the time, George Eltgroth, the newly hired patent attorney for EMCC, hoped to derive some benefit from the racetrack owner's request. Eltgroth had been a patent attorney for Bendix Corporation in Baltimore and knew executives from many Baltimore-based organizations including American Totalisator.

Eltgroth succeeded in convincing the vice president of Totalisator, Henry Straus, that there was considerable advantage to backing an organization that might otherwise prove to be a source of future competition in the totalisator field.[34] Straus was very impressed with Eckert and Mauchly's computer work. Although his company was owned by the Munn brothers, major investment decisions were left to Straus, and he became the main impetus behind Totalisator's investment interests in EMCC.

On August 6, 1948, Straus agreed to provide financial support to Eckert and Mauchly,[35] and four days later EMCC signed a contract with American Totalisator. The terms of the contract reflected Straus's view that EMCC would function most effectively if control remained with Eckert and Mauchly. This was precisely the sort of support that Eckert and Mauchly had hoped for. Henry Straus became chairman of the nine-person board of EMCC, and three of his associates were also elected to the board. Eckert and Mauchly remained board members and retained control of 54 percent of the voting common stock; an additional 6 percent was held by EMCC employees.

American Totalisator agreed to make capital contributions of approximately $500,000 in return for 40 percent of the voting common stock of EMCC. Upon execution of the contract, American Totalisator would advance EMCC $50,000, lend an additional $62,000 in notes to mature in January 1950, and purchase 40 percent of the common stock for $438,000 by June 30, 1950.

The support supplied by American Totalisator kept EMCC solvent for fourteen months, during which time the BINAC was completed and development on the UNIVAC continued. By September 30, 1949, EMCC was a thriving organization, with 134 employees, a new office building on Ridge Avenue in North Philadelphia, and six contracts for UNIVAC systems totaling $1,200,000.[36]

One month later, on October 25, 1949, Henry Straus and an associate, Gene Johnson, were killed when Straus's twin-engine airplane crashed near Baltimore.[37] Since Straus was the prime force behind Totalisator's support, his death brought an abrupt end to that company's interest in EMCC. The loans were to mature in January 1950, making EMCC's financial situation critical.

Several sources, including Mauchly himself, have claimed that Straus's death was the primary cause of EMCC's insolvency.[38] It is questionable, however, whether the American Totalisator Company could have supplied the additional hundreds of thousands, if not millions, of dollars necessary for Eckert and Mauchly to retain control of their corporation. The EMCC Report to Shareholders of December 31, 1949, indicates that additional funds would have been necessary in any event:

It is now apparent that even if the American Totalisator Company were to continue to supply operating capital in return for preferred stock up to the limit contemplated in their contract with us, we would not have adequate funds to carry through the test period of the first UNIVAC.[39]

As a direct result of Straus's death, Eckert and Mauchly spent the remaining months of 1949 seeking financing from loan companies and research foundations. Finally, they sought to sell their corporation to a major manufacturer of calculating equipment, such as IBM, National Cash Register, or Remington Rand.[40] Other organizations, among them Philco, Burroughs, and Hughes Aircraft, expressed an interest in purchasing EMCC.[41] When all the loans were denied, it became clear that EMCC would have to sell to the first bidder.[42]

EMCC and Remington Rand

The major manufacturers of tabulating equipment as well as other companies with an interest in investing in electronic digital computers had had many opportunities in 1949 to observe Eckert and Mauchly's progress. The many demonstrations of various equipment were always accompanied by publicity releases and invitations to interested parties. The BINAC demonstrations in August 1949 were witnessed by representatives of many organizations, including IBM and Remington Rand.[43] When Eckert and Mauchly approached these organizations in an effort to sell the corporation, their work was already well known.

IBM was interested in hiring Eckert and Mauchly but would not consider the purchase of their corporation. Thomas Watson, Sr., was still not convinced that electronic digital computers would have any significant commercial market. Further, purchase of EMCC by IBM might result in antitrust litigation, a matter about which IBM was extremely sensitive.[44]

Testing unit for mercury memory tank. *Left to right*, John Mauchly, General Leslie Groves, and Presper Eckert. Courtesy Smithsonian Institution.

NCR and Remington Rand, the other two major manufacturers of tabulating equipment, expressed considerable interest in purchasing EMCC, but they needed time to make an offer. At that point, the plight of Eckert and Mauchly was so desperate that they were ready to consider the first reasonable offer.

On February 1, 1950, Remington Rand agreed to purchase the Eckert-Mauchly Computer Corporation. American Totalisator was to receive $438,000 for its 40 percent share of EMCC stock. A total of $100,000 was to be paid to Eckert and Mauchly and to the employees holding stock. Eckert and Mauchly were each guaranteed a salary of $18,000 for eight years, which was 20 percent more than the $15,000 they were receiving. Most of the other employees of EMCC also received similar increases. Finally, Remington Rand agreed to pay EMCC annually, for eight years, 59 percent of the net profits received from the patents with a minimum annual guarantee of $5,000.[45]

The Eckert-Mauchly Computer Corporation was designated a subsidiary of Remington Rand and functioned as a separate division. Remington Rand's director of advanced research, General Leslie R. Groves, formerly of the Manhattan Project, was put in charge of the overall operations of this division. The division's main objective was, of course, to build the UNIVAC.

The purchase agreement marked Remington Rand's entry into the electronic digital computing field. Two years later, it also bought Engineering Research Associates of St. Paul, Minnesota, which had become a successful manufacturer of scientific computers. These acquisitions gave Remington Rand a substantial lead in the computing field. They also marked a major milestone in the history of electronic digital computers. The large, established corporation finally entered the computer market after substantial development had occurred and the existence of a commercial market had been established.[46] In short, the early 1950s marked the beginning of the era of the commercial computer, with Remington Rand and then IBM as the first two major manufacturers.

A contemporary *Business Week* article reflected a general lack of enthusiasm about Remington Rand's acquisition. Under the heading "Remington Rand Scores," the journal noted: "The salesmen will find the market to be fairly limited. The UNIVAC is not the kind of machine that every office could use . . . It is of value chiefly to companies which deal in a great many figures or in highly complicated mathematical formulas."[47]

From the outset, Remington Rand recognized that EMCC had seriously underestimated the overhead and development costs for the UNIVAC.[48] In order to resolve some of these financial difficulties, it sought to adjust the price on the existing UNIVAC contracts—three for the government, one for Prudential, and two for A. C. Nielsen.

Remington Rand's lawyers attempted to renegotiate the government contracts. "We freely admit at this time that the contract should have been on a cost plus fixed fee basis," they wrote NBS. "We now request that consideration be given toward adjusting the contract price to reimburse us in part for the added cost suffered as a result of improvements made in the original design."[49]

NBS was amenable to the idea of renegotiating, but could find no legal way of doing so. It invited Remington Rand's attorneys to seek some means for providing such assistance, but at this point the attorneys threatened to cancel the contracts entirely unless additional funds were forthcoming. Rankled by this posture, NBS countered with its own threat to take legal action if the terms of the contracts were not met. By June 1950 Remington Rand decided it had no choice but to continue manufacturing the three UNIVACs for the government at the original price.[50]

Remington Rand's aggressive posture was more effective in the company's dealings with Nielsen and Prudential. James Rand, president of the company, and General Groves realized that they could not make any profit on UNIVACs sold for less than $500,000 each.* The Prudential and Nielsen contracts called for UNIVACs to be delivered for approximately $150,000 each. Rather than sustain this considerable loss, Remington Rand sought to have the two parties cancel the contracts.

Remington Rand threatened to sue in order to cancel the existing Nielsen and Prudential contracts. The company's attorneys argued that, win or lose, they were prepared to tie the matter up in extensive litigation for many years; by the time the suit was settled, the UNIVAC would be obsolete and of no value to either party. Rather than incur the added legal costs, both Nielsen and Prudential canceled their contracts in 1951. Monies expended by the two companies were returned.[51]

EMCC's technical staff continued to function under Eckert's supervision in Philadelphia. Mauchly, however, was transferred to the Sales Department when a security check revealed that he did not have facilities clearance. The old security problem that plagued Mauchly several years before had never been fully resolved and to avoid any embarrassments, Remington Rand transferred him. In 1958, Remington Rand asked Mauchly to move to New York to work more closely with its sales force there. Because he was unwilling to make such a move he resigned and later formed his own company.[52]

On March 31, 1951, the Census Bureau accepted the first UNIVAC.

---

*The ultimate cost of constructing the UNIVAC is difficult to ascertain, but an official estimate is $930,000. See Martin H. Weik, "A Survey of Domestic Electronic Digital Computing Systems," Ballistics Research Laboratory Report 971, 1955, UPA.

John Mauchly, 1979. Fabian Bachrach photograph, courtesy Kay Mauchly.

Within eighteen months, the other two UNIVACs for which the government had contracted were delivered. In the end, forty-six UNIVAC I's were built for both government and commercial use.

In the interim Nielsen and Prudential signed contracts with IBM for its first fully electronic commercial computer, the 701. It appears that IBM actively began to develop and market electronic computers only after Remington Rand entered the field.

UNIVAC: The First Commercial Computer System

In many ways the UNIVAC was a refinement of the technology developed in the ENIAC and EDVAC. The ENIAC used 18,000 vacuum tubes for circuitry and data representation. The UNIVAC minimized the use of vacuum tubes, which had the dual disadvantages of burning out fairly frequently and of generating heat and thus requiring extensive cooling and ventilating equipment. As originally conceived, the UNIVAC was to use only 1,500 tubes; the more than 5,000 tubes required by the final design still represented a decided improvement over the ENIAC.[53]

The memory in the UNIVAC was based on the mercury delay line conceived by Eckert while he was working on a radar project at the Moore School in the early 1940s. Originally developed for use in the EDVAC, by 1951 it had also been successfully utilized in the EDSAC at Cambridge University, in the Pilot ACE, in the SEAC developed by NBS, and in the BINAC.

The memory of the UNIVAC could store 1,000 twelve-digit characters, with each storage position capable of holding either a number or an alphabetic character. The ENIAC had a capacity for storing only 20 numbers in accumulators.[54]

The ENIAC operated in parallel; the UNIVAC with its mercury-delay-line memory was a serial machine. The 2.25 megahertz pulse rate of the UNIVAC was so fast that it more than compensated for any loss of speed incurred by the shift from parallel to serial operation. A report from the Electronic Control Company in 1947 summed up the difference in operation: "In the ENIAC all digits of a given number were operated upon simultaneously; in the UNIVAC each digit in turn passes through the same circuits. Duplication of equipment is thereby avoided but as a result it is necessary to use a higher fundamental pulse rate in order to maintain the same computing speed."[55] The UNIVAC could perform an addition or subtraction in less than 600 microseconds, a multiplication in 2,500 microseconds, and a division in 4,000 microseconds.

The UNIVAC was designed to be far more compact than the oversized ENIAC. Although the original specifications called for a device that was to measure 8.0 feet by 3.0 feet by 6.5 feet, the completed UNIVAC processor stood 14.5 feet by 7.5 by 9.0 feet, still a great improvement.[56]

A distinct feature of the system as a whole was its ability to store and retrieve data on magnetic tape. This contribution was no less revolutionary than the mercury delay line memory.[57]

Until 1950 the most widely used medium for recording data was the punch card. The computational devices developed by IBM, Remington Rand, and other manufacturers all used cards as input. Even the ENIAC, by far the fastest computational device in 1946, relied on punch-card equipment to read cards as input and punch cards as output. Because the card devices were much slower than the processor itself, they had a serious, adverse effect on the overall speed of the ENIAC.

The only alternative to punch cards during the immediate postwar period

---

UNIVAC

Specifications from Martin Weik, BRL Report No. 971.

Manufacturer

Remington Rand Division Sperry Rand Corporation 315 Fourth Avenue New York 10, N.Y.

Operating Agencies

The following agencies supplied survey information:
Army Map Service, Washington 25, D.C.
AEC Computing Facility, New York Univ., N.Y.
Radiation Laboratory, Univ. of California, Livermore, California
Department of the Air Force, HQUSAF, Washington 25, D.C., Attn: DCS Comptroller
HQ Air Material Command, Wright-Patterson AFB, Ohio
Pictures were furnished by the USAF and the Univ. of California, RL.

General System

Application General Purpose, Mapping, Geodesy, Research and services in mathematical sciences, AEC reactor design problems. Weapons development. Air Force Programming Computations. Logistical business-type problem solution
Timing   Synchronous
Operation   Sequential

Numerical System

Internal number system: Decimal
Decimal digits per word: 11 plus sign 12 alphanumeric
Decimal digits per instruction: 6
Decimal digits per instruction not decoded: 1
Instructions per word: 2
Total no. of instructions decoded: 63
Total no. of instructions used: 45
Arithmetic system: Fixed point
Instruction type: One address code
Number range: -1 to $+1$
Floating point performed by subroutines supplied with computer. Words may be made up of alphabetic, numeric and typewriter characters.
AMS and USAF report 64 and 46 instructions decoded and 40 and 46 instructions used, respectively.

Arithmetic Unit

Add time
   (excluding storage access):   120 microsec
Multiply time
   (excluding storage access):   1800 microsec
Divide time
   (excluding storage access):   3600 microsec
Construction: Vacuum tubes
Number of rapid access word registers: 4
Basic pulse repetition rate: 2.25 megacycles/sec.
Multiply and divide times depend upon numerical value of multiplier, dividend, and divisor respectively.
All quantities processed by the computer are in units of 11 digits plus a sign. Time includes simultaneous computation in duplicate circuits and comparison of results for identity.

was punched paper tape. The advantage of paper tape was that data were recorded on continuous strips, obviating the need for eighty- or ninety-column layouts. Both punched paper tape and cards, however, used mechanical devices to sense holes; such devices seriously limited the overall speed of any electronic device.

Eckert and Mauchly had entered the commercial computing field with the intention of attracting customers who were using IBM equipment and punch-card media. One of their strategies was to offer customers a superior input-output medium. As Mauchly explained in a memorandum to Edmund Berkeley in March 1947:

. . . so far as we know our own plans for the use of magnetic tape and our requirements for the tape control mechanism call for speeds which are higher than anything considered elsewhere. Higher input speeds can of course be obtained by photoelectric

---

Storage

Media	Words	Digits	Microsec Access
Acoustic Delay			
Line-Hg	1000	12,000	400 max
Magnetic Tape	120,000	1,440,000	

1500 foot magnetic tapes are used.

Input

Media/Speed
Magnetic Tape: 12,800 char/sec. read-in speed 100 inches/second
Metallic tape: 1/2 inch wide in lengths of 100, 200, 500 or 1500 feet, recorded at densities of 20, 50, 120 or 128 char/inch.
Input Media are prepared by:
Unityper I Keypunching
Records at 20 char/inch. Loop controlled. When used with Printing Unit produces printed copy.
Unityper II Keypunching
Records at 50 char/inch. Printed copy produced simultaneously.
Card-to-Tape-Converter 240 cards/min. instantaneous conversion.
80 column punched card input 120 char/inch.
90 Column Card-to-Tape Converter 240 card/min.
90 column punched card input 120 char/inch.
Tape Operated Unityper II (prototype) 6-10 char/sec. Converts 5 channel punched paper tape to 7 channel (plus sprocket channel) magnetic tape recording.
Punched Paper Tape to Magnetic Tape Converter
200 char/sec.
High Speed Conversion.
Magnetic Tape Recording of Unityper II verified by:

Verifier Keypunching
Verifies original recording; provides for correcting mistakes on original recording; produces printed copy simultaneously with the other two functions.
Magnetic tape recording of Card-to-Tape Converters verified internally.

Output

Media/Speed
Magnetic Tape: 12,800 char/sec with speed 100 inches/sec. Recorded at 128 char/inch
Output Equipment using Magnetic Tape input:
Uniprinter 10-11 char/sec. Converts recording on magnetic tape to desired printed format.
High Speed Printer 600 lines/min. adjustable to 200 and 400 if desired. 120 char/line; 130 char/line maximum with repetition of characters.
Card Punching Printer (Delivery—October 1956). Will print on both sides of a card and will punch the card.
Tape-To-Card Converter 120 cards/min. Converts magnetic tape recording to 80 column punched cards. Detachable plugboard provides for field rearrangement.
Tape to 90 Column Card Converter—Delivery 8 months.
Converts to 90 column punched cards; otherwise similar to Tape-To-Card Converter.
Rad Lab—Buffer storage Hg 3500 microsec/60 words.
USAF-AMC- Typewriter not used for normal input-output.

verifier

uniservos

unityper II

high-speed printer

tape-to-card
converter

The UNIVAC tape system, *above*, included the supervisory control, the central processing unit, the UNITYPER, and several UNISERVOs. Contemporary promotional photographs courtesy Smithsonian Institution.

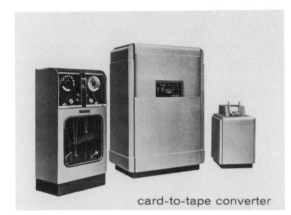

card-to-tape converter

uniprinter

reading of photographic film or even punched paper tape, and for certain special purposes, systems using this kind of equipment have great advantages. However, the erasability of magnetic tape constitutes such an enormous advantage for almost every application that this kind of external memory is a necessity for a general purpose machine . . . the compactness with which information can be stored on a magnetic tape is comparable to that of non-erasable media such as photographic film.[58]

They set out to develop a magnetic tape that could be used as both input and output with the UNIVAC. Unlike the plastic tape used with the BINAC, which was not very durable, the UNIVAC tape, called UNITAPE, was metallic. Initially, the tape was to be one-quarter-inch wide with a thickness of from 0.001 to 0.003 inches. As constructed, however, the width of the tape was one-half inch.[59] Approximately 1,200 feet of tape was wound on one reel. The tape could store 100–120 decimal digits per inch so one reel could store more than a million characters of data, the equivalent of tens of thousands of cards.

In addition to compactness, magnetic tape had other advantages: Records could be as long as desired instead of being restricted to eighty or ninety characters as with cards, tapes were relatively easy to store, and they were very durable.[60] The main disadvantage of tape was that data could not be read by people, only machines.

While there was no need for card processing at all with the UNIVAC system, companies with current card files could convert to a magnetic tape system or purchase a card-to-tape converter and, if desired, a tape-to-card converter so that processed data could be returned to the card format. This procedure, unnecessary as it was, allayed many of the fears and apprehensions of organizations accustomed to using cards.[61]

The UNIVAC system consisted of the central processor and the purchaser's choice of the following components: UNISERVOS, Supervisory Typewriters, UNITYPERS (numeric only), UNITYPERS (alphabetic and numeric), UNIPRINTERS, and Reproducers. The peripheral equipment could be purchased in any quantity or configuration desired.

The UNISERVO was the device that read data to and from magnetic tape. The speed with which it operated revolutionized input-output processing. Eckert and Mauchly's original goal was 10,000 decimal digits per second, but as finally designed, the input-output rate per second was 7,200 characters[62] or the equivalent of ninety IBM cards per second.

Originally eight UNISERVOs were considered a maximum for the UNIVAC system, but this was later expanded to ten. The UNISERVO could read tape forward or backward, but recording was limited to forward motion only.[63]

The Supervisory Typewriter was a console device that enabled the operator to control the system manually. A panel of selector switches and indicator lights could be used for diagnosing a system problem or for communicating an operator request to the system. This typewriter could also simultaneously produce a printed copy of all information being recorded on magnetic tape at ten characters per second.

The UNITYPER was a keyboard device used for manually recording data on magnetic tape. An operator depressed keys as on a typewriter keyboard, and the characters were automatically converted to magnetized bits on the tape.[64] The keyboard could be either all numeric or a combination of alphabetic and numeric characters. Although a correction feature allowed a field to be erased and retyped, the ability of an operator to recognize errors was limited.[65]

The UNIPRINTER was a device for printing information that had been processed by the computer. All controls for such printing were maintained on magnetic tape; the margins and tabulator stops, however, could be manually preset.

The Reproducer was a special device for duplicating tapes. Because no processing was required, it could reproduce data at the rate of 10,000 decimal digits per second.

The initial programming of the UNIVAC was performed in a machine language code with a set of approximately thirty instructions. A letter was used to represent an operation code and memory locations were expressed as three decimal digits. The programming capability was constantly updated.[66] Even before the early 1950s, Mauchly conceived of the possibility of coding in a symbolic language later called Short Code.[67]

An Assessment of Eckert and Mauchly's Organization

To assess Eckert and Mauchly's overall success is difficult. Technologically, they were able to develop and market an electronic computer for commercial use years before their competition. As businessmen, however, they were far less astute. Competing in a field where only major corporations with a significant amount of capital for research and development normally succeeded, they were unable to estimate accurately the requirements of a complex research and development effort. Because of their inexperience in business, they made many mistakes that established corporations would probably not have made. For instance, as Eckert and Mauchly themselves acknowledged later, their contracts with the government would have proven far more beneficial if they had been on a cost-plus-fixed-fee basis.

Shortly after Remington Rand purchased the corporation in February 1950, George Eltgroth, attorney for EMCC, summarized the corporation's failings in a letter to a friend:

We lost $179,000 on BINAC as we delivered for $100,000 an instrument which cost us $279,000 to build . . . These figures are significant since no one else in this country has ever produced an operating electronic digital computer at a cost of even $1,000,000. A reason, of course, was the major underestimation by the technical men who founded the corporation of the cost of doing business. For example, they talked seriously of overheads of the order of 25% and 40% whereas our operating experience has indicated values of 125%, the normal expected factor in a business of this type with our particular accounting set up. The situation was aggravated by a failure to appreciate the time required to button up such a complex engineering accomplishment.[68]

EMCC was repeatedly frustrated by the fact that "our largest problems are at present not technical ones but rather the securing of adequate capital so as to assure the government as well as others that we can carry out the contracts which we make."[69]

Moreover, Mauchly's willingness to allow the technical staff to determine business policy was an additional reason for EMCC's problems. Eckert's dominance appeared pervasive, at least in the 1948–1949 period. That UNIVAC production rather than BINAC research and development was emphasized in 1948–1949 is one case in point. There were other instances when Mauchly sought engineering advice on business problems where entrepreneurial input would have been more appropriate:

I am convinced that we are losing a hell of a lot of valuable time by reason of the fact that we are slow in making some necessary decisions . . . We cannot sell machines without first setting a price on them and that goes for our stock. I feel that the main reason why we have not as yet advanced very far in our effort to raise capital is that we have been unwilling to stick our necks out and put a definite price on our stock.[70]

Eckert's uncompromising stand on BINAC design priorities indicates that he believed engineering decisions should take priority over business concerns. In this regard, Eckert's dominance (as well as Mauchly's submission to it), while a distinct asset technologically, was a barrier to the success of their business.[71]

Another difficulty was Eckert's predilection as an inventor to focus on improving a device, sometimes at the expense of bringing it to fruition. As late as 1949, after the UNIVAC design had already been approved, Eckert thought that changing the memory from a mercury delay type to an electrostatic one would have decided advantages. The main advantages of this form of memory, which uses patterns of charges to represent binary numbers, are its speed and its ability to process digits in parallel rather than serial fashion.[72] Both the Whirlwind computer at MIT and the Institute for Advanced Study computer utilized this form of memory.

Eckert prepared a report for NBS specifying detailed plans for constructing an electrostatic memory,[73] but representatives of NBS objected to a major design change at such a late date.[74] The changes were not incorporated, but the fact that Eckert was willing to scrap previous design work at this juncture illustrates, to some extent, his lack of business sense.

In light of EMCC's efforts to stay solvent and its ultimate fate, the attempts of Henry Halladay, the Honeywell attorney in the litigation with Sperry Rand, to depict Eckert and Mauchly as partners who attempted to "rig" the computer market is somewhat ironic. Pointing out that the case was an antitrust as well as a patent matter, Halladay claimed that "it revolves around the attempt of the defendants and their predecessors in interest, including the partnership of Eckert and Mauchly, to so rig the computer market as to be in a position to dictate the terms upon which competition would be permitted."[75]

Considering the lack of experience and sophistication of Eckert and Mauchly in business matters, that they achieved as much as they did is, indeed, significant. Moreover, had they not made the attempt, it is likely that the commercial use of electronic digital computers would have been delayed for some time.[76] None of the major electronics companies or calculating equipment manufacturers in the United States, with the exception of Raytheon, had seriously attempted to develop similar equipment for commercial use.

Finally, whatever the financial difficulties and compromises in design experienced by Eckert and Mauchly in producing the UNIVAC, it was a revolutionary achievement marking the culmination of one period in computer history and the start of a new one.

8   In Retrospect

It is clear that Eckert and Mauchly's work was significantly influenced by academic, industrial, and governmental forces. It is equally clear that the influence of these social factors upon the development of the ENIAC, EDVAC, BINAC, and UNIVAC was not simple or uniform but multifaceted and complex.

The academic institution that had the greatest influence on the two inventors was the Moore School of Electrical Engineering, which both fostered and inhibited their work. The school's influence in turn was affected by governmental forces.

During the war the university provided an unusually favorable environment for the development of such devices. After the war, however, when the Moore School was concerned about how to deal with postwar government funding as a source of regular support, the attitudes of administrators toward the computer projects shifted. Moreover, the decision by Eckert and Mauchly to seek financial gain from their inventions was deemed incompatible with university policy and therefore was unacceptable to the Moore School.

The motivations of Eckert and Mauchly and their desire to develop large-scale computers meant that they had to establish their own commercial organization. Although it is not always the case that financial gain and academic interests are incompatible, the administrators at the Moore School *perceived* them to be incompatible. The school was unable to reconcile its beliefs on this matter with the potential benefits to be derived from being the preeminent computer center in the United States. Eckert and Mauchly therefore resigned from the school's staff and formed their own company, signaling the birth of the computer industry.

The failure of large corporations to take the initiative in developing computers during the immediate postwar period meant that if these devices were to be developed at all, the government would have to become the principal financing agent. Thus, the government's financial support of electronic digital computers both during and after the war was largely responsible for the very existence of many early projects. Various federal agencies were particularly impressed with Eckert and Mauchly's work, but despite their enthusiasm and willingness to provide funding, their influence was not nearly as great as it could have been. Bureaucratic delays in signing contracts and forwarding payments, problems with security clearance, and frequent requests for accountability all served to inhibit the Eckert-Mauchly Computer Corporation's progress. Moreover, these bureaucratic problems forced the two men to seek additional support from the private sector. Their decision to build the BINAC certainly affected progress on the UNIVAC and resulted in user dissatisfaction with both projects.

Although large corporations and academic institutions could adjust to the limitations imposed by the government, EMCC, a small business with a precarious financial position, could not. Hence, without adequate support from the academic and governmental spheres, Eckert and Mauchly were not skilled enough as businessmen, nor was their company large enough or financially secure enough to compete and succeed in the free market. Their eventual take-over by a large company was then the only way for their ideas to reach fruition and for a profit to be derived.

The plight of Eckert and Mauchly suggests that a high-technology field like computer development could not have succeeded without the intervention of large corporations and supports David Noble's claim in *America by Design* that the development of modern technology cannot be separated from the rise of corporate capitalism.[1]

Within the context of Mauchly and Eckert's experience, the most relevant of Noble's claims is that technology does not develop and survive in an autonomous fashion, but is integrally related to, and indeed dependent on, the social forces at play.[2]

Regardless of the vision and motives of the two men, in the end the group that derived the most benefit from electronic digital computers was, in fact, the large corporations owned and operated by what Noble would term the "dominant class in society."[3] It is no overstatement to suggest that the construction of a large-scale computer, no matter how competent the engineers involved, was at that time not feasible unless performed under the aegis of a large industrial or academic institution, or by the government itself.

Science and Technology

The relationship between science and technology has been complex and dynamic and continues to be a subject of debate among historians.[4] The interaction between Eckert and Mauchly and their relationship to the scientific and engineering communities illuminate this interrelationship but do not provide any universal construct governing the process.

One theory addressed by historians is the notion that technological change is generally a direct result or outgrowth of new scientific discoveries. In his work on high-voltage transmission systems Thomas Parke Hughes has challenged this theory. Hughes claims that invention is more frequently a response to technological need than to new scientific theories or discoveries.[5]

Evidence presented in the first few chapters above substantiates Hughes's conclusion. It is clear that the invention of electronic digital computers was not directly dependent on recent scientific discoveries and was in response to a technological need. Electron theory, the basis for electronics, was not a new concept in 1943; the scientific theories necessary to develop computers were formulated by 1919. Moreover, the ENIAC was very much a response to the inadequacies of the differential analyzer. Similarly, the EDVAC was a response to the inadequacies of the ENIAC.

In his paper on the ENIAC, Hughes points out:

The invention of the differential analyzer emerged from a setting comparable to the circumstances in which ENIAC was later introduced. In both cases, the general development of technology created a reverse salient in an expanding front. The concept, reverse salient, conveys the image of an advancing line punctuated by segments in which the advance has been significantly retarded. These retarded segments are reverse salients and are often seen as situations that must be improved upon if the advance is to continue. Uncoordinated advancing technological systems have reverse salients calling for response in order that technological advance may continue. In the case of the invention of the differential analyzer, it was primarily a response to a reverse salient in the advanced front of electrical engineering technology; in the case of ENIAC . . . it was a response to a reverse salient in the rapidly advancing front of military ordnance technology.[6]

In short, the major factors affecting the technological development of computers were frequently not scientific but social, administrative, even political ones.

Scientific need, however, as opposed to scientific discovery, was a significant factor in providing the climate or frame of reference necessary for technological development. It is no mere coincidence that many of the major inventors and innovators in the computer field from 1930 to 1943, and afterwards as well, were scientists who were in need of tools or equipment to promote scientific advance. Stibitz, Aiken, von Neumann, Atanasoff, Wallace Eckert, and Mauchly all held Ph.D. degrees in scientific disciplines. They each built or adapted computational equipment for a specific scientific purpose. Although the history of the Eckert and Mauchly computers supports Hughes's claim that scientific discovery does not always provide a necessary or sufficient condition for technological advance, science sometimes does, as in this case, play a significant role in creating a need for technology.

Values of Scientists and Technologists

Another major theory relating to the interaction of science and technology is that scientists and technologists subscribe to the same values. Hughes, in studying power transmission systems, concluded that research engineers in that field seem to have used "a method that should be styled scientific." According to Hughes:

The authors they cited and the periodicals they used and for which they wrote represented original knowledge; the engineers consciously or unconsciously used and attempted to formulate general statements or laws; mathematics was an analytical tool and a language for them; hypotheses were formulated by them and experiments were designed for the laboratory or in nature to test these hypotheses . . . research engineers' use of the scientific method may be one of the closest links of technology and science.[7]

The conclusions drawn from examining the work of Mauchly and Eckert do not, however, support this claim. In the case of computer development, the norms of science and technology were somewhat dissimilar, and in some instances they even clashed. Scientists like von Neumann, Goldstine, and Burks, for example, conformed to academic standards by writing and publishing articles and reports as a method of either establishing priority or disseminating their findings. Most of the engineers, on the other hand, did not publish, and in the few cases where they did, it was only after a new device had been operational for some time.

Scientists associated with the Eckert-Mauchly computers considered the economic motives of the two men a violation of academic and scientific norms. Hughes himself has noted that

With respect to patents, there is a difference between the style of scientists and technologists. Ten or twenty patents may be worthless economically, but they are an ornament for an engineer, whereas it may be almost a disgrace for a scientist to have patents.[8]

Hughes has suggested that the methods of research undertaken by scientists and technologists are also similar. In the case of the Eckert-Mauchly organization, however, the evidence does not support this view. Eckert as the supervising engineer was fundamentally, indeed almost exclusively, interested in producing operating computers. He had little interest in the theoretical basis for design or in the application of these devices. Although he took part in discussions on decimal versus binary notation, serial versus parallel transmission, and so on, he was far more interested in realizing specific design principles than in providing a theoretical construct. In this sense, he relied heavily on the experimental method. Von Neumann, on the other hand, and Mauchly as well, was only peripherally interested in the actual technology. Von Neumann's main concern was the theoretical construct which could be applied to a wide variety of computers. His method of research was far more deductive than inductive. While it may well be that in many cases the differences between the scientific and technological methods of inquiry are minimal, in this instance, Eckert as chief engineer and von Neumann and Mauchly as science advisors and consultants differed considerably in their approaches.[9]

A study by Edwin Layton of the science-technology interaction focuses on the distinctions rather than the similarities between the disciplines and is therefore more applicable to the development of the Eckert-Mauchly computer. He sees science and engineering as "different social organisms" or "subcultures," each "with its own membership and values, its own rituals and perceptions."[10] Layton also points out: "Nor do engineers accept the priority of theory over practice." According to Layton:

> Though most engineers have been willing to accept an identity as applied scientists, there has been at least some dissent. There is, in fact, a second engineering ideology, which defines the engineer's role in terms of design which may or may not be considered part of "science." Indeed most engineering publications and most engineering practices are probably better understood in terms of design than science.[11]

Hence, the normative systems in scientific and technological fields are frequently different enough, as in the Eckert-Mauchly case, to warrant the emphasis on their dissimilarity as opposed to their similarity. However, the concerns of scientists and technologists for priority and preeminence sometimes cause them to act in very similar ways, indicating that a sharp dichotomy between the two fields may, in some instances, be more myth than reality.

Further, instead of opposing each other, the practical needs of the technologist and the theoretical orientation of the scientist sometimes complement each other. The case of the stored-program concept certainly seems to support this view, despite the sharp divergence of opinion that now exists on this issue. More importantly, the relationship of Eckert, the engineer, and Mauchly, the scientist (albeit an atypical one), demonstrates how the integration of these perspectives can be extremely effective from a technological point of view.

The Relationship Between Invention and Innovation

The nature of technological advance is frequently seen as having two dimensions, one broadly characterized as "invention"—the idea, the material advance—and one even more broadly characterized as innovation—the application of invention, or the forces that lead to the integration of that advance within society. A major aim of this book has been to demonstrate that innovative components have played an integral role in the development of the Eckert-Mauchly computers, that Mauchly was in large part responsible for this innovative contribution, and that the forces of invention and innovation were dynamically interrelated.

Despite a general consensus by historians on this dual nature of technological advance, many scholars disagree about the overall import of each of these two factors. The historian of ideas is, in general, concerned with the history of invention and sees technological development mainly as the unfolding of ideas, with innovation a secondary concern.[12] Economic historians, on the other hand, are generally concerned with the applications of technological advance and consider the inventive process secondary. Joseph Schumpeter's classic work, *The Theory of Economic Development*, illustrates this perspective:

As long as they are not carried into practice, inventions are economically irrelevant . . . Although entrepreneurs of course may be inventors, just as they may be capitalists, they are inventors not by nature of their function but by coincidence and vice versa . . . It is therefore not advisable, and it may be downright misleading to stress the element of invention as much as many writers do.[13]

Social historians, in general, are only peripherally interested in technological developments per se; they see technology primarily in terms of its relationship to society.[14]

The electronic digital computer is a specific case in the history of technology that requires analysis in terms that integrate all three orientations—intellectual, economic, and social. Invention and innovation, as integrally related forces, cannot be effectively separated. Thomas M. Smith, in an article on the research and development phase of Project Whirlwind, states:

We all find it useful to speak analytically of the R & D process, on occasion, in terms of its early, or creative and inventive, phase; in terms of its middle, or developmental, phase; and in terms of its production for market, or innovations, phase. And we all agree that the middle phase overlaps with the phases on either side of it in such a way that no sharp lines can be drawn.[15]

Simplistic models that define the inventor as the creator and the innovator as the entrepreneur also do not suffice. In the case of the Eckert-Mauchly computers, Mauchly was mainly interested in the innovative aspects of the development work. He was keenly aware at an early stage of the feasibility of electronic digital computers. Later, he focused on their potential applications and on the potential profits to be derived, but his entrepreneurial and administrative abilities were, in general, not on a par with his innovative vision.

"Innovation," as used in this book, encompasses the adaptation of ideas in an intellectual sense so that they are rendered practical, the adaptation of ideas in a social sense so that they are rendered useful, and the adaptation of ideas in an economic sense so that they are rendered profitable. It is within this framework that the term "innovator" best applies to Mauchly.

Questions of Priority: Atanasoff

The *Honeywell* v. *Sperry Rand* case was in many ways responsible for bringing some of the controversial issues surrounding the Eckert-Mauchly computers to the forefront, as well as for creating additional ones. One basis for Honeywell's claim that the ENIAC patent was invalid was the prior invention of the Atanasoff-Berry computer.

Prior to this court action John Vincent Atanasoff's name was not well known to most computer scientists, or even to most participants in the Eckert-Mauchly organization. Hence, as a direct result of Honeywell's claim and the fact that the court held in favor of that claim, Atanasoff is frequently depicted as the main influence on Mauchly and, through Mauchly, the entire history of computers. Goldstine, for instance, gives the following account:

Atanasoff contemplated storing the coefficients of an equation in capacitors located on the periphery of a cylinder rotating at one revolution per second and using punch cards for the storage of intermediate results. He apparently had a prototype of his machine working "early in 1940." This machine was, it should be emphasized, probably the first use of vacuum tubes to do digital computation and was a special-purpose machine . . .

This machine never saw the light of day as a serious tool for computation since it was somewhat premature in its engineering conception and limited in its logical one. Nonetheless it must be viewed as a great pioneering effort. Perhaps its chief importance was to influence the thinking of another physicist who was much interested in the computational process, John W. Mauchly.

Atanasoff is similarly depicted by Goldstine as having been the prime agent in fostering Mauchly's interest in electronic computers: "During 1941, Mauchly was so stimulated by his conversations with Atanasoff that he sketched in his laboratory notebook various emendations to Atanasoff's ideas."[16] Goldstine's apparent support of Honeywell's claim regarding Atanasoff's priority has been addressed in Chapter 2 above.

The Atanasoff-Berry Computer. Courtesy John V. Atanasoff.

In that chapter, I indicated that in the late 1930s John Mauchly recognized that a need existed for electronic digital computers and was able to foresee their widespread applicability. In 1940, he met Atanasoff. Like Mauchly, Atanasoff recognized that it was possible to construct an electronic digital computer; indeed, he built a model of such a device. The existence of this prototype, or model, convinced Mauchly that such a device was, in fact, feasible.

Thus, in 1940, when these men met, they were both interested in constructing an electronic digital computer for scientific use; moreover, Atanasoff had already begun such a project. The influence of Atanasoff on Mauchly seems to have ended at that point. During the war, Atanasoff abandoned his computer project; in fact, he never completed the actual device. Mauchly, on the other hand, recognized that wartime was a most propitious period for building a computer. In the summer of 1941 he enrolled in a war-training course at the Moore School and later accepted a position there in an effort to learn more about electronics and to gain a closer association with experts in that field.

Atanasoff was interested in developing a computer for solving very specific types of problems, that is, systems of linear equations. Mauchly was interested in developing a computer for solving a wide variety of problems in meteorology, physics, and commercial areas as well.

It is relevant to note the differences in physical characteristics of the computers developed by the two men. The Atanasoff-Berry computer was a compact, cabinet-size model equipped with a rotating drum memory device and designed to incorporate over 300 vacuum tubes when finished. The machine never was fully operational.

The ENIAC, on the other hand, was a huge machine of 30 large units containing over 18,000 vacuum tubes. It occupied an entire room. Accepted as operational by the Army in June 1946, it remained in use at the Moore School until November, when it was disassembled for shipping to Aberdeen. Once reassembled in July 1947, it remained in operation more than eight years, until October 1955. During this period, it solved many problems for the Army, other government agencies, and university people generally.

Thus, Goldstine's claim regarding the influence of Atanasoff on Mauchly's work fails to come to terms with the question of innovation. Mauchly's vision and his adaptation of Atanasoff's work, combined with his own work in the field, represented this innovative component.

The question of priority, then, is clearly an issue. It is obvious that, in some sense, Eckert and Mauchly's work was not without precedent. The two men were "scooped" in a way by Charles Babbage (1792–1871), the first known inventor to conceive of a programmable computer; by Howard Aiken and George Stibitz, who developed digital computers, albeit electromechanical ones; by Wallace Eckert and Leslie Comrie, who recognized that punch-card digital equipment had its place in scientific applications; by Vannevar Bush, Harold Hazen, and Samuel Caldwell, who constructed electrical and electronic computers, albeit analog ones; by NCR, RCA, and other large corporations, which developed electronic counters for the National Defense Research Committee; and by John Atanasoff, who constructed a model of an electronic digital computer for solving systems of linear equations. Most inventions are, in some sense, based on technologies intrinsic to other inventions. But, as in other episodes in the history of technology, the inventors who demonstrate applicability as well as creativity and who bring ideas to fruition are frequently the ones who gain recognition.[17] Eckert and Mauchly's successful completion of the ENIAC was directly related to their ability to convince the government of the applicability of such a machine. Hence, the recognition to which they are entitled is based, in part, on the invention of the first fully operational electronic digital computer and their innovative ability to demonstrate its practicality for wartime use.

The question of priority, however, is frequently given too much consideration by some historians. Such a question serves no real purpose in understanding the dynamics of technological development. Louis C. Hunter suggests that

Historians have been too prone to compensate for the wide gaps in our knowledge by playing up the achievements of the few men whose names have come down to us. There is reason to believe that if the returns were all in, the accomplishments of a Fulton, a Shreve, an Evans or a French [inventors of steamboats] would assume a quite modest position beside the collective contribution of scores of master mechanics, ship carpenters, and shop foremen in whose hands the detailed work of construction, adaption and innovation largely rested.[18]

Similarly, the support provided by highly skilled engineers both at the Moore School and at their company was of fundamental importance in the development of all the Eckert-Mauchly computers.

The Stored-Program Concept

Another issue relating to the Eckert-Mauchly computers that has given rise to controversy is the priority claims over the stored-program concept. This controversy has wider significance since it is really part of the issue of John von Neumann's role in the history of electronic digital computers.

For a beginning, it is important to reiterate that the ideas intrinsic to the ENIAC and the EDVAC were very much a result of a group effort. Mauchly may be credited with the initial concept and with an appreciation for its applicability. Eckert may be credited with the invention of key components such as the electronic ring counter for the ENIAC and the mercury delay line for the EDVAC. Moreover, he was responsible for the overall supervision of engineering operations for all four machines. But the integration of

The ENIAC, with portable function table matrices on right. Courtesy Smithsonian Institution.

features, the development of concepts, and particularly the logical design for the EDVAC were group efforts.

Von Neumann's emergence on the scene in 1944 served to heighten the significance of the ENIAC and EDVAC projects and to alter the group dynamics. His attention to the logical design of computers in general shifted the focus of the Eckert-Mauchly group. Among other things, this shift highlighted the importance of developing a stored-program computer, a concept that actually preceded von Neumann's involvement.

Goldstine comments on von Neumann's influence:

> He was among all members of the group at the Moore School, *the* indispensable one. Everyone there was indispensable as regards some part of the project—Eckert, for example, was unique in his invention of the delay line as a memory device—but only von Neumann was essential to the entire task.[19]

To suggest, unequivocally, that von Neumann was the one essential person in the Moore School group indicates Goldstine's predilection to value scientific contributions over engineering ones and to give primary credit to von Neumann's work.

The stored-program concept has been attributed to von Neumann largely as a result of the June 1945 "First Draft of a Report on the EDVAC" (printed as an appendix to this book). As indicated in Chapter 4 above, there has been a good deal of controversy regarding von Neumann's name on the report as sole author and the right of his colleagues to distribute the report without giving appropriate credit to others. Since many of the ideas formulated in the draft were a result of general discussions at the Moore School, they were neither the property nor the exclusive creation of any single person. Goldstine agrees that "all members of the discussion group shared their ideas with each other without restraint and therefore all deserve credit. Eckert and Mauchly unquestionably led on the technical side and von Neumann on the logical" and excuses the failure of von Neumann to credit others as follows:

> It has been said by some that von Neumann did not give credit in his "First Draft" to others. The reason for this was that the document was intended by von Neumann as a working paper for use in clarifying and coordinating the thinking of the group and was not intended for publication.[20]

Since scientists, as opposed to engineers, focus on writing reports and papers to establish a frame of reference for ideas, Goldstine sees von Neumann's motives as entirely appropriate. Despite the caveats regarding the draft report, Goldstine claims that von Neumann's own ideas predominated in it:

> This report represents a masterful analysis and synthesis by him of all the thinking that had gone into the EDVAC from the fall of 1944 through the spring of 1945. Not everything in there is his, but the crucial parts are . . . Von Neumann was the first person, as far as I am concerned, who understood explicitly that a computer performed logical functions and that the electrical aspects were ancillary.[21]

Clearly Goldstine regards the scientist's focus on "analysis and synthesis" as more significant than the engineer's focus on "electrical aspects." Although the evidence presented in Chapter 4 does not support Goldstine's perspective, von Neumann's contribution to the Moore School projects should not be understated. His presence legitimized development work on electronic digital computers for engineers, mathematicians, and the government in the postwar period. His theory of logical design set the stage for a whole series of computers constructed in the so-called "von Neumann tradition." Goldstine's statement on these influences appears at first glance to be a reasonable assessment:

Prior to von Neumann people certainly knew that circuits had to be built to effect the various arithmetic and control functions, but they concentrated primarily on the electrical engineering aspects. These aspects were of course of vital importance, but it was von Neumann who first gave a logical treatment to the subject, much as if it were a conventional branch of logic or mathematics.[22]

But a major conclusion of this book is that the stored-program concept was not the invention of von Neumann alone. It is more appropriate to state, as Goldstine himself does, that von Neumann "elucidated" this concept:

In his famous report he proposed a repertoire of instructions for the EDVAC, and in a subsequent letter he worked out detailed programming for a *sort and merge* routine. This represents a milestone, since it is the first elucidation of the now famous stored program concept together with a completely worked-out illustration.[23]

Perhaps the most valid account of von Neumann's contribution to logical design and to the stored-program concept is given by Maurice Wilkes:

The computing field owes a very great debt to von Neumann. He *appreciated* [emphasis added] at once the possibilities of what became known as logical design and the potentialities implicit in the stored program principle. That von Neumann should bring his great prestige and influence to bear was important, since the new ideas were too revolutionary for some, and powerful voices were being raised to say that the ultrasonic memory would not be reliable enough, and that to mix instructions and numbers in the same memory was going against nature.[24]

Wilkes's comments indicate that von Neumann understood the importance of the stored-program concept and that he was singularly effective at legitimizing stored-program computers as scientific instruments. Wilkes's perspective, then, appears to be somewhat more objective than Goldstine's.

The Moore School's Decline

There is no doubt that the administrators and educators at the Moore School provided the climate necessary for the youthful engineers to develop the first electronic digital computer. This contribution is particularly significant in light of the fact that there were larger and better known engineering schools and corporations that had made great strides in developing computational equipment and that seemed the logical places for the growth of new ideas for computers.

The early lead gained by the Moore School in developing these devices raises the question why this engineering school failed to maintain its pre-eminence in the field. Indeed, the speed with which it lost that preeminence is itself striking. The Moore School was the only institution in the United States that was building an electronic digital computer from 1943 to 1945. By 1946, many of the main participants in this development had left and the institution was no longer a prime force in the field.

Goldstine suggests the following reasons for this decline:

First perhaps may be the failure on the part of the senior staff of the Moore School—Brainerd excepted—to appreciate the overwhelming importance the computer was to have to electrical engineering as a discipline. It is my surmise that while these professors saw that the school had done an excellent piece of war work, they did not see the implications of these devices for the future. As we have already mentioned, none of them was close technically to the situation, but all saw or heard the fireworks arising from intellectual credits and patents. Perhaps, therefore, they were "turned off" by the disruptive aspects that they witnessed.

It may also be that the dean felt intuitively that a major effort in computers was too large and disruptive a program for the orderly life of a school dedicated to teaching the young.[25]

Most of Goldstine's assessments of this issue are borne out in the material discussed in previous chapters. The Moore School's inability, or unwillingness, to deal decisively with the issue of postwar government funding was a fundamental factor in the school's decline as a computing center. The school's failure to come to terms with the conflicting norms of academics like Brainerd and of profit-oriented engineers like Eckert was another major factor that compromised its position in the computing field.

Goldstine suggests that "perhaps it was the strong impetus at the Institute for Advanced Study, more than any other reason, which served to end the hegemony of the Moore School in the field of computing."[26] Here, again, Goldstine tends to underestimate the value of Eckert and Mauchly's contribution to the school's work and to overemphasize von Neumann's role. The Moore School did not appear to decline relative to the rising influence of von Neumann and the institute. The Moore School declined as a center for computing research because of the departure of Eckert and Mauchly.

The Significance of the BINAC

Although many people have claimed that the BINAC was never fully operational, the evidence presented in Chapter 5 indicates that the BINAC, at the time of its acceptance test, was a working computer. Once moved to California, however, it failed to operate properly for some time. Moreover, it was not possible to use the BINAC as an airborne computer, as some have claimed was meant to be its primary function.

The Eckert-Mauchly organization considered the BINAC a second-order priority. Had the firm focused its efforts on the development of smaller scale mathematical devices like the BINAC, rather than on the far more elaborate, large-scale UNIVAC, it might have sold more machines at a lower cost and with less overhead. Such a policy decision might well have kept Eckert and Mauchly's company solvent, but it was not the policy they pursued. BINAC was less a failure in its own right than a casualty of their larger policy failures.

Indifference of Large Firms in the 1940s

Such major industrial firms as NCR, RCA, and IBM were engaged in small-scale research on the feasibility of electronic counters and electronic digital computers in the early 1940s. During the late 1940s, these organizations demonstrated an interest in the work of Eckert and Mauchly and in other groups designing computers. Such firms did not, however, undertake major computer projects for commercial purposes during the immediate postwar period.[27] According to Henry Tropp:

The National Cash Register Company offers a particularly intriguing industrial "might have been." NCR actually had an electronic computing device constructed during the late 1930s. It was a high-speed arithmetic machine which could add, subtract and multiply electronically, and presumably this machine could have become the first commercial electronic computer had the company wished to pioneer in this field. However, NCR management was not interested in automatic computing per se, but only in improving its existing line of office equipment.[28]

Tropp goes on to cite other examples of major industrial firms that failed to take any initiative in developing electronic devices:

If one examines the environment at major U.S. corporations during the 1930s and early 1940s, there is a striking lack of interest in any aspect of automatic computing. I have yet to see a publication from that period that reveals an interest in putting research and development funds into finding better ways of doing automatic computation. At Bell Laboratories, for instance, Stibitz's Model I Calculator might well have been the last in the series if it hadn't been for the pressure of wartime needs and the accompanying government support. IBM was similarly uninterested in advancing the computer art . . . The company seems to have been primarily interested in improving existing products and building a strong patent position for possible future applications. I have been able to discern no evidence of a vision of IBM—or any other corporation—in those days that was comparable to that held by Aiken, Mauchly, Stibitz, Atanasoff, J. Presper Eckert or Wallace Eckert.[29]

IBM's failure to undertake any research projects in this area is particularly surprising, since it was the major manufacturer of calculating equipment and

UNIVAC central processing unit displaying mercury-delay-line memory tanks. Courtesy Smithsonian Institution.

was the company which would be most affected by the availability of commercial computers. Moreover, IBM had already demonstrated its interest in computational research and development by funding the academic projects of Howard Aiken and Wallace Eckert. Yet no work on electronic digital computers was undertaken by that organization in the 1940s despite inter-office memos written by IBM engineers recommending such work. Moreover, when Eckert and Mauchly sought to sell their ill-fated company, IBM showed little interest. William Rodgers, the author of a biography of Thomas Watson, Sr., states:

The builders of ENIAC went to the Watson Laboratory to discuss with men there the possibility of joining resources and talent to put their new UNIVAC on the market. Eckert and Mauchly wanted a contract with IBM and the Watson Laboratory and to be taken into the company or empowered to produce the computer under some financial arrangement to be agreed upon. Eckert and Mauchly, with a professional reputation among their peers as great as Aiken's in scientific respects, were nearly broke. While they possessed the UNIVAC, they were without resources . . . Watson Laboratory scientists, impressed by the men and the UNIVAC, were enthusiastic about Eckert and Mauchly's proposals and recommended negotiations. But word came uptown from galactic headquarters to brush them off. There was, in the words of Watson's decision relayed to the Laboratory, "no reasonable interaction possible between Eckert-Mauchly and IBM."[30]

Because of IBM's policy of barring independent scholars access to its archives, the reasons for the company's belated entry into the field are difficult to assess. It may be that IBM recognized that once development work was completed by others, it could capture the market by simply adapting the new technology. This would save the company the money and effort necessary to develop this new technology itself. On the other hand, it may be that fear of antitrust regulations kept large organizations like IBM from undertaking expensive research and development efforts. The risk of possibly gaining an early virtual monopoly on computers might not have been worth the financial benefits to be derived.

Rather than point to IBM's belated entry into the computer field, Goldstine (who was at one time director of mathematical sciences at IBM's Thomas Watson Research Center) focuses on its "early" start:

In my opinion it was Thomas Watson, Jr. who played the key role in moving IBM into the electronic computer field . . . He exerted considerable pressure on IBM to move it in the direction of adapting electronic techniques to the business machine field. He *early* [emphasis added] sensed the importance scientific computing would have to the entire field.[31]

Goldstine's appraisal of this matter is, I believe, somewhat less than objective. Although the younger Watson may have sensed the prospects early, the fact remains that IBM made a late entry, not an early start, in the computer field.

Summary

The controversial issues relating to Atanasoff's contribution to Mauchly's work, the stored-program concept, the Moore School's loss of preeminence in the computer field, the significance of the BINAC, and the failure of large corporations to develop computers in the 1940s have all been addressed by Goldstine and others who have written on the history of computing. A major objective of this book was to treat these issues as objectively as possible. The conclusions drawn are in many cases radically different from those which have heretofore been provided by others. Of perhaps greater significance is the effort in this study to relate these issues to larger questions in the history of technology, and by so doing, to provide an appropriate historical perspective on the development of the electronic digital computer.

APPENDIX

First Draft
of a
Report on the
EDVAC

John von Neumann

Contract No. W-670-ORD-4926 between the United States Army Ordnance Department and the University of Pennsylvania.

CONTENTS

180 APPENDIX

CONTENTS

First Draft
of a
Report on the
EDVAC

John von Neumann

1.0 Definitions

1.1 The considerations which follow deal with the structure of a *very high speed automatic digital computing system,* and in particular with its *logical control.* Before going into specific details, some general explanatory remarks regarding these concepts may be appropriate.

1.2 An *automatic computing system* is a (usually highly composite) device, which can carry out instructions to perform calculations of a considerable order of complexity—e.g. to solve a non-linear partial differential equation in 2 or 3 independent variables numerically.

The instructions which govern this operation must be given to the device in absolutely exhaustive detail. They include all numerical information which is required to solve the problem under consideration: Initial and boundary values of the dependent variables, values of fixed parameters (constants), tables of fixed functions which occur in the statement of the problem. These instructions must be given in some form which the device can sense: Punched into a series of punchcards or on teletype tape, magnetically impressed on steel tape or wire, photographically impressed on motion picture film, wired into one or more, fixed or exchangeable plugboards—this list being by no means necessarily complete. All these procedures require the use of some code, to express the logical and the algebraical definition of the problem under consideration, as well as the necessary numerical material (cf. above).

Once these instructions are given to the device, it must be able to carry them out completely and without any need for further intelligent human intervention. At the end of the required operations the device must record the results again in one of the forms referred to above. The results are numerical data; they are a specified part of the numerical material produced by the device in the process of carrying out the instructions referred to above.

1.3 It is worth noting, however, that the device will in general produce essentially more numerical material (in order to reach the results) than the (final) results mentioned. Thus only a fraction of its numerical output will have to be recorded as indicated in 1.2, the remainder will only circulate in the interior of the device, and never be recorded for human sensing. This point will receive closer consideration subsequently, in particular in [*not completed*].

1.4 The remarks of 1.2 on the desired automatic functioning of the device must, of course, assume that it functions faultlessly. Malfunctioning of any device has, however, always a finite probability—and for a complicated device and a long sequence of operations it may not be possible to keep this possibility negligible. Any error may vitiate the entire output of the device. For the recognition and correction of such malfunctions intelligent human intervention will in general be necessary.

However, it may be possible to avoid even these phenomena to some extent. The device may recognize the most frequent malfunctions automatically, indicate their presence and location by externally visible signs, and then stop. Under certain conditions it might even carry out the necessary correction automatically and continue. (Cf.[*not completed*].)

2.0 Main Subdivision of the System

2.1 In analyzing the functioning of the contemplated device, certain classificatory distinctions suggest themselves immediately.

2.2 First: Since the device is primarily a computer, it will have to perform the elementary operations of arithmetic most frequently. There are addition, subtraction, multiplication and division: $+, -, \times, \div$. It is therefore reasonable that it should contain specialized organs for just these operations.

It must be observed, however, that while this principle as such is probably sound, the specific way in which it is realized requires close scrutiny. Even the above list of operations: $+, -, \times, \div$, is not beyond doubt. It may be extended to include such operation as $\sqrt{}, \sqrt[3]{}$, sgn, $| \ |$, also $^{10}\log$, $^{2}\log$, ln, sin and their inverses, etc. One might also consider restricting it, e.g. omitting $\div$ and even $\times$. One might also consider more elastic arrangements. For some operations radically different procedures are conceivable, e.g. using successive approximation methods or function tables. These matters will be gone into in [*not completed*]. At any rate a *central arithmetical* part of the device will probably have to exist, and this constitutes *the first specific part: CA*.

2.3 Second: The logical control of the device, that is the proper sequencing of its operations, can be most efficiently carried out by a central control organ. If the device is to be *elastic*, that is as nearly as possible *all purpose*, then a distinction must be made between the specific instructions given for and defining a particular problem, and the general control organs which see to it that these instructions—no matter what they are—are carried out. The former must be stored in some way—in existing devices this is done as indicated in 1.2—the latter are represented by definite operating parts of the device. By the *central control* we mean this latter function only, and the organs which perform it form *the second specific part: CC*.

2.4 Third: Any device which is to carry out long and complicated sequences of operations (specifically of calculations) must have a considerable memory. At least the four following phases of its operation require a memory:

(a) Even in the process of carrying out a multiplication or a division, a series of intermediate (partial) results must be remembered. This applies to a lesser extent even to additions and subtractions (when a carry digit may have to be carried over several positions), and to a greater extent to $\sqrt{\ }, \sqrt[3]{\ }$, if these operations are wanted. (Cf. [*not completed*].)

(b) The instructions which govern a complicated problem may constitute a considerable material, particularly so, if the code is circumstantial (which it is in most arrangements). This material must be remembered.

(c) In many problems specific functions play an essential role. They are usually given in the form of a table. Indeed in some cases this is the way in which they are given by experience (e.g. the equation of state of a substance in many hydrodynamical problems). In other cases they may be given by analytical expressions, but it may nevertheless be simpler and quicker to obtain their values from a fixed tabulation, than to compute them anew (on the basis of the analytical definition) whenever a value is required. It is usually convenient to have tables of a moderate number of entries only (100–200) and to use interpolation. Linear and even quadratic interpolation will not be sufficient in most cases, so it is best to count on a standard of cubic or biquadratic (or even higher order) interpolation, c.f. [*not completed*].

Some of the functions mentioned in the course of 2.2 may be handled in this way: ^{10}lg, ^{2}lg, ln, sin and their inverses, possibly also $\sqrt{\ }, \sqrt[3]{\ }$. Even the reciprocal might be treated in this manner, thereby reducing $\div$ to $\times$.

(d) For partial differential equations the initial conditions and the boundary conditions may constitute an extensive numerical material, which must be remembered throughout a given problem.

(e) For partial differential equations of the hyperbolic or parabolic type, integrated along with a variable t, the (intermediate) results belonging to the cycle t must be remembered for the calculation of the cycle $t + dt$. This material is much of the type (d), except that it is not put into the device by human operators, but produced (and probably subsequently again removed and replaced by the corresponding data for t + dt) by the device itself, in the course of its automatic operation.

(f) For total differential equations (d), (e) apply too, but they require smaller memory capacities. Further memory requirements of the type (d) are required in problems which depend on given constants, fixed parameters, etc.

(g) Problems which are solved by successive approximations (e.g. partial differential equations of the elliptic type, treated by relaxation methods) require a memory of the type (e): The (intermediate) results of each approximation must be remembered, while those of the next one are being computed.

(h) Sorting problems and certain statistical experiments (for which a very high speed device offers an interesting opportunity) require a memory for the material which is being treated.

2.5 To sum up the third remark: The device requires a considerable memory. While it appears that various parts of this memory have to perform functions which differ somewhat in their nature and considerably in their purpose, it is nevertheless tempting to treat the entire memory as one organ, and to have its parts even as interchangeable as possible for the various functions enumerated above. This point will be considered in detail cf. [*not completed*].

At any rate the total *memory* constitutes *the third specific part of the device: M*.

2.6 The three specific parts CA, CC, (together C), and M correspond to the *associative* neurons in the human nervous system. It retains to discuss the equivalents of the *sensory* or *afferent* and the *motor* or *efferent* neurons. These are the *input* and the *output* organs of the device, and we shall now consider them briefly.

In other words: All transfers of numerical (or other) information between the parts C and M of the device must be affected by the mechanisms contained in these parts. There remains, however, the necessity of getting the original definitory information from outside into the device, and also of getting the final information, the results, from the device into the outside.

By the outside we mean media of the type described in 1.2: Here information can be produced more or less directly by human action (typing, punching, photographing light impulses produced by keys of the same type, magnetizing metal tape or wire in some analogous manner, etc.), it can be statically stored, and finally sensed more or less directly by human organs.

The device must be endowed with the ability to maintain the input and output (sensory and motor) contact with some specific medium of this type (cf. 1.2): That medium will be called the *outside recording medium of the device: R.* Now we have:

2.7 Fourth: The device must have organs to transfer (numerical or other) information from R into its specific parts C and M. These organs form its *input*, the *fourth specific part: I.* It will be seen that it is best to make all transfers from R (by I) into M, and never directly into C (cf. [*not completed*]).

2.8 Fifth: The device must have organs to transfer (presumably only numerical information) from its specific parts C and M into R. These organs form its *output*, the *fifth specific part: O.* It will be seen that it is again best to make all transfers from M (by O) into R, and never directly from C (cf.[*not completed*]).

2.9 The output information, which goes into R, represents, of course, the final results of the operation of the device on the problem under consideration. These must be distinguished from the intermediate results, discussed e.g. in 2.4, (e)–(g), which remain inside M. At this point an important question arises: Quite apart from its attribute of more or less direct accessibility to human action and perception R has also the properties of a memory. Indeed, it is the natural medium for long time storage of all the information obtained by the automatic device on various problems. Why is it then necessary to provide for another type of memory within the device M? Could not all, or at least some functions of M—preferably those which involve great bulks of information—be taken over by R?

Inspection of the typical functions of M, as enumerated in 2.4, (a)–(h), shows this: It would be convenient to shift (a) (the short-duration memory required while an arithmetical operation is being carried out) outside the device, i.e. from M into R. (Actually (a) will be inside the device, but in CA rather than in M. Cf. the end of 12.2.) All existing devices, even the existing desk computing machines, use the equivalent of M at this point. However (b) (logical instructions) might be sensed from outside, i.e. by I from R, and the same goes for (c) (function tables) and (e), (g) (intermediate results). The latter may be conveyed by O to R when the device produces them, and sensed by I from R when it needs them. The same is true to some extent of (d) (initial conditions and parameters) and possibly even of (f) (intermediate results from a total differential equation). As to (h) (sorting and statistics), the situation is somewhat ambiguous: In many cases the possibility of using M accelerates matters decisively, but suitable blending of the use of M with a longer range use of R may be feasible without serious loss of speed and increase the amount of material that can be handled considerably.

Indeed, all existing (fully or partially automatic) computing devices use R—as a stack of punchcards or a length of teletype tape—for all these purposes (excepting (a), as pointed out above). Nevertheless it will appear that a really high speed device would be very limited in its usefulness, unless it can rely on M, rather than on R, for all the purposes enumerated in 2.4, (a)–(h), with certain limitations in the case of (e), (g), (h), (cf. [*not completed*]).

3.0 Procedure of Discussion

3.1 The classification of 2.0 being completed, it is now possible to take up the five specific parts into which the device was soon to be subdivided, and to discuss them one by one. Such a discussion must bring out the features required for each one of these parts in itself, as well as in their relations to each other. It must also determine the specific procedures to be used in dealing with numbers from the point of view of the device, in carrying out arithmetical operations, and providing for the general logical control. All questions of timing and of speed, and of the relative importance of various factors, must be settled within the framework of these considerations.

3.2 The ideal procedure would be, to take up the five specific parts in some definite order, to treat each one of them exhaustively, and go on to the next one only after the predecessor is completely disposed of. However, this seems hardly feasible. The desirable features of the various parts, and the decisions based on them, emerge only after a somewhat zigzagging discussion. It is therefore necessary to take up one part first, pass after an incomplete discussion to a second part, return after an equally incomplete discussion of the latter with the combined results to the first part, extend the discussion of the first part without yet concluding it, then possibly go on to a third part, etc. Furthermore, these discussions of specific parts will be mixed with discussions of general principles, of arithmetical procedures, of the elements to be used, etc.

In the course of such a discussion the desired features and the arrangements which seem best suited to secure them will crystallize gradually until the device and its control assume a fairly definite shape. As emphasized before, this applies to the physical device as well as to the arithmetical and logical arrangements which govern its functioning.

3.3 In the course of this discussion the viewpoints of 1.4, concerned with the detection, location, and under certain conditions even correction, of malfunctions must also receive some consideration. That is, attention must be given to facilities for *checking* errors. We will not be able to do anything like full justice to this important subject, but we will try to consider it at least cursorily whenever this seems essential (cf.[*not completed*]).

4.0 Elements, Synchronism Neuron Analogy

4.1 We begin the discussion with some general remarks:

Every digital computing device contains certain relay-like *elements*, with discrete equilibria. Such an element has two or more distinct states in which it can exist indefinitely. These may be perfect equilibria, in each of which the element will remain without any outside support, while appropriate outside stimuli will transfer it from one equilibrium into another. Or, alternatively, there may be two states, one of which is an equilibrium which exists when there is no outside support, while the other depends for its existence upon the presence of an outside stimulus. The relay action manifests itself in the emission of stimuli by the element whenever it has itself received a stimulus of the type indicated above. The emitted stimuli must be of the same kind as the received one, that is, they must be able to stimulate other elements. There must, however, be no energy relation between the received and the emitted stimuli, that is, an element which has received one stimulus, must be able to emit several of the same intensity. In other words: Being a relay the element must receive its energy supply from another source than the incoming stimulus.

In existing digital computing devices various mechanical or electrical devices have been used as elements: Wheels, which can be locked into any one of ten (or more) significant positions, and which on moving from one position to another transmit electric pulses that may cause other similar wheels to move; single or combined telegraph relays, actuated by an electromagnet and opening or closing electric circuits; combinations of these two elements;—and finally there exists the plausible and tempting possibility of using vacuum tubes, the grid acting as a valve for the cathode-plate circuit. In the last mentioned case the grid may also be replaced by deflecting organs, i.e. the vacuum tube by a cathode ray tube—but it is likely that for some time to come the greater availability and various electrical advantages of the vacuum tubes proper will keep the first procedure in the foreground.

Any such device may time itself autonomously, by the successive reaction times of its elements. In this case all stimuli must ultimately originate in the input. Alternatively, they may have their timing impressed by a fixed clock, which provides certain stimuli that are necessary for its functioning at definite periodically recurrent moments. This clock may be a rotating axis in a mechanical or a mixed, mechanico-electrical device; and it may be an electrical oscillator (possibly crystal controlled) in a purely electrical device. If reliance is to be placed on synchronisms of several distinct sequences of operations performed simultaneously by the device, the clock impressed timing is obviously preferable. We will use the term *element* in the above defined technical sense, and call the device *synchronous* or *asynchronous*, according to whether its timing is impressed by a clock or autonomous, as described above.

4.2 It is worth mentioning, that the neurons of the higher animals are definitely elements in the above sense. They have all-or-none character, that is two states: Quiescent and excited. They fulfill the requirements of 4.1 with an interesting variant: An excited neuron emits the standard stimulus along many lines (axons). Such a line can, however, be connected in two different ways to the next neuron: First: In an *excitatory synapsis*, so that the stimulus causes the excitation of that neuron. Second: In an *inhibitory synapsis*, so that the stimulus absolutely prevents the excitation of the neuron by any stimulus on any other (excitatory) synapsis. The neuron also has a definite reaction time, between the reception of a stimulus and the emission of the stimuli caused by it, the *synaptic delay*.

Following W. Pitts and W. S. MacCulloch ("A logical calculus of the ideas immanent in nervous activity", *Bull. Math. Biophysics,* vol. 5 [1943], pp. 115–133) we ignore the more complicated aspects of neuron functioning: Thresholds, temporal summation, relative inhibition, changes of the threshold by after effects of stimulation beyond the synaptic delay, etc. It is, however, convenient to consider occasionally neurons with fixed thresholds 2 and 3, that is neurons which can be excited only by (simultaneous) stimuli on 2 or 3 excitatory synapses (and none on an inhibitory synapsis). Cf. [*not completed*].

It is easily seen, that these simplified neuron functions can be imitated by telegraph relays or by vacuum tubes. Although the nervous system is presumably asynchronous (for the synaptic delays), precise synaptic delays can be obtained by using synchronous setups. Cf. [*not completed*].

4.3 It is clear that a very high speed computing device should ideally have vacuum tube elements. Vacuum tube aggregates like counters and scalers have been used and found reliable at reaction times (synaptic delays) as short as a microsecond ($= 10^{-6}$ seconds), this a performance which no other device can approximate. Indeed: Purely mechanical devices may be entirely disregarded and practical telegraph relay reaction times are of the order of 10 milliseconds ($= 10^{-2}$ seconds) or more. It is interesting to note that the synaptic time of a human neuron is of the order of a milliseconds ($= 10^{-3}$ seconds).

In the considerations which follow we will assume accordingly, that the device has vacuum tubes as elements. We will also try to make all estimates of numbers of tubes involved, timing, etc. on the basis, that the types of tubes used are the conventional and commercially available ones. That is, that no tubes of unusual complexity or with fundamentally new functions are to be used. The possibilities for the use of new types of tubes will actually become clearer and more definite after a thorough analysis with the conventional types (or some equivalent elements, cf.[*not completed*]) has been carried out.

Finally it will appear that a synchronous device has considerable advantages (cf.[*not completed*]).

5.0 Principles Governing the Arithmetical Operations

5.1 Let us now consider certain functions of the first specific part: the central arithmetical part CA.

The element in the sense of 4.3, the vacuum tube used as a current valve or *gate,* is an all-or-none device, or at least it approximates one: According to whether the grid bias is above or below cut-off; it will pass current or not. It is true that it needs definite potentials on all its electrodes in order to maintain either state, but there are combinations of vacuum tubes which have perfect equilibria: Several states in each of which the combination can exist indefinitely, without any outside support, while appropriate outside stimuli (electric pulses) will transfer it from one equilibrium into another. These are the so called *trigger circuits*, the basic one having two equilibria and containing two triodes or one pentode. The trigger circuits with more than two equilibria are disproportionately more involved.

Thus, whether the tubes are used as gates or as triggers, the all-or-none, two equilibrium arrangements are the simplest ones. Since these tube arrangements are to handle numbers by means of their digits, it is natural to use a system of arithmetic in which the digits are also two valued. This suggests the use of the binary system.

The analogs of human neurons, discussed in 4.2–4.3 are equally all-or-none elements. It will appear that they are quite useful for all preliminary, orienting considerations on vacuum tube systems (cf. [*not completed*]). It is therefore satisfactory that here too, the natural arithmetical system to handle is the binary one.

5.2 A consistent use of the binary system is also likely to simplify the operations of multiplication and division considerably. Specifically it does away with the decimal multiplication table, or with the alternative double procedure of building up the multiples by each multiplier or quotient digit by additions first, and then combining these (according to positional value) by a second sequence of additions or subtractions. In other words: Binary arithmetics has a simpler and more one-piece logical structure than any other, particularly than the decimal one.

It must be remembered, of course, that the numerical material which is directly in human use, is likely to have to be expressed in the decimal system. Hence, the notations used in R should be decimal. But it is nevertheless preferable to use strictly binary procedures in CA, and also in whatever numerical material may enter into the central control CC. Hence M should store binary material only.

This necessitates incorporating decimal-binary and binary-decimal conversion facilities into I and O. Since these conversions require a good deal of arithmetical manipulating, it is most economical to use CA, and hence for coordinating purposes also CC, in conjunction with I and O. The use of CA implies, however, that all arithmetics used in both conversions must be strictly binary. For details cf. [*not completed*].

5.3 At this point there arises another question of principle.

In all existing devices where the element is not a vacuum tube the reaction time of the element is sufficiently long to make a certain telescoping of the steps involved in addition, subtraction, and still more in multiplication and division, desirable. To take a specific case consider binary multiplication. A reasonable precision for many differential equation problems is given by carrying 8 significant decimal digits, that is by keeping the relative rounding-off errors below $10^{-8.}$ This corresponds to 2^{-27} in the binary system that is to carrying 27 significant binary digits. Hence a multiplication consists of pairing each one of 27 multiplicand digits with each one of 27 multiplier digits, and forming product digits 0 and 1 accordingly, and then positioning and combining them. These are essentially $27^2 = 729$ steps, and the operations of collecting and combining may about double their number. So 1000–1500 steps are essentially right.

It is natural to observe that in the decimal system a considerably smaller number of steps obtains: $8^2 = 64$ steps, possibly doubled, that is about 100 steps. However, this low number is purchased at the price of using a multiplication table or otherwise increasing or complicating the equipment. At this price the procedure can be shortened by more direct binary artifices, too, which will be considered presently. For this reason it seems not necessary to discuss the decimal procedure separately.

5.4 As pointed out before, 1000–1500 successive steps per multiplication would make any non vacuum tube device inacceptably slow. All such devices, excepting some of the latest special relays, have reaction times of more than 10 milliseconds, and these newest relays (which may have reaction times down to 5 milliseconds) have not been in use very long. This would give an extreme minimum of 10–15 seconds per (8 decimal digit) multiplication, whereas this time is 10 seconds for fast modern desk computing machines, and 6 seconds for the standard I.B.M. multipliers. (For the significance of these durations, as well as of those of possible vacuum tube devices, when applied to typical problems, cf. [*not completed*].)

The logical procedure to avoid these long durations, consists of *telescoping operations*, that is of carrying out simultaneously as many as possible. The complexities of carrying prevent even such simple operations as addition or subtraction to be carried out at once. In division the calculation of a digit cannot even begin unless all digits to its left are already known. Nevertheless considerable simultaneisations are possible: In addition or subtraction all pairs of corresponding digits can be combined at once, all first carry digits can be applied together in the next step, etc. In multiplication all the partial products of the form (multiplicand) $\times$ (multiplier digit) can be formed and positioned simultaneously—in the binary system such a partial product is zero or the multiplicand, hence this is only a matter of positioning. In both addition and multiplication the above mentioned accelerated forms of addition and subtraction can be used. Also, in multiplication the partial products can be summed up quickly by adding the first pair together simultaneously with the second pair, the third pair, etc.; then adding the first pair of pair sums together simultaneously with the second one, the third one, etc.; and so on until all terms are collected. (Since $27 \leqq 2^5$, this allows to collect 27 partial sums—assuming a 27 binary digit multiplier—in 5 addition times. This scheme is due to H. Aiken.)

Such accelerating, telescoping procedures are being used in all existing devices. (The use of the decimal system, with or without further telescoping artifices is also of this type, as pointed out at the end of 5.3. It is actually somewhat less efficient than purely diadic procedures. The arguments of 5.1–5.2 speak against considering it here.) However, they save time only at exactly the rate at which they multiply the necessary equipment, that is the number of elements in the device: Clearly if a duration is halved by systematically carrying out two additions at once, double adding equipment will be required (even assuming that it can be used without disproportionate control facilities and fully efficiently), etc.

This way of gaining time by increasing equipment is fully justified in non vacuum tube element devices, where gaining time is of the essence, and extensive engineering experience is available regarding the handling of involved devices containing many elements. A really all-purpose automatic digital computing system constructed along these lines must, according to all available experience, contain over 10,000 elements.

5.5 For a vacuum tube element device on the other hand, it would seem that the opposite procedure holds more promise.

As pointed out in 4.3, the reaction time of a not too complicated vacuum tube device can be made as short as one microsecond. Now at this rate even the unmanipulated duration of the multiplication, obtained in 5.3 is acceptable: 1000–1500 reaction times amount to 1.0–1.5 milliseconds, and this is so much faster than any conceivable non vacuum tube device, that it actually produces a serious problem of keeping the device balanced, that is to keep the necessarily human supervision beyond its input and output ends in step with its operations. (For details of this cf. [*not completed*].)

Regarding other arithmetical operations like this can be said: Addition and subtraction are clearly much faster than multiplication. On a basis of 27 binary digits (cf. 5.3), and taking carrying into consideration, each should take at most twice 27 steps, that is about 30–50 steps or reaction times. This amounts to 0.03–0.05 milliseconds. Division takes, in this scheme where shortcuts and telescoping have not been attempted in multiplying and the binary system is being used, about the same number of steps as multiplication. (cf. [*not completed*] .) Square rooting is usually and in this scheme too, not essentially longer than dividing.

5.6 Accelerating these arithmetical operations does therefore not seem necessary—at least not until we have become thoroughly and practically familiar with the use of very high speed devices of this kind, and also properly understood and started to exploit the entirely new possibilities for numerical treatment of complicated problems which they open up. Furthermore it seems questionable whether the method of acceleration by telescoping processes at the price of multiplying the number of elements required would in this situation achieve its purpose at all: The more complicated the vacuum tube equipment—that is, the greater the number of elements required—the wider the tolerances must be. Consequently any increase in this direction will also necessitate working with longer reaction times than the above mentioned one of one microsecond. The precise quantitative effects of this factor are hard to estimate in a general way—but they are certainly much more important for vacuum tube elements than for mechanical or for telegraph relay ones.

Thus it seems worthwhile to consider the following viewpoint: The device should be as simple as possible, that is, contain as few elements as possible. This can be achieved by never performing two operations simultaneously, if this would cause a significant increase in the number of elements required. The result will be that the device will work more reliably and the vacuum tubes can be driven to shorter reaction times than otherwise.

5.7 The point to which the application of this principle can be profitably pushed will, of course, depend on the actual physical characteristics of the available vacuum tube elements. It may be, that the optimum is not at a 100% application of this principle and that some compromise will be found to be optimal. However, this will always depend on the momentary state of the vacuum tube technique, clearly the faster the tubes are which will function reliably in this situation, the stronger the case is for uncompromising application of this principle. It would seem that already with the present technical possibilities the optimum is rather nearly at this uncompromising solution.

It is also worth emphasizing that up to now all thinking about high speed digital computing devices has tended in the opposite direction: Towards acceleration by telescoping processes at the price of multiplying the number of elements required. It would therefore seem to be more instructive to try to think out as completely as possible the opposite viewpoint: That one of absolutely refraining from the procedure mentioned above, that is of carrying out consistently the principle formulated in 5.6.

We will therefore proceed in this direction.

6.0 E-elements

6.1 The considerations of 5.0 have defined the main principles for the treatment of CA. We continue now on this basis, with somewhat more specific and technical detail.

In order to do this it is necessary to use some schematic picture for the functioning of the standard element of the device: Indeed, the decisions regarding the arithmetical and the logical control procedures of the device, as well as its other functions, can only be made on the basis of some assumptions about the functioning of the elements.

The ideal procedure would be to treat the elements as what they are intended to be: as vacuum tubes. However, this would necessitate a detailed analysis of specific radio engineering questions at this early stage of the discussion, when too many alternatives are still open, to be treated all exhaustively and in detail. Also, the numerous alternative possibilities for arranging arithmetical procedures, logical control, etc., would superpose on the equally numerous possibilities for the choice of types and sizes of vacuum tubes and other circuit elements from the point of view of practical performance, etc. All this would produce an involved and opaque situation in which the preliminary orientation which we are now attempting would be hardly possible.

In order to avoid this we will base our considerations on a hypothetical element, which functions essentially like a vacuum tube—e.g. like a triode with an appropriate associated RLC-circuit—but which can be discussed as an isolated entity, without going into detailed radio frequency electromagnetic considerations. We re-emphasize: This simplification is only temporary, only a transient standpoint, to make the present preliminary discussion possible. After the conclusions of the preliminary discussion the elements will have to be reconsidered in their true electromagnetic nature. But at that time the decisions of the preliminary discussion will be available, and the corresponding alternatives accordingly eliminated.

6.2 The analogs of human neurons, discussed in 4.2–4.3 and again referred to at the end of 5.1, seem to provide elements of just the kind postulated at the end of 6.1. We propose to use them accordingly for the purpose described there: as the constituent elements of the device, for the duration of the preliminary discussion. We must therefore give a precise account of the properties which we postulate for these elements.

The element which we will discuss, to be called an *E-element*, will be represented to be a circle $\bigcirc$, which receives the excitatory and inhibitory stimuli, and emits its own stimuli along a line attached to it: $\bigcirc\!\!-\!\!-$. This axis may branch: $\bigcirc\!\!\prec$, $\bigcirc\!\!+\!\!\tau$. The emission along it follows the original stimulation by a *synaptic delay*, which we can assume to be a fixed time, the same for all E-elements, to be denoted by t. We propose to neglect the other delays (due to conduction of the stimuli along the lines) aside of t. We will mark the presence of the delay t by an arrow on the line: $\bigcirc\!\!\succ$, $\bigcirc\!\!\succ\!\!\prec$. This will also serve to identify the origin and the direction of the line.

6.3 At this point the following observation is necessary. In the human nervous system the conduction times along the lines (axons) can be longer than the synaptic delays, hence our above procedure of neglecting them aside of t would be unsound. In the actually intended vacuum tube interpretation, however, this procedure is justified: t is to be about a microsecond, an electromagnetic impulse travels in this time 300 meters, and as the lines are likely to be short compared to this, the conduction times may indeed be neglected. (It would take an ultra high-frequency device—t $\cong 10^{-8}$ seconds or less—to vitiate this argument.)

Another point of essential divergence between the human nervous system and our intended application consists in our use of a well defined dispersionless synaptic delay t, common to all E-elements. (The emphasis is on the exclusion of a dispersion. We will actually use E-elements with a synaptic delay 2t, cf.[*not completed*].) We propose to use the delays t as absolute units of time which can be relied upon to synchronize the functions of various parts of the device. The advantages of such an arrangement are immediately plausible, specific technical reasons will appear in [*not completed*].

In order to achieve this, it is necessary to conceive the device as synchronous in the sense of 4.1. The central clock is best thought of as an electrical oscillator, which emits in every period t a short, standard pulse of a length t' of about $1/5t–1/2t$. The stimuli emitted nominally by an E-element are actually pulses of the clock, for which the pulse acts as a gate. There is clearly a wide tolerance for the period during which the gate must be kept open, to pass the clock-pulse without distortion. Cf. Figure 1. Thus the opening of the gate can be controlled by any electric delay device with a mean delay time t, but considerable permissible dispersion. Nevertheless the effective synaptic delay will be t with the full precision of the clock, and the stimulus is completely renewed and synchronized after each step. For a more detailed description in terms of vacuum tubes, cf. [*not completed*].

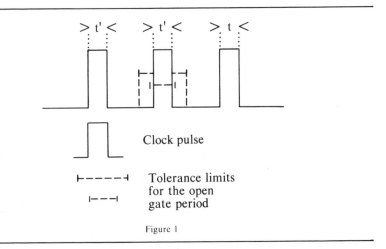

Clock pulse

Tolerance limits
for the open
gate period

Figure 1

6.4 Let us now return to the description of the E-elements.

An E-element receives the stimuli of its antecedents across excitatory synapses: —◯〉—, or inhibitory synapses: —◯〉—. As pointed out in 4.2, we will consider E-elements with thresholds 1, 2, 3, that is, which get excited by these minimum numbers of simultaneous excitatory stimuli. All inhibitory stimuli, on the other hand, will be assumed to be absolute. E-elements with the above thresholds will be denoted by ◯, ②, ③, respectively.

Since we have a strict synchronism of stimuli arriving only at times which are integer multiples of t, we may disregard phenomena of tiring, facilitation, etc. We also disregard relative inhibition, temporal summation of stimuli, changes of threshold, changes synapses, etc. In all this we are following the procedure of W. Pitts and W. J. MacCulloch (cf. loc. cit. 4.2). We will also use E-elements with double synaptic delay 2t: ◯⟫, and mixed types: ◯⟩⟨ .

The reason for our using these variants is, that they give a greater flexibility in putting together simple structures, and they can all be realized by vacuum tube circuits of the same complexity.

It should be observed, that the authors quoted above have shown, that most of these elements can be built up from each other. Thus ◯⟫ is clearly equivalent to ◯⟩◯⟩, and in the case of ②⟩ at least = ②⟫ is equivalent to the network of Figure 2. However, it would seem to be misleading in our application, to represent these functions as if they required 2 or 3 E-elements, since their complexity in a vacuum tube realization is not essentially greater than that of the simplest E-element ◯⟩, cf. [*not completed*].

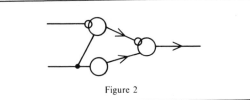

Figure 2

We conclude by observing that in planning networks of E-elements, all backtracks of stimuli along the connecting lines must be avoided. Specifically: The excitatory and the inhibitory synapses and the emission points—that is the three connections on ⟋◯⟩ —will be treated as one-way valves for stimuli—from left to right in the above picture. But everywhere else the lines and their connections ╳ will be assumed to pass stimuli in all directions. For the delays ⟶ either assumption can be made, this last point does not happen to matter in our networks.

6.5 Comparison of some typical E-element networks with their vacuum tube realizations indicates, that it takes usually 1–2 vacuum tubes for each E-element. In complicated networks, with many stimulating lines for each E-element, this number may become somewhat higher. On the average, however, counting 2 vacuum tubes per E-element would seem to be a reasonable estimate. This should take care of amplification and pulse-shaping requirements too, but of course not of the power supply. For some of the details, cf. [*not completed*].

7.0 Circuits for the Arithmetical Operations $+$, $\times$

7.1 For the device—and in particular for CA—a real number is a sequence of binary digits. We saw in 5.3, that a standard of 27 binary digit numbers corresponds to the convention of carrying 8 significant decimal digits, and is therefore satisfactory for many problems. We are not yet prepared to make a decision on this point (cf., however, [*not completed*]), but we will assume for the time being that the standard number has about 30 digits.

When an arithmetical operation is to be performed on such numbers, they must be present in some form in the device, and more particularly in CA. Each (binary) digit is obviously representable by a stimulus at a certain point and time in the device, or more precisely, the value 1 for that digit can be represented by the presence and the value 0 by the absence of that stimulus. Now the question arises, how the 30 (binary) digits of a real number are to be represented together. They could be represented simultaneously by 30 (possible) stimuli at 30 different positions in CA, or all 30 digits of one number could be represented by (possible) stimuli at the same point, occurring during 30 successive periods τ in time.

Following the principle of 5.6—to place multiple events in temporal succession rather than in (simultaneous) spacial juxtaposition—we choose the latter alternative. Hence a number is represented by a line, which emits during 30 successive periods t the stimuli corresponding to its 30 (binary) digits.

7.2 In the following discussions we will draw various networks of E-elements, to perform various functions. These drawings will also be used to define *block symbols*. That is, after exhibiting the structure of a particular network, a block symbol will be assigned to it, which will represent it in all its further applications—including those where it enters as a constituent into a higher order network and its block symbol. A block symbol shows all input and ouput lines of its network, but not their internal connections. The input lines will be marked $\succ$—, and the output lines —•. A block symbol carries the abbreviated name of its network (or its function), and the number of E-elements in it as an index to the name. Cf. e.g. Figure 3 below.

7.3 We proceed to describe an *adder* network: Figure 3. The two addends come in on the input lines a′, a″, and the sum is emitted with a delay 2τ against the addend inputs on the output line s. (The dotted extra input line c is for a special purpose which will appear in 8.2.) The carry digit is formed by $\textcircled{2}$. The corresponding digits of the two addends together with the proceeding carry digit (delay τ!) excite each one of $\bigcirc$ (left), $\textcircled{2}$, $\textcircled{3}$, and an output stimulus (that is a sum digit 1) results only when $\bigcirc$ is excited without $\textcircled{2}$, or when $\textcircled{3}$ is excited—that is when the number of 1's among the three digits mentioned is odd. The carry stimulus (that is a carry digit 1) results, as pointed out above, only when $\textcircled{2}$ is excited—that is when there are at least two 1's among the three digits mentioned. All this constitutes clearly a correct procedure of binary addition.

In the above we have made no provisions for handling the *sign* of a number, nor for the positioning of its *binary point* (the analog of the *decimal point*). These concepts will be taken up in [*not completed*], but before considering them we will carry out a preliminary discussion of the multiplier and the divider.

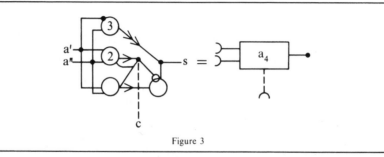

Figure 3

7.4 A multiplier network differs qualitatively from the adder in this respect: In addition every digit of each addend is used only once, in multiplication each digit of the multiplicand is used as many times as there are digits in the multiplier. Hence the principle of 5.6. (cf. also the end of 7.1) requires, that both factors be remembered by the multiplier network for a (relatively) considerable time: Since each number has 30 digits, the duration of the multiplication requires remembering for at least $30^2 = 900$ periods τ. In other words: It is no longer possible, as in the adder, to feed in the two factors on two input lines, and to extract in continuous operation the product on the output line—the multiplier needs a memory (cf. 2.4. a).

In discussing this memory we need not bring in M—this is a relatively small memory capacity required for immediate use in CA, and it is best considered in CA.

7.5 The E-elements can be used as memory devices: An element which stimulates itself, ⟨⟩⟶, will hold a stimulus indefinitely. Provided with two input lines rs, cs for receiving and for clearing (forgetting) this stimulus, and with an output line os to signalize the presence of the stimulus (during the time interval over which it is remembered), it becomes the network of Figure 4.

rs ——⟨⟩⟶ ——— os = ⟩⟩ [m₁] —•

Figure 4

It should be noted that this $\boxed{m_1}$ corresponds to the actual vacuum tube trigger circuits mentioned at the beginning of 5.1. It is worth mentioning that $\boxed{m_1}$ contains one E-element, while the simplest trigger circuits contain one or two vacuum tubes (cf. loc. cit.), in agreement with the estimates of 6.5.

Another observation is that $\boxed{m_1}$ remembers only one stimulus, that is one binary digit. If k-fold memory capacity is wanted, then k blocks $\boxed{m_1}$ are required, or a cyclical arrangement of k E-elements:

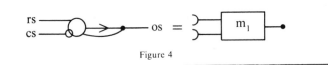

This cycle can be provided with inputs and outputs in various ways, which can be arranged so that whenever a new stimulus (or rather the fact of its presence or absence, that is a binary digit) is received for remembering—say at the left end of the cycle—the old stimulus which should take its place—coming from the right end of the cycle—is automatically cleared. Instead of going into these details, however, we prefer to keep the cycle open:

and provide it with such terminal equipment (at both ends, possibly connecting them) as may be required in each particular case. This simple line is shown again in Figure 5. Terminal equipment, which will normally cycle the output os at $\boxed{lk}$'s right and back into the input at its left end, but upon stimulation at s suppress (clear) this returning of the output os and connect instead the input with the line rs, is shown in Figure 6.

7.6 $\boxed{lk}$, with the terminal equipment of Figure 6, is a perfect memory organ, but without it, in the form of Figure 5, it is simply a delay organ. Indeed, its sole function is to retain any stimulus for k periods t and then remit

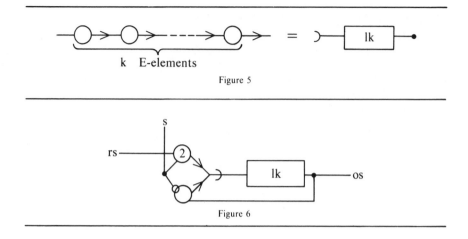

Figure 5

Figure 6

it, and to be able to do this for successive stimuli without any interference between them.

This being so, and remembering that each E-element represents (one or two) vacuum tubes, it would seem wasteful to use k – 2k vacuum tubes to achieve nothing more than a delay kτ. There exist delay devices which can do this (in our present situation τ is about a microsecond and k is about 30) more simply. We do not discuss them here, but merely observe that there are several possible arrangements (cf. 12.5). Accordingly, we replace the block ⟮lk⟯ of Figure 5 by a new block ⟮dl (k)⟯ , which is to represent such a device. It contains no E-element, and will itself be treated as a new element.

We observe, that is, ⟮dl (k)⟯ is a linear delay circuit, stimuli can backtrack through it (cf. the end of 6.4). To prevent this, it suffices to protect its ends by E-elements, that is to achieve the first and the last τ delay by —◯)— or to use it in some combination like Figure 6, where the E-elements of the associated network provide this protection.

7.7 We can now describe a *multiplier* network.

Binary multiplication consists of this: For each digital position in the multiplier (going from left to right), the multiplicand is shifted by one position to the right, and then it is or is not added to the sum of partial products already formed, according to whether the multiplier digit under consideration is 1 or 0.

Consequently the multiplier must contain an auxiliary network, which will or will not pass the multiplicand into the adder, according to whether the multiplier digit in question is 1 or 0. This can be achieved in two steps: First, a network is required, which will emit stimuli during a certain interval of τ

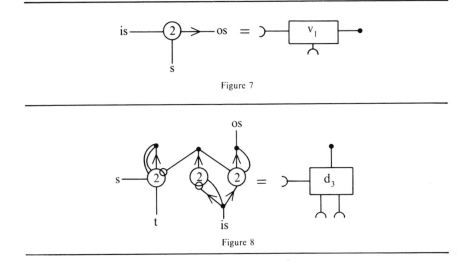

Figure 7

Figure 8

periods (the interval in which the multiplicand is wanted), provided that a certain input (connected to the organ which contains the multiplier) was stimulated at a certain earlier moment (when the proper multiplier digit is emitted). Such a network will be called a *discriminator*. Second, a valve is required which will pass a stimulus only if it is also stimulated on a second input it possesses. These two blocks together solve our problem: The discriminator must be properly controlled, its output connected to the second input of the valve, and the multiplicand routed through the valve into the adder. The valve is quite simple: Figure 7. The main stimulus is passed from (is) to (os), the second input centers at s.

A *discriminator* is shown on Figure 8. A stimulus at the input t defines the moment at which the stimulus, which determines whether the later emission (at os) shall take place at all, must be received at the inputs. If these two stimuli coincide, the left (2) is excited. Considering its feedback, it will remain excited until it succeeds in stimulating the middle (2). The middle (2) is connected to (is) in such a manner that it can be excited by the left (2) only at a moment at which (is) is stimulated, but at whose predecessor (is) was not stimulated—that is at the beginning of a sequence of stimuli at (is). The middle (2) then quenches the left (2), and together with (is) excites the right (2). The middle (2) now becomes and stays quiescent until the end of this sequence of stimuli and (is) and beyond this, until the beginning of the next sequence. Hence the left (2) is isolated from the two other (2), and thereby is ready to register the s, t stimuli for the next (is) sequence. On the other hand the feedback of the right (2) is such, that it will stay excited for the duration of this (is) sequence, and emit stimuli at os. There is clearly a delay 2τ between the input at (is) and the output at os.

Now the *multiplier* network can be put together: Figure 9. The multiplicand circulates through ⎡dl I⎤ , the multiplier through ⎡dl II⎤ , and the sum of partial products (which begins with the value 0 and is gradually built up to the complete product) through ⎡dl III⎤ . The two inputs t, t' receive the timing stimuli required by the discriminator (they correspond to t, as in Figure 8).

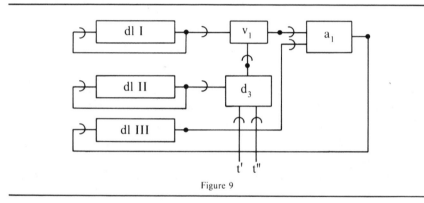

Figure 9

7.8 The analysis of 7.7 avoided the following essential features of the multiplier: (a) The *timing* network which controls the inputs t, t', and stimulates them at the proper moments. It will clearly have to contain ⎡dl⎤ -like elements. (b) The k (delay lengths) of the ⎡dl I⎤ – ⎡dl III⎤ . These too have certain functions of synchronization: Each time when the adder functions (that is in each interval it – ft) the multiplicand and the partial product sum (that is the outputs of ⎡dl I⎤ and of ⎡dl III⎤) must be brought together in such a manner, that the former is advanced by τ (moved by one position to the right) relatively to the latter, in comparison with their preceding encounter.

Also, if the two factors have 30 digits each, the product has 60 digits. Hence ⎡dl III⎤ should have about twice the k of ⎡dl I⎤ and ⎡dl II⎤ , and a cycle in the former must correspond to about two cycles in the latter. (The timing stimuli on t and t' will be best regulated in phase with ⎡dl III⎤ .) On the other hand, it is advisable to make provisions for rounding the product off to the standard number digits, and thereby keep the k of ⎡dl III⎤ near

30. (c) The networks required to get the multiplicand and the multiplier into $\boxed{\text{dl I}}$ and $\boxed{\text{dl II}}$ (from other parts of the device), and to get the product out of $\boxed{\text{dl III}}$. (d) The networks required to handle the signs and the binary point positions of the factors. They are obviously dependent upon the way in which these attributes are to be dealt with arithmetically (cf. the end of 7.3 and [*not completed*]).

All these points will be dealt with subsequently. The questions connected with (d)—arithmetical treatment of sign and binary point—must be taken up first, since the former is needed for subtraction, and hence for division too, and the latter is important for both multiplication and division.

8.0 Circuits for the Arithmetical Operation $-$, $\div$

8.1 Until now a number x was a sequence of (about 30) binary digits, with no definition of sign or binary point. We must now stipulate conventions for the treatment of these concepts.

The extreme left digit will be reserved for the sign, so that its values 0,1 express the signs $+$, $-$, respectively. If the binary point is between the digital positions i and $i + 1$ (from the left), then the positional value of the sign digit is 2^{i-1}. Hence without the sign convention the number x would lie in the interval $0 \leqq x < 2^i$, and with the sign convention the subinterval $0 \leqq x < 2^{i-1}$ is unaffected and corresponds to non negative numbers, while the interval $2^{i-1} \leqq x < 2^i$ corresponds to negative numbers. We let the latter x represent a negative x', so that the remaining digits of x are essentially the complements to the digits of $-x'$. More precisely: $2^{i-1} - (- x') = -2^{i-1}$, that is $x^1 = x - 2^i$. To $-2^{i-1} \leqq x' < 0$.

In other words: The digital sequences which we use represent, without the sign convention, the interval $0 \leqq x < 2^i$, and with the sign convention the interval $-2^{i-1} \leqq x < 2^{i-1}$. The second interval is correlated to the first one by subtracting 2^i if necessary—that is their correspondence is module 2^i.

Since addition and subtraction leave relations module 2^i unaffected, we can ignore these arrangements in carrying out additions and subtractions. The same is true for the position of the binary point: If this is moved from i to i', then each number is multiplied by $2^{i'-i}$, but addition and subtraction leave this relation invariant too. (All these things are, of course, the conventional decimal procedures.)

Thus we need not add anything to the addition procedure of 7.3, and it will be correct to set up a subtraction procedure in the same way. The multiplication procedure of 7.7, however, will have to be reconsidered, and the same caution applies to the division procedure to be set up.

8.2 We now set up a *subtractor* network. We can use the adder (cf. 7.3) for this purpose, if one addend—say the first one—is fed in the negative. According to the above this means that this addend x is replaced by $2^i - x$. That is, each digit of x is replaced by its complement, and a unit of the extreme right digital position is then added to this addend—or just as well as an extra addend.

This last operation can be carried out by stimulating the extra input c of the adder (cf. Figure 3) at that time. This takes automatically care of all carries which may be caused by this extra addition.

The complementation of each digit can be done by a valve which does the opposite of that of Figure 7: When stimulated at s, it passes the complement of the main stimulus from (is) to os: Figure 10. Now the *subtractor* network is shown on Figure 11. The subtrahend and the minuend come in on the input lines s, m, and the difference is emitted with a delay 3τ against the inputs on the output line d. The two inputs t', t'' receive the necessary timing stimuli: t' throughout the period of subtraction, t'' at its first t (corresponding to the extreme right digital position, cf. above).

8.3 Next we form a *divider* network, in the same preliminary sense as the multiplier network of 7.7.

Binary division consists of this: For each digital position in the quotient (going from left to right), the divisor is subtracted from the partial remainder (of the dividend) already formed; but which has been shifted left by one position, preceding this subtraction. If the resulting difference is not negative (that is, if its extreme left digit is 0) then the next quotient digit is 1, and the next partial remainder (the one to be used for the following quotient digit, before the shift left referred to above.) If the difference is negative (that is, if its extreme left digit is 1) then the next quotient digit is 0, and the next par-

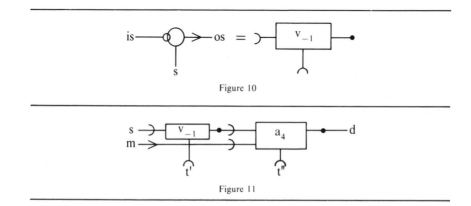

Figure 10

Figure 11

tial remainder (in the same sense as above) is the preceding partial remainder, but in its shifted position.

The alternative in division is therefore comparable to that one in multiplication (cf. 7.7), with this notable difference: In multiplication it was a matter of passing or not passing an addend: the multiplicand, in division the question is which of two minuends to pass: the (shifted) preceding partial remainder, or this quantity minus the divisor. Hence we now need two valves where we needed one in multiplication. Also, we need a discriminator which is somewhat more elaborate than that one of Figure 8: It must not only pass a sequence of stimuli from is to os if there was a stimulus at s at the moment defined by the stimulation of t, but it must alternatively pass that sequence from is to another output os' if there was no stimulus at s at the moment in question. Comparison of Figure 8 with Figure 12 shows, that the latter possesses the desired properties. The delay between is and os or os' is now 3τ.

Now the *divider* network can be put together: Figure 13. The divisor circulates through $\boxed{\text{dl I}}$, while the dividend is originally in $\boxed{\text{dl III}}$, but is replaced, as the division progresses, by the successive partial remainders. The valve $\boxed{v_{-1}}$ routes the divisor negatively into the adder. The two valves $\boxed{v_1}$ immediately under it select the partial remainder (cf. below) and send it from their common output line on one hand unchanged into $\boxed{\text{dl II}}$ and on the other hand into the adder, from where the sum (actually the difference) goes into $\boxed{\text{dl III}}$. The timing must be such as to produce the required one position shift left. Thus $\boxed{\text{dl II}}$ and $\boxed{\text{dl III}}$ contain the two numbers from among which the next partial remainder is to be selected. This selection is done by the discriminator $\boxed{d_4}$ which governs the two valves controlling the (second addend) input of the adder (cf. above). The sign digit of the resulting sum controls the discriminator, the timing stimulus at t must coincide with its appearance (extreme left digit of the sum). t' must be stimulated during the period in which the two addends (actually minuend and subtrahend) are to enter the adder (advanced by 3t). t'' must receive the extra stimulus required in subtraction (t'' in Figure 11) coinciding with the extreme right digit of the difference. The quotient is assembled in $\boxed{\text{dl IV}}$, for each one of its digits the necessary stimulus is available at the second output of the discriminator (os' in Figure 10) it is passed into $\boxed{\text{dl IV}}$ through the lowest valve $\boxed{v_1}$, timed by a stimulus at t'''.

8.4 The analysis of 8.3 avoided the same essential features of the divider, which 7.7 omitted for the multiplier, and which were enumerated in 7.8:

(a) The *timing* network which controls the inputs t, t' t'', t'''.

(b) The k (delay lengths) of the $\boxed{\text{dl I}}$ – $\boxed{\text{dl IV}}$. The details differ from those in 7.8, (b), but the problem is closely parallel.

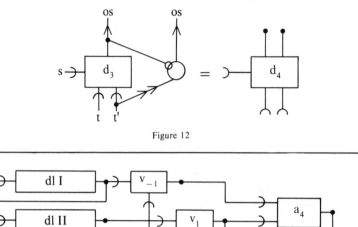

Figure 12

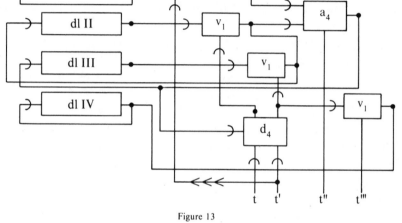

Figure 13

(c) The networks required to get the dividend and the divisor into
dl III and dl I , and to get the quotient out of dl IV .

(d) The networks required to handle signs and binary point positions.

As in the case of multiplication all these points will be dealt with subsequently.

9.0 The Binary Point

9.1 As pointed out at the end of 8.1, the sign convention of 8.1 as well as
the binary point convention, which has not yet been determined, have no influence on addition and subtraction, but their relationship to multiplication
and division is essential and requires consideration.

It is clear from the definitions of multiplication and of division, as given at
the beginning of 7.7 and of 8.3 respectively, that they apply only when all

numbers involved are non-negative. That is, when the extreme left digit (of multiplicand and multiplier, or dividend and divisor) is 0. Let us therefore assume this for the present (this subject will be taken up again in [*not completed*]), and consider the role of the binary point in multiplication and division.

9.2 As pointed out in 7.8, (b), the product of the 30 digit numbers has 60 digits, and since the product should be a number with the same standard number of significant digits as its factors, this necessitates omitting 30 digits from the product.

If the binary point is between the digital positions i and $i + 1$ (from the left) in one factor, and between j and $j + 1$ in the other, then these numbers lie between 0 and 2^{i-1} and between 0 and 2^{j-1} (the extreme left digit is 0, cf. 9.1). Hence the product lies between 0 and 2^{i+j-2}. However, if it is known to lie between 0 and 2^{k-1} ($1 \leqq k \leqq i + j - 1$), then its binary point lies between k and $k + 1$. Then of its 60 digits the first $i + j - 1 - k$ (from the left) are 0 and are omitted, and so it is only necessary to omit the $31 - i - j + k$ last digits (to the right) by some rounding-off process.

This shows, that the essential effect of the positioning of the binary point is, that it determines which digits among the supernumerary ones in a product are to be omitted.

If $k < i + j - 1$, then special precautions must be taken so that no two numbers are ever multiplied for which the product is $> 2^{k-1}$ (it is only limited by $\leqq 2^{1+j-2}$). This difficulty is well known in planning calculations on IBM or other automatic devices. There is an elegant trick to get around this difficulty, due to G. Stibitz, but since it would complicate the structure of CA somewhat, we prefer to carry out the first discussion without using it. We prefer instead to suppress this difficulty at this point altogether by an arrangement which produces an essentially equivalent one at another point. However, this means only that in planning calculations the usual care must be exercised, and it simplifies the device and its discussion. This procedure, too, is in the spirit of the principle of 5.6.

This arrangement consists in requiring $k = 1 + j - 1$, so that every multiplication can always be carried out. We also want a fixed position for the binary point, common to all numbers: $1 = j = k$. Hence $i = j = k = 1$, that is: The binary point is always between the two first digital positions (from the left). In other words: The binary point follows always immediately after the sign digit.

Thus all non-negative numbers will be between 0 and 1, and all numbers (of either sign) between -1 and 1. This makes it clear once more that the multiplication can always be carried out.

9.3 The caution formulated above is, therefore, that in planning any calculation for the device, it is necessary to see to it, that all numbers which occur in the course of the calculation should always be between −1 and 1. This can be done by multiplying the numbers of the actual problem by appropriate (usually negative) powers of 2 (actually in many cases powers of 10 are appropriate, cf. [*not completed*]), and transforming all formulae accordingly. From the point of view of planning it is no better and no worse, than the familiar difficulty of positioning the decimal point in most existing automatic devices. It is necessary to make certain compensatory arrangements in I and O, cf. [*not completed*].

Specifically the requirement that all numbers remain between −1 and 1, necessitates to remember these limitations in planning caculations:

(a) No addition or subtraction must be performed if its result is a number not between −1 and 1 (but of course between −2 and 2).

(b) No division must be performed if the divisor is less (in absolute value) than the dividend.

If these rules are violated, the adder, subtractor and divider will still produce results, but these will not be the sum difference and quotient respectively. It is not difficult to include checking organs which signalize all infractions of the rules (a), (b), (cf. [*not completed*]).

9.4 In connection with multiplication and division some remarks about rounding-off are necessary.

It seems reasonable to carry both these operations one digit beyond what is to be kept—under the present assumptions to the 31st digit—and then omit the supernumerary digit by some rounding process. Just plain ignoring that digit would, as is well known, cause systematical rounding-off errors biased in one direction (towards 0). The usual Gaussian decimal procedure of rounding off to the nearest value of the last digit kept, and in case of a (supernumerary digit) S to the even one means in the binary system this: Digit pairs (30th and 31st) 00,10 are rounded to 0,1; 01 is rounded to 00; 11 is rounded by adding 01. This requires addition, with carry digits and their inconveniences. Instead one may follow the equivalent of the decimal procedure of rounding 5's to the nearest odd digit, as suggested by J. W. Mauchly. In the binary system this means that digit pairs (30th and 31st) 00, 01, 10, 11 are rounded to 0, 1, 1, 1.

This rounding-off rule can be stated very simply: The 30th digit is rounded to 1 if either the 30th or the 31st digit was 1, otherwise it is rounded to 0.

A *rounding-off valve* which does this is shown on Figure 14. A digit (stimulus) is passed from is to os while s is stimulated, but when s' is also stimulated, the digit is combined with its predecessor (that is the one to its left) according to the above rounding-off rule.

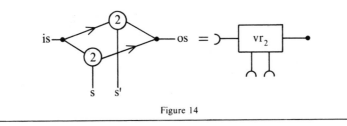

Figure 14

10.0 Circuit for the Arithmetical Operation $\sqrt{\ }$. Other Operations

10.1 A *square rooter* network can be built so that it differs very little from the divider. The description which follows is preliminary in the same sense as those of the multiplier and the divider networks in 7.7 and 8.3.

Binary square rooting consists of this: For each digital position in the square root (going from left to right), the square root a (as formed up to that position) is used to form 2a + 1, and this 2a + 1 is subtracted from the partial remainder (of the radicand) already formed, but which has been shifted left by two positions (adding new digits 0 if the original digits are exhausted), before this subtraction. If the resulting difference is not negative (that is, if its extreme left digit is 0) then the next square root digit is 1, and the next partial remainder (the one to be used for the following quotient digit, before the double shift left referred to above) is the difference in question. If the difference is negative (that is, if its extreme left digit is 1) then the next square root digit is 0, and the next partial remainder (in the same sense as above) is the preceding partial remainder, but in its doubly shifted position.

This procedure is obviously very similar to that one used in division (cf. 8.3), with the following differences: First: The simple left shifts (of the partial remainder) are replaced by double ones (with possible additions of new digits 0). Second: The quantity which is being subtracted is not one given at the start (the dividend), but one that is determined by the result obtained so far: 2a + 1 if a is the square root up to the position under consideration.

The first difference is a rather simple matter of timing, requiring no essential additional equipment. The second difference involves a change in the connection, but also no equipment. It is true, that 2a + 1 must be formed from a, but this is a particularly simple operation in the binary system: 2a is formed by a shift left, and since 2a + 1 is required for a subtraction, the final +1 can be taken into account by omitting the usual correction of the extreme right digit in subtraction (cf. 8.2, it is the stimulus on t'' in Figure 11 which is to be omitted).

Now the *square rooter* network can be put together: Figure 15. The similarity with the divider network of Figure 13 is striking. It will be noted that ⌐dl I⌐ is not needed. The radicand is originally in ⌐dl III⌐ , but is replaced, as the square rooting progresses, by the successive partial remainders. The valve ⌐v_{-1}⌐ routes the square root a (as formed up to that position) negatively into the adder—the timing must be such as to produce a shift left, thereby replacing a by 2a, and the absence of the extra correcting pulse for subtraction (t'' in Figures 11 and 13, cf. the discussion above) replaces it by 2a + 1. The two valves ⌐v_1⌐ immediately under it select the partial remainder (cf. below) and send it from their common output line on one hand unchanged into ⌐dl II⌐ and on the other hand into the adder, from where the sum (actually the difference) goes into ⌐dl III⌐ . The timing must be such as to produce the required double position shift left. Thus ⌐dl II⌐ and ⌐dl III⌐ contain the two numbers from among which the next

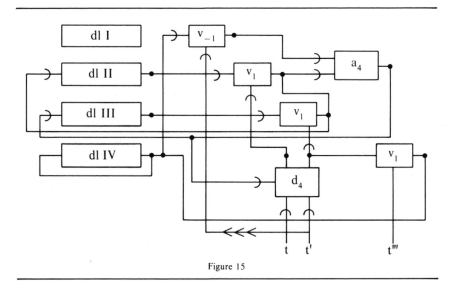

Figure 15

partial remainder is to be selected. This selection is done by the discriminator ⌐d_4⌐ which governs the two valves controlling the (second addend) input of the adder (cf. the discussion of Figure 12 in 8.3). The sign digit of the resulting sum controls the discriminator, the timing stimulus at t must coincide with its appearance (extreme left digit of the sum) t' must be stimulated during the period during which the two addends (actually minuend and subtrahend) are to enter the adder (advanced by 3t). The square root is assembled in dl IV , for each one of its digits the necessary stimulus is available at the second output of the discriminator (os' in Figure 12), it is passed into dl IV through the lowest valve v_1 , timed by a stimulus at t'''.

10.2 The concluding remarks of 8.4 concerning the divider apply essentially unchanged to the square rooter.

The rules of 9.3 concerning the sizes of numbers entering into various operations are easily extended to cover square rooting: The radicand must be non negative and the square root which is produced will be non negative. Hence square rooting must only be performed if the radicand is between 0 and 1, and the square root will also lie between 0 and 1.

The other remarks in 9.3 and 9.4 apply to square rooting too.

10.3 The networks which can add, subtract, multiply, divide and square root having been described, it is now possible to decide how they are to be integrated in CA, and which operations CA should be able to perform.

The first question is, whether it is necessary or worthwhile to include all the operations enumerated above: $+, -, \times, \div, \sqrt{}$.

Little need be said about $+, -$: These operations are so fundamental and so frequent, and the networks which execute them are so simple (cf. Figures 3 and 11), that it is clear that they should be included.

With $\times$ the need for discussion begins, and at this stage a certain point of principle may be brought out. Prima facie it would seem justified to provide for a multiplier, since the operation $\times$ is very important, and the multiplier of Figure 9—while not nearly as simple as the adder of Figure 3—is still very simple compared with the complexity of the entire device. Also, it contains an adder and therefore permits to carry out $+, -$ on the same equipment as $\times$, and it has been made very simple by following the principle formulated in 5.3–5.7.

There are nevertheless possible doubts about the stringency of these considerations. Indeed multiplication (and similarly division and square rooting) can be reduced to addition (or subtraction or halving—the latter being merely a shift to the right in the binary system) by using (preferably base 2) logarithm and antilogarithm tables. Now function tables will have to be incorporated into the complete device anyhow, and logarithm-antilogarithm tables are among the most frequently used ones—why not use them then to eliminate $\times$ (and $\div, \sqrt{}$) as special operations? The answer is, that no function table can be detailed enough to be used without interpolation (this would under the conditions contemplated, require $2^{30} \cong 10^9$ entries!), and interpolation requires multiplication! It is true that one might use a lower precision multiplication in interpolating, and gain a higher precision one by this procedure—and this could be elaborated to a complete system of multiplication by successive approximations. Simple estimates show, however, that such a procedure is actually more laborious than the ordinary arithmetical one for multiplication. Barring such procedures, one can therefore state, that function tables can be used for simplifying arithmetical (or any other) operations only after the operation $\times$ has been taken care of, not before! This, then, would seem to justify the inclusion of $\times$ among the operation of CA.

Finally we come to $\div$ and $\sqrt{}$. These could now certainly be handled by function tables: Both $\div$ and $\sqrt{}$ with logarithm-antilogarithm ones, $\div$ also with reciprocal tables (and $\times$). There are also well known, fast convergent iterative processes: For the reciprocal

$$u \leftarrow 2u - au^2 = (2 - au)u$$

(two operations $\times$ per stage, this converges to $1/a$), for the square root

$$u \leftarrow \frac{3}{2}u - 2au^3 = \left\{\frac{3}{2} - (2au)u\right\}u$$

(three operations $\times$ per stage, this converges to $1/\sqrt{4a}$, hence it must be multiplied by 2a at the end, to give $\sqrt{a}$).

However, all these processes require more or less involved logical controls and they replace $\div$ and $\quad$ by not inconsiderable numbers of operations of $\times$. Now our discussions of $\times$, $\div$, $\sqrt{}$ show, that each one of these operations lasts, with 30 (binary) digit numbers (cf. 7.1), order of $30^2 t$, hence it is wasteful in time to replace $\div$, $\sqrt{}$ by even a moderate number of $\times$. Besides the saving in equipment is not very significant: The divider of Figure 13 exceeds the multiplier of Figure 9 by above 50% in equipment, and it contains it as a part so that duplications are avoidable. (Cf. [*not completed*].) The square rooter is almost identical with the divider, as Figure 15 and its discussion show.

Indeed the justification of using trick methods for $\div$, $\sqrt{}$, all of which amount to replacing them by several $\times$, exists only in devices where $\times$ has been considerably abbreviated. As mentioned in 5.3–5.4 the duration of $\times$ and also of $\div$ can be reduced to a much smaller number of τ than what we contemplate. As pointed out loc. cit., this involves telescoping and simultaneising operations, and increasing the necessary equipment very considerably. We saw, that such procedures are indicated in devices with elements which do not have the speed and the possibilities of vacuum tubes. In such devices the further circumstance may be important, that $\times$ can be more efficiently abbreviated than $\div$ (cf. 5.4), and it may therefore be worthwhile to resort to the above mentioned procedures, which replace $\div$, $\sqrt{}$ by several $\times$. In a vacuum tube device based on the principles of 5.3–5.7, however, $\times$, $\div$,$\sqrt{}$ are all of the same order of duration and complication and the direct arithmetical approach to all of them therefore seems to be justified, in preference to the trick methods discussed above.

Thus all operations $+$, $-$, $\times$, $\div$,$\sqrt{}$ would seem to deserve inclusion as such in CA, more or less in the form of the networks of Figures 3, 11, 9, 13, 15, remembering that all these networks should actually be merged into one, which consists essentially of the elements of the divider, Figure 13. The whole or appropriate parts of this network can then be selected by the action of suitably disposed controlling E-elements, which act as valves on the necessary connections, to make it carry out the particular one among the operations $+$, $-$, $\times$, $\div$,$\sqrt{}$ which is desired. (Cf. [*not completed*].) For additional remarks on specific operations and general logical control, cf. [*not completed*].

10.4 The next question is, what further operations (besides $+$, $-$, $\times$, $\div$,$\sqrt{}$) would be included in CA?

As pointed out in the first part of 10.3 once $\times$ is available, any other function can be obtained from function tables with interpolation. (For the details cf. [*not completed*]). Hence it would seem that beyond $\times$ (and $+$, $-$ which came before it), no further operations need be included as such in CA. Actually $\div$,$\sqrt{}$ were nevertheless included, and the direct arithmetical approach was used for them—but here we had the excuse that the arithmetical procedures involved had about the same duration as those of $\times$, and required an increase of only about 50% in equipment.

Further operations, which one might consider, will hardly meet these specifications. Thus the cube root differs in its arithmetical treatment essentially from the square root, as the latter requires the intermediate operation $2a + 1$ (cf. 10.1), which is very simple, particularly in the binary system while the former requires at the same points the intermediate operation $3a^2 + 3a + 1 = 3a(a + 1) + 1$, which is much more complicated, since it involves a multiplication. Other desirable operations—like the logarithm, the trigonometric functions, and their inverses—allow hardly any properly arithmetical treatment. In these cases the direct approach involves the use of their power series, for which the general logical control facilities of the device must be adequate. On the other hand the use of function tables and interpolation, as suggested above is in most cases more effective than the direct power series approach.

These considerations make the inclusion of further algebraical or analytical operations in CA unnecessary. There are however some quite elementary operations, which deserve to be included for logical or organizational rea-

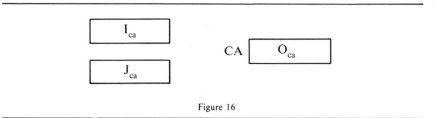

Figure 16

sons. In order to discuss these it is necessary to consider the functioning of CA somewhat more closely, although we are not yet ready to do full justice to the viewpoints brought up in 7.8 and at the end of 10.3.

11.0 Organization of CA. Complete List of Operations

11.1 As pointed out at the end of 10.3 CA will be organized essentially as a divider, with suitable controls to modify its action for the requirements of the other operations. (It will also contain controls for the purposes enumerated in 7.8.) This implies that it will in general deal with two real number variables, which go into the memory organs $\boxed{dl\ I}$, $\boxed{dl\ II}$ of the divider network of Figure 13. (These should coincide with the $\boxed{dl\ I}$, $\boxed{dl\ II}$ of the multiplier, Figure 9. The square rooter, Figure 15, needs no $\boxed{dl\ I}$, but it makes the same use of $\boxed{dl\ II}$. The adder and subtractor were not connected on Figures 3 and 11 to such memory organs, but they will have to be when the organization of CA is completed.) So we must think of CA as having two input organs, $\boxed{dl\ I}$ and $\boxed{dl\ II}$, and of course one output organ. (The latter has not been correlated with the adder and subtractor. For the multiplier it is $\boxed{dl\ III}$, for the divider and square rooter it is $\boxed{dl\ IV}$. These things too will have to be adjusted in the final organization of CA.) Let us denote these two inputs of CA by I_{ca} and J_{ca}, and the output by O_{ca} (each of them with its attached memory organ), schematically shown on Figure 16.

Now the following complex of problems must be considered: As mentioned before, particularly in 2.5, an extensive memory M forms an essential part of the device. Since CA is the main internal operating unit of the device (M stores, CC administers, and I, O maintain the connections with the outside, cf. the analysis in 2.0), the connections for transfers between M and CA are very important. How are these connections to be organized?

It is clearly necessary to be able to transfer from any part of M to CA, i.e. to I_{ca}, J_{ca}, and conversely from CA, i.e. from O_{ca}, to any part of M. Direct connections between various parts of M do therefore not seem to be necessary: It is always possible to transfer from one part of M to the other via CA.

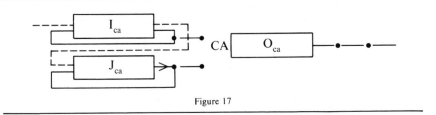

Figure 17

(Cf., however, [*not completed*].) These considerations give rise to two questions: First: Is it necessary to connect each part of M with both I_{ca} and J_{ca} or can this be simplified? Second: How are the transfers from one part of M to an other part of M to be handled, where CA is only a through station?

The first question can be answered in the light of the principle of 5.6—to place multiple events in a temporal succession rather than in (simultaneous) spacial juxtaposition. This means that two real numbers which go from M into I_{ca} and J_{ca} will have to go there in two successive steps. This being so, it is just as well to route each real number first into I_{ca}, and to move it on (within CA) from I_{ca} to J_{ca} when the next real number comes (from M) into I_{ca}. We restate:

Every real number coming from M into CA is routed into I_{ca}. At the same time the real number previously in I_{ca} is moved on to J_{ca}, and the real number previously in J_{ca} is necessarily cleared, i.e. forgotten. It should be noted, that I_{ca} and J_{ca} can be assumed to contain memory organs of the type discussed in 7.6. (Cf. Figure 6, there, cf. also the various ⌐dl⌐ in the ×, ÷,√networks in Figures 9, 13, 15) in which the real numbers they hold are circulating. Consequently the connections of I_{ca} and J_{ca} in CA are those indicated in Figure 17: The lines – – – conduct when a real number (from M) enters CA, the lines —— conduct at all other times. The connections of I_{ca} and J_{ca} with the operating parts of CA are supposed to branch out from the two terminals —•. The output O_{ca} connects with the outside (relatively to CA, i.e. with M) by the line –·—··–, which conducts when a result leaves CA (for M). The circulating connections of O_{ca} and its connections with the operating parts of CA are not shown, nor the E-elements which control the connections shown (nor, of course, the operating parts of CA). (For the complete description of CA cf. [*not completed*].)

11.2 With the help of Figures 16, 17 the second question is also easily answered. For a transfer from one part of M to another part of M, going through CA, the portion of the route inside CA is clearly a transfer from I_{ca} or J_{ca} to O_{ca}. Denoting the real numbers in I_{ca}, J_{ca} by x, y, this amounts to "combining" x, y to either x or y, since the "result" of any operation performed by CA (like $+$, $-$, $\times$, $\div$,√) is supposed to appear at O_{ca}. This operation is trivial and a special case e.g. of addition: If x (or y) is wanted it suffices to get zero in the place of y (or x)—i.e. into I_{ca} (or J_{ca})—and then apply the operation. On the other hand, however, it seems preferable to introduce these operations as such: First: "Getting zero into I_{ca} (or J_{ca})" is unnecessarily time consuming. Second: The direct transfer from I_{ca} (or J_{ca}) to O_{ca}, which these operations require is easily effected by a small part of the CA network visualized at the beginning of 11.1. Third: We propose to introduce both operations (for I_{ca} as well as for J_{ca}), because it will appear that each can play a separate useful role in the internal administration of CA (cf. below).

We introduce accordingly two new operations: i and j, corresponding to direct transfers from I_{ca} or J_{ca} to O_{ca}.

These two operations have these further uses: It will be seen (cf. [*not completed*]) that the output of CA (from O_{ca}) can be fed back directly into the input of CA (to I_{ca}, this moves the contents of I_{ca} into J_{ca} and clears J_{ca}, of 11.1). Now assume that I_{ca}, J_{ca} contain the real numbers x, y, and that i or j is applied, in conjunction with this feedback. Then the contents of I_{ca} J_{ca} are replaced by x, x or y, x. I.e. from the point of view of any other two variable operations $(+, -, \div,$ i.e. $x + y, x - y, sy, x/y)$ the variables x, y have been replaced by x, x or y, x. Now the latter is an important manipulation for the unsymmetric operations $(x - y, x/y)$, and the former is important for the symmetric operations $(x + y, xy)$ since it leads to doubling and squaring. Both manipulations are frequent enough in ordinary algebra, to justify a direct treatment by means of the operations i, j.

11.3 A further necessary operation is connected with the need to be able to sense the sign of a number, or the order relation between two numbers, and to choose accordingly between two (suitably given) alternative courses of action. It will appear later, that the ability to choose the first or the second one of two given numbers u, v, in dependence upon such an alternative, is quite adequate to mediate the choice between any two given alternative courses of action. (Cf. [*not completed*].) Accordingly, we need an operation which can do this: Given four numbers x, y, u, v, it "forms" u if x = y. (This senses the order relation between x, y. If we put y = 0, it senses the sign of x.)

In this form the operation has four variables: x, y, u, v. (In the sign form it has three variables: x, u, v.) Now the scheme for the CA network chosen at the beginning of 11.1, which was essentially that one of the divider, had room for two variables only, and this is equally true for the discussion of the inputs of CA in 11.1. Hence four (or three) variables are too many. Consequently it is necessary to break our operation up into two variable operations—and then we might as well do this with the more general (four rather than three variables) form.

It is plausible to begin with a (partial) operation which merely decides whether $x \geqq y$ or $x < y$ and remembers this, but without taking any action yet. This is best done by forming $x - y$, and then remembering its sign digit only, i.e. its first digit (from the left). (Cf. 8.1. This digit is 0 for $x - y \geqq 0$, i.e. $x \geqq y$, and it is 1 for $x - y < 0$, i.e. $x < y$.) Thus this (partial) operation is essentially in the nature of a subtraction, and it can therefore present no additional difficulties in a CA which can subtract. Now it seems best to arrange things so, that once this operation has been performed, CA will simply wait until two new numbers u, v have been moved into I_{ca}, J_{ca} (thus clearing x, y out—if u, v are to occupy I_{ca}, J_{ca}, respectively, then v must be fed in first and u second), and then transfer (without any further instructions) u or v into O_{ca} (i.e. perform i or j) according to whether the sign digit referred to above was 0 or 1.

We introduce accordingly such an operation: s. It is most convenient to arrange things so, that after x, y have occupied I_{ca}, J_{ca}, a subtraction is ordered and provisions made that the result $x - y$ should remain in O_{ca}. Then x, y must be displaced from I_{ca}, J_{ca} by u, v and s ordered. s will sense whether the number in O_{ca} is $\geqq 0$ or < 0 (i.e. $x \geqq y$ or $x < y$), clear it from O_{ca}, and "form" accordingly u or v in O_{ca}. The operation preceding s need, by the way, not be subtraction: It might be addition or i or j. Accordingly the number in O_{ca}, which provides the criterion for s will not be $x - y$, but $x + y$ or x or y. I.e. s will form u or v according to whether the multiplication or the division, and the former might indeed be sometimes useful. For details of these operations cf. [*not completed*].

11.4 Combining the conclusions of 10.3, 10.4, 11.2, 11.3 a list of eight operations of CA obtains: $+$, $-$, $\times$, $\div$, $\sqrt{}$, i, j, s. To these two more will have to be added, because of the necessity of converting numbers between the binary and the decimal systems, as indicated at the end of 5.2. Thus we need a decimal-to-binary conversion and a binary-to-decimal conversion db, bd. The networks which carry out these two operations will be discussed in [*not completed*].

This concludes for the moment the discussion of CA. We have enumerated the ten operations which it must be able to perform. The questions of 7.8, the general control problems of 11.1, and the specific networks for db, bd still remain to be disposed of. But it is better to return to these after various other characteristics of the device have been decided upon. We postpone therefore their discussion and turn now to other parts of the device.

12.0 Capacity of the Memory M. General Principles

12.1 We consider next the third specific part: the memory M.

Memory devices were discussed in 7.5, 7.6, since they are needed as parts of the $\times$, $\div$, networks (cf. 7.4, 7.7 for $\times$, 8.3 for $\div$, 10.2 for $\sqrt{}$) and hence of CA itself (cf. the beginning of 11.1). In all these cases the devices considered had a *sequential* or *delay* character, which was in most cases made cyclical by suitable terminal organs. More precisely:

The blocks $\boxed{\text{lk}}$ and $\boxed{\text{dl (k)}}$ in 7.5, 7.6 are essentially *delays*, which hold a stimulus that enters their input for a time kt, and then emit it. Consequently they can be converted into cyclical memories, which hold a stimulus indefinitely, and make it available at the output at all times which differ from each other by multiples of kt. It suffices for this purpose to feed the output back into the input: ⌐$\boxed{\text{lk}}$⌐ or ⌐$\boxed{\text{dl (k)}}$⌐ . Since the period kt contains k fundamental periods t, the capacity of such a memory device is k stimuli. The above schemes lack the proper input, clearing and output facilities, but these are shown on Figure 6. It should be noted that in Figure 6 the cycle around $\boxed{\text{lk}}$ goes through one more E-element, and therefore the period of this device is actually (k + 1) t, and its capacity correspondingly k + 1 stimuli. (The $\boxed{\text{lk}}$ of Figure 5 may, of course, be replaced by a $\boxed{\text{dl (k)}}$ cf. 7.6.)

Now it is by no means necessary, that memory be of this cyclical (or delay) type. We must therefore before making a decision concerning M, discuss other possible types and the advantages and disadvantages of the cyclical type in comparison with them.

12.2 Preceding this discussion, however, we must consider the *capacity* which we desire in M. We did already mention above this concept of capacity for M or a part of M: It is the number of stimuli which this organ can remember, or more precisely, the number of occasions for which it can remember whether or not a stimulus was present. The presence or absence of a stimulus (at a given occasion, i.e., on a given line in a given moment) can be used to express the value 1 or 0 for a binary digit (in a given position). Hence the capacity of a memory is the number of binary digits (the values of) which it can retain. In other words:

The *(capacity) unit of memory* is the ability to retain the value of one binary digit.

We can now express the "cost" of various types of information in these memory units.

Let us consider first the memory capacity required to store a standard (real) number. As indicated in 7.1, we shall fix the size of such a number at 30 binary digits (at least for most uses, cf. [*not completed*]). This keeps the relative rounding-off errors below 2^{-30}, which corresponds to 10^{-9}, i.e., carrying 9 significant decimal digits. Thus a standard number corresponds to 30 memory units. To this must be added one unit for its sign (cf. the end of 9.2) and it is advisable to add a further unit in lieu of a symbol which characterizes it as a number (to distinguish it from an order, cf. [*not completed*]). In this way we arrive to $32 = 2^5$ units per number.

The fact that a number requires 32 memory units, makes it advisable to subdivide the entire memory in this way: First, obviously, into *units*, second into groups of 32 units, to be called *minor cycles*. (For the major cycles cf. [*not completed*].) Each standard (real) number accordingly occupies precisely one minor cycle. It simplifies the organization of the entire memory, and various synchronization problems of the device along with it, if all other constants of the memory are also made to fit into this subdivision into minor cycles.

Recalling the classification (a)–(h) of 2.4 for the presumptive contents of the memory M, we note: (a), according to our present ideas belongs to CA and not to M (it is handled by | dl I | to | dl IV |, cf. the beginning of 11.1) (c)–(g), and probably (h) also, consist of standard numbers. (b) on the other hand consists of the operation instructions which govern the functioning of the device, to be called *standard orders*. It will therefore be necessary to formulate the standard orders in such a manner, that each one should also occupy precisely one minor cycle, i.e. 32 units. This will be done in [*not completed*].

12.3 We are now in a position to estimate the capacity requirements of each memory type (a)–(h) of 2.4.

Ad (a): Need not be discussed since it is taken care of in CA (cf. above). Actually, since it requires | dl I | to | dl IV | each of which must hold essentially a standard number, i.e. 30 units (with small deviations, cf. [*not completed*]), this corresponds to 120 units. Since this is not in M, the organization into minor cycles does not apply here, but we note that 120 units correspond to 4 minor cycles. Of course some other parts of CA are memory organs too, usually with capacities of one or a few units: e.g. the discriminators of Figures 8 and 12. The complete CA actually contains / more | dl |organs, corresponding to - / units, i.e. - 0 minor cycles (cf. [*not completed*]).

Ad (b): The capacity required for this purpose can only be estimated after the form of all standard orders has been decided upon, and several typical problems have been formulated—"set up"—in that terminology. This will be done in [*not completed*]. It will then appear, that the capacity requirements of (b) are small compared to those of some of (c)–(h), particularly to those of (c).

Ad (c): As indicated loc. cit., we count on function tables of 100–200 entries. A function table is primarily a switching problem, and the natural numbers of alternatives for a switching system are the powers of 2. (Cf. [*not completed*].) Hence $128 = 2^7$ is a suitable number of entries. Thus the relative precision obtained directly for the variable is 2^{-7}. Since a relative precision of 2^{-30} is desired for the result, and $(2^{-7})^4 > 2^{-30}$, $(2^{-7})^5 << 2^{-30}$, the interpolation, error must be fifth order, i.e. the interpolation biquadratic. (One might go to even higher order interpolation, and hence fewer entries in the function table. However, it will appear that the capacity requirements of (c) are even for 128 entries small compared e.g. to those of (c).) With biquadratic interpolation five table values are needed for each interpolation: Two above and two below the rounded off variable. Hence 128 entries allow actually the use of 124 only, and these correspond to 123 intervals, i.e. a relative precision 123^{-1} for the variable. However even $123^{-5} << 2^{-30}$ (by a factor of about $1/25$).

Thus a function table consists of 128 numbers, i.e. it requires a capacity of 128 minor cycles. The familiar mathematical problems hardly ever require more than five function tables (very rarely that much), i.e. a capacity of 640 minor cycles seems to be a safe overestimate of the capacity required for (c).

Ad (d): These capacities are clearly less than or at most comparable to those required by (e). Indeed the initial values are the same thing as the intermediate values of (f), except that they belong to the first value of t. And in a partial differential equation with n + 1 variables, say $x_1, \ldots, x_n$ and t, the intermediate values of a given t—to be discussed under (e)—as well as the initial values or the totality of all boundary values for all t correspond all three to n-dimensional manifolds (in the (n + 1) -dimensional space) of $x_1, \ldots, x_n$ and t; hence they are likely to involve all about the same number of data.

Another important point is, that the initial values and the boundary values are usually given—partly or wholly—by a formula—or by a moderate number of formulae; i.e., unlike the intermediate values of (e), they need not be remembered as individual numbers.

Ad (e): For a partial differential equation with two variables, say x and t, the number of intermediate values for a given t is determined by the number of x-lattice points used in the calculation. This is hardly ever more than 150, and it is unlikely that more than 5 numerical quantities should be associated with each point.

In typical hydrodynamical problems, where x is a Lagrangeian label-coordinate, 50–100 points are usually a light estimate, and 2 numbers are required at each point: A position-coordinate and a velocity. Returning to the higher estimate of 150 points and 5 numbers at each point gives 750 numbers, i.e. it requires a capacity of 750 minor cycles. Therefore 1,000 minor cycles seem to be a safe overestimate of the capacity required for (e) in two variable (x and t) problems.

For a partial differential equation with three variables, say x, y and t, the estimate is harder to make. In hydrodynamical problems, at least, important progress could be made with 30 × 30 or 40 × 20 or similar numbers of x, y lattice points say — 1,000 points. Interpreting x, y again in Lagrangeian labels shows, that at least 4 numbers are needed at each point: Two position coordinates and two velocity components. We take 6 numbers per point to allow for possible other non hydrodynamical quantities. This gives 6,000 numbers, i.e. it requires a capacity of 6,000 minor cycles for (e) in hydrodynamical three variable (x, y and t) problems.

It will be seen (cf. [*not completed*]), that a memory capacity of 6,000 minor cycles—i.e. of 200,000 units—is still conveniently feasible but that essentially higher capacities would be increasingly difficult to control. Even 200,000 units produce somewhat of an unbalance—i.e. they make M bigger than the other parts of the device put together. It seems therefore unwise to go further, and to try to treat four variable (x, y, z and t) problems.

It should be noted that two variable (x and t) problems include all linear or circular symmetric plane or spherical symmetric spacial transient problems, also certain general plane or cylinder symmetric spacial stationary problems (they must be hyperbolic, e.g. supersonic, t is replace by y). Three variable problems (x, y and t) include all spacial transient problems. Comparing this enumeration with the well known situation of fluid dynamics, elasticity, etc., shows how important each one of these successive stages is: Complete freedom with two variable problems; extension to four variable problems. As we indicated, the possibilities of the practical size for M draw the natural limit for the device contemplated at present between the second and the third alternatives. It will be seen that considerations of duration place the limit in the same place (cf. [*not completed*]).

Ad (f): The memory capacities required by a total differential equation with two variables—i.e to the lower estimate of (e).

Ad (g): As pointed out in (g) in 2.4, these problems are very similar to those of (e), except that the variable t now disappears. Hence the lower estimate of (e) (1,000 minor cycles) applies when a system of (at most 5) one-variable functions (of x) is being sought by successive approximation or relaxation methods, while the higher estimate of (e) (6,000 minor cycles) applies when a system of (at most 6) two-variable functions (of x, y) is being sought. Many problems of this type, however, deal with one function only—this cuts the above estimates considerably (to 200 or 1,000 minor cycles). Problems in which only a system of individual constants is being sought by successive approximations require clearly smaller capacities: They compare to the preceding problems like (f) to (e).

Ad (h): These problems are so manifold, that it is difficult to plan for them systematically at this stage.

In sorting problems any device not based freely on permutable record elements (like punchcards) has certain handicaps (cf. [*not completed*]), besides this subject can only be adequately treated after an analysis of the relation of M and of R has been made (cf. 2.9 and [*not completed*]). It should be noted, however, that the standard punchcard has place for 80 decimal digits, i.e. 9 9-digit decimal numbers, that is 9 numbers in our present sense, i.e. 9 minor cycles. Hence the 6,000 minor cycles considered in (e) correspond to a sorting capacity of 700 fully used cards. In most sorting problems the 80 columns of the cards are far from fully used—this may increase the equivalent sorting capacity of our device proportionately above 700. This means, that the device has a non negligible, but certainly not impressive sorting capacity. It is probably only worth using on sorting problems of more than usual mathematical complexity.

In statistical experiments the memory requirements are usually small: Each individual problem is usually of moderate complexity, each individual problem is independent (or only dependent by a few data) from its predecessors; and all that need be remembered through the entire sequence of individual problems are the numbers of how many problems successively solved had their results in each one of a moderate number of given distinct classes.

12.4 The estimates of 12.3 can be summarized as follows: The needs of (d)–(h) are alternative, i.e. they cannot occur in the same problem. The highest estimate reached here was one of 6,000 minor cycles, but already 1,000 minor cycles would permit to treat many important problems. (a) need not be considered in M. (b) and (c) are cumulative, i.e. they may add to (d)–(h) in the same problem. 1,000 minor cycles for each, i.e. 2,000 together, seem to be a safe overestimate. If the higher value 6,000 is used in (d)–(h), these 2,000 may be added for (b)–(c). If the lower value 1,000 is used in (d)–(h), it seems reasonable to cut the (b)–(c) capacity to 1,000. (This amounts to assuming fewer function tables and somewhat less complicated "set ups." Actually even these estimates are generous, cf. [*not completed*].) Thus total capacities of 8,000 or 2,000 minor cycles obtain.

It will be seen that it is desirable to have a capacity of minor cycles which is a power of two (cf. [*not completed*]). This makes the choices of 8,000 or 2,000 minor cycles of a convenient approximate size: They lie very near to powers of two. We consider accordingly these two total memory capacities: 8,192 = 2^{13} or 2,048 = 2^{11} minor cycles, i.e. 262,272 = 2^{18} or 65,536 = 2^{16} units. For the purposes of the discussions which follow *we will use the first higher estimate.*

This result deserves to be noted. It shows in a most striking way where the real difficulty, the main bottleneck of an automatic very high speed computing device lies: At the memory. Compared to the relative simplicity of CA (cf. the beginning of 11.1 and [*not completed*]), and to the simplicity of CC and of its "code" (cf. [*not completed*]), M is somewhat impressive: The requirements formulated in 12.2, which were considerable but by no means fantastic, necessitate a memory M with a capacity of about a quarter million units! Clearly the practicality of a device as is contemplated here depends most critically on the possibility of building such an M, and on the question of how simple such an M can be made to be.

12.5 How can an M of a capacity of 2^{18} or 250,000 units be built?

The necessity of introducing delay elements of very great efficiency, as indicated in 7.5, 7.6 and 12.1, becomes now obvious: One E-element, as shown on Figure 4, has a unit memory capacity, hence any direct solution of the problem of construction M with the help of E-elements would require as many E-elements as the desired capacity of M—indeed, because of the necessity of switching and gating about four times more (cf. [*not completed*]). This is manifestly impractical for the desired capacity of 250,000—or, for that matter, for the lower alternative in 12.5, of 65,000.

We therefore return to the discussion of the cyclical or delay memory, which was touched upon in 12.1. (Another type will be considered in 12.6.)

Delays $\boxed{\text{dl (k)}}$ can be built with great capacities k, without using any E-elements at all. This was mentioned in 7.6, together with the fact that even linear electric circuits of this type exist. Indeed, the contemplated τ of about one microsecond requires a circuit passband of 3–5 megacycles (remember Figure 1!) and then the equipment required for delays of 1–3 microseconds—i.e. k = 1, 2, 3—is simple and cheap, and that for delays up to 30–35 microseconds—i.e. k = 30, . . . , 35—is available and not unduly expensive or complicated. Beyond this order of k, however, the linear electric circuit approach becomes impractical.

This means that the delays $\rightarrow$ $\rangle\rangle$ $\rangle\rangle\rangle$ which occur in all E-networks of Figures 3–15 can be easily made with linear circuits. Also, that the various ⃞dl⃞ of CA (cf. Figures 9, 13, 15, and the beginning of 11.1), which should have k values 30, and of which only a moderate number will be needed (cf. (a) in 12.3), can be reasonably made with linear circuits. For M itself, however, the situation is different.

M must be made of ⃞dl⃞ organs, of a total capacity 250,000. If these were linear circuits, of maximum capacity 30 (cf. above), then 8,000 such organs would be required, which is clearly impractical. This is also true for the lower alternative of 12.5, capacity 65,000, since even then 2,000 such organs would be necessary.

Now it is possible to build ⃞dl⃞ organs which have an electrical input and output, but not a linear electrical circuit in between, with k values up to several thousand. Their nature is such that a 4 stage amplification is needed at the output, which, apart from its amplifying character, also serves to reshape and resynchronize the output pulse. I.e. that last stage gates the clock pulse (cf. 6.3) using a non linear part of a vacuum tube characteristic which goes across the cutoff; while all other stages effect ordinary amplification, using linear parts of vacuum tube characteristics. Thus each one of these ⃞dl⃞ requires 4 vacuum tubes at its output, it also requires 4 E-elements for switching and gating (cf. [*not completed*]). This gives probably 10 or fewer vacuum tubes per ⃞dl⃞ organ. The nature of these ⃞dl⃞ organs is such, that a few hundred of them can be built and incorporated into one device without undue difficulties—although they will then certainly constitute the greater part of the device (cf. [*not completed*]).

Now the M capacity of 250,000 can be achieved with such ⃞dl⃞ devices, each one having a capacity 1,000–2,000, by using 250–125 of them. Such numbers are still manageable (cf. above), and they require about 8 times more, i.e. 2,500–1,250 vacuum tubes. This is a considerable but perfectly practical number of tubes—indeed probably considerably lower than the upper limit of practicality. The fact that they occur in identical groups of 10 is also very advantageous. (For details cf. [*not completed*].) It will be seen that the other parts of the device of which CA and CC are electrically the most complicated, require together <<1,000 vacuum tubes. (Cf. [*not completed*].) Thus the vacuum tube requirements of the device are controlled essentially by M, and they are of the order of 2,000–3,000. (Cf. loc. cit. above.) This confirms the conclusion of 12.4, that the decisive part of the device, determining more than any other part its feasibility, dimensions and cost, is the memory.

We must now decide more accurately what the capacity of each ⃞dl⃞ should be—within the limits which were found to be practical. A combination of a few very simple viewpoints leads to such a decision.

12.6 We saw above that each ⬚dl⬚ organ requires about 10 associated vacuum tubes, essentially independently of its length. (A very long ⬚dl⬚ might require one more stage of amplification, i.e. 11 vacuum tubes.) Thus the number of ⬚dl⬚ organs, and not the total capacity determines the number of vacuum tubes in M. This would justify using as few ⬚dl⬚ organs as possible, i.e. of as high individual capacity as possible. Now it would probably be feasible to develop ⬚dl⬚'s of the type considered with capacities considerably higher than the few thousand mentioned above. There are, however, other considerations which set a limit to increases of ⬚dl⬚ .

In the first place, the considerations at the end of 6.3 show, that the definition of ⬚dl⬚'s delay time must be a fraction t' of t (about 1/5–1/2), so that each stimulus emerging from ⬚dl⬚ may gate the correct clock pulse for the output. For a capacity k, i.e. a delay kt, this is relative precision 5k–2k, which is perfectly feasible for the device in question when k is as large as 1,000, but becomes increasingly uncertain when k increases beyond 10,000. However, this argument is limited by the consideration that as the individual ⬚dl⬚ capacity increases, correspondingly fewer such organs are needed, and therefore each one can be made with correspondingly more attention and precision.

Next, there is another more sharply limiting consideration. If each ⬚dl⬚ has the capacity k, then 250,000/k of them will be needed, and 250,000/k amplifying switching and gating vacuum tube aggregates are necessary. Without going yet into the details of these circuits, the individual ⬚dl⬚ and its associated circuits can be shown schematically in Figure 18. Note, that Figure 6 showed the block SG in detail but the block A not at all. The actual arrangement will differ from Figure 6 in some details, even regarding SG, (cf.[*not completed*]). Since ⬚dl⬚ is to be used as a memory its output must be fed back—directly or indirectly—into its input. In an aggregate of many ⬚dl⬚ organs—which M is going to be—we have a choice to feed each ⬚dl⬚ back into itself, or to have longer cycles of ⬚dl⬚'s: Figure 19 (a) and (b), respectively. It should be noted, that (b) shows a cycle which

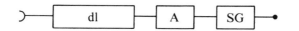

A: Amplification
SG: Switching and Gating

Figure 18

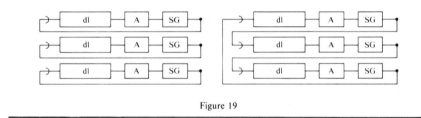

Figure 19

has a capacity that is a multiple of the individual ⎢ dl ⎢ 's capacity—i.e. this is a way to produce a cycle which is free of the individual ⎢ dl ⎢ 's capacity limitations. This is, of course, due to the reforming of the stimuli traversing this aggregate at each station A. The information contained in the aggregate can be observed from the outside at every station SG, and it is also here that it can be intercepted, cleared, and replaced by other information from the outside. (For details cf. [*not completed*].) Both statements apply equally to both schemes (a) and (b) of Figure 19. Thus the entire aggregate has its inputs, outputs, as well as its switching and gating controls at the stations SG—it is here that all outside connections for all these purposes must be made.

To omit an SG on the scheme (a) would be unreasonable: It would make the corresponding ⎢ dl ⎢ completely inaccessible and useless. In the scheme (b), on the other hand, all SG but one could be omitted (provided that all A are left in place): The aggregate would still have at least one input and output that can be switched and gated and it would therefore remain organically connected with the other parts of the device—the outside in the sense used above.

We saw in the last part of 12.5, that each A and each SG required about the same number of vacuum tubes (4), hence the omission of an SG represents a 50% savings on the associated equipment at that junction.

Now the number of SG stations required can be estimated. (It is better to think in terms of scheme (b) of Figure 19 in general, and to turn to (a) only if all SG are known to be present, cf. above.) Indeed: Let each ⎢ dl ⎢ have a capacity k, and let there be an SG after every l of them. Then the aggregate between any two SG has the capacity $k' = kl$. (One can also use scheme (b) with aggregates of l ⎢ dl ⎢ 's each and one SG each.) Hence $250,000/k'$ SG's are needed altogether, and the switching problem of M is a $250,000/k'$ way one. On the other hand every individual memory unit passes a position SG only at the end of each $k't$ period. I.e. it becomes accessible to the other parts of the device only then. Hence if the information contained in it is required in any other part of the device, it becomes necessary to wait for it—this waiting time being at most k't, and averaging 1/2 k't.

This means that obtaining an item of information from M consumes an average time 1/2 k't. This is, of course, not a time requirement per memory unit: Once the first unit has been obtained in this way all those which follow after it (say one or more minor cycles) consume only their natural duration, t. On the other hand this variable waiting time (maximum k't, average 1/2 k't), must be replaced in most cases by a fixed waiting time k't, since it is usually necessary to return to the point in the process at which the information was desired, after having obtained that information—and this amounts altogether to a precise period k't. (For details cf.[*not completed*].) Finally, this wait k't is absent, if the part of M in which the desired information is contained follows immediately upon the point at which that information is wanted and the process continues from there. We can therefore say: *The average time of transfer from a general position in M is k't.*

Hence the value of k' must be obtained from the general principles of balancing the time requirements of the various operations of the device. The considerations which govern this particular case are simple:

In the process of performing the calculations of a mathematical problem a number in M will be required in the other parts of the device in order to use it in some arithmetical operations. It is exceptional if all these operations are linear, i.e. $+$, $-$, normally $\times$, and possible $\div$, $\sqrt{}$, will also occur. It should be noted that substituting a number u into a function f given by a function table, so as to form f(u), usually involves interpolation—i.e. one $\times$ if the interpolation is linear, which is usually not sufficient, and two to four $\times$'s if it is quadratic to biquadratic, which is normal. (Cf. e.g. (c) in 12.3.) A survey of several problems, which are typical for various branches of computing mathematics, shows that an average of two $\times$ (including $\div$, $\sqrt{}$) per number obtained from M is certainly not too high. (For examples cf. [*not completed*].) Hence every number obtained from M is used for two multiplication times or longer, therefore the waiting time required for obtaining it is not harmful as long as it is a fraction of two multiplication times.

A multiplication time is of the order of 30^2 times t (cf. 5.3, 7.1 and 12.2, for $\div$, $\sqrt{}$ cf. 5.5) say 1,000t. Hence our condition is that k't must be a fraction of 2,000t. Thus k' $\cong$ 1,000 seems reasonable. Now a $\boxed{dl}$ with k' $\cong$ 1,000 is perfectly feasible (cf. the second part of 12.5), hence k' = k' $\cong$ 1000, l = 1 is a logical choice. In other words: Each $\boxed{dl}$ has a capacity k $\cong$ 1,000 and has an SG associated with it, as shown on Figures 18, 19.

This choice implies that the number of ⌷ dl ⌷'s required is 250,000/k ~ 250 and the number of vacuum tubes in their associated circuits is about 10 times more (cf. the end of 12.5), i.e. 2,500.

12.7 The factorization of the capacity—250,000 into—250 ⌷ dl ⌷ organs of a capacity—1,000 each can also be interpreted in this manner: The memory capacity 250,000 presents prima facie a 250,000-way switching problem, in order to make all parts of this memory immediately accessible to the other organs of the device. In this form the task is unmanageable for E-elements (e.g. vacuum tubes, cf. however 12.8). The above factorization replaces this by a 250-way switching problem, and replaces for the remaining factor 1,000 the (immediate, i.e. synchronous) switching by a temporal succession—i.e. by a wait of 1000t.

This is an important general principle: A $c = hk$-way switching problem can be replaced by a k-way switching problem and an h-step temporal succession—i.e. a wait of ht. We had $d = 250,000$ and chose $k = 1,000$, $h = 250$. The size of k was determined by the desire to keep h down without letting the waiting time kt grow beyond one multiplication time. This gave k 1,000, and proved to be compatible with the physical possibilities of a ⌷ dl ⌷ of capacity k.

It will be seen, that it is convenient to have k, h, and and hence also c, powers of two. The above values for these quantities are near such powers, and accordingly we choose:

Total capacity of M:	$c = 262,144 = 2^{18}$.
Capacity of a ⌷ dl ⌷ organ:	$k = 1,024 = 2^{10}$.
Number of ⌷ dl ⌷ organs in M:	$h = 256 = 2^8$.

The two first capacities are stated in memory units. In terms of minor cycles of $32 = 2^5$ memory units each:

Total capacity of M in minor cycles:	$c/32 = 8,192 = 2^{13}$.
Capacity of a ⌷ dl ⌷ organ in minor cycles:	$k/32 = 32 = 2^5$.

12.8 The discussions up to this point were based entirely on the assumption of a delay memory. It is therefore important to note that this need not be the only practicable solution for the memory problem—indeed, that there exists an entirely different approach which may even appear prima facie to be more natural.

The solution to which we allude must be sought along the lines of the *iconoscope*. This device in its developed form remembers the state of 400 by $500 = 200,000$ separate points, indeed it remembers for each point more than one alternative. As it is well known, it remembers whether each point has been illuminated or not, but it can distinguish more than two states: Besides light and no light it can also recognize—at each point—several intermediate degrees of illumination. These memories are placed on it by a light beam, and subsequently sensed by an electron beam, but it is easy to see that small changes would make it possible to do the placing of the memories by an electron beam also.

Thus a single iconoscope has a memory capacity of the same order as our desideratum for the entire M (250,000), and all memory units are simultaneously accessible for input and output. The situation is very much like the one described at the beginning of 12.5, and there characterized as impracticable with vacuum tube-like E-elements. The iconoscope comes nevertheless close to achieving this: It stores 200,000 memory units by means of one dielectric plate: The plate acts in this case like 200,000 independent memory units—indeed a condenser is a perfectly adequate memory unit, since it can hold a charge if it is properly switched and gated (and it is at this point that vacuum tubes are usually required). The 250,000-way switching and gating is done (not by about twice 250,000 vacuum tubes, which would be the obvious solution, but) by a single electron beam—the switching action proper being the steering (deflecting) of this beam so as to hit the desired point on the plate.

Nevertheless, the iconoscope in its present form is not immediately usable as a memory in our sense. The remarks which follow bring out some of the main viewpoints which will govern the use of equipment of this type for our purposes.

(a) The charge deposited at a "point" of the iconoscope plate, or rather in one of the elementary areas, influences the neighboring areas and their charges. Hence the definition of an elementary area is actually not quite sharp. This is within certain limits tolerable in the present use of the iconoscope, which is the production of the visual impression of a certain image. It would, however, be entirely unacceptable in connection with a use as a memory, as we are contemplating it, since this requires perfectly distinct and independent registration and storage of digital or logical symbols. It will probably prove possible to overcome this difficulty after an adequate development—but this development may be not inconsiderable and it may necessitate reducing the number of elementary areas (i.e. the memory capacity) considerably below 250,000. If this happens, a correspondingly greater number of modified iconoscopes will be required in M.

(b) If the iconoscope were to be used with 400 by 500 = 200,000 elementary areas (cf. above), then the necessary switching, that is the steering of the electron beam would have to be done with very considerable precision:

Since 500 elementary intervals must be distinguished in both directions of linear deflection, a minimum relative precision of $1/2 \times 1/500 = .1\%$ will be necessary in each linear direction. This is a considerable precision, which is rarely and only with great difficulties achieved in "electrical analogy" devices, and hence a most inopportune requirement for our digital device. A more reasonable, but still far from trivial, linear precision of, say, .5% would cut the memory capacity to 10,000 (since 100 by 100 = 10,000, $1/2 \times 1/100 = .5\%$).

There are ways to circumvent such difficulties, at least in part, but they cannot be discussed here.

(c) One main virtue of the iconoscope memory is that it permits rapid switching to any desired part of the memory. It is entirely free of the octroyed temporal sequence in which adjacent memory units emerge from a delay memory. Now while this is an important advantage in some respects, the automatic temporal sequence is actually desirable in others. Indeed, when there is no such automatic temporal sequence it is necessary to state in the logical instructions which govern the problem precisely at which location in the memory any particular item of information that is wanted is to be found. However, it would be unbearably wasteful if this statement had to be made separately for each unit of memory. Thus the digits of a number, or more generally, all units of a minor cycle should follow each other automatically. Further, it is usually convenient that the minor cycles expressing the successive steps in a sequence of logical instructions should follow each other automatically. Thus it is probably best to have a standard sequence of the constituent memory units as the basis of switching, which the electron beam follows automatically, unless it receives a special instruction. Such a special instruction may then be able to interrupt this basic sequence, and to switch the electron beam to a different desired memory unit (i.e. point on the iconoscope plate).

This basic temporal sequence on the iconoscope plate corresponds, of course, to the usual method of automatic sequential scanning with the electron beam—i.e. to a familiar part of the standard iconoscope equipment. Only the above-mentioned exceptional voluntary switches to other points require new equipment.

To sum up: It is not the presence of a basic temporal sequence of memory units which constitutes a weakness of a delay memory as compared to an iconoscope memory, but rather the inability of the former to break away from this sequence in exceptional cases (without paying the price of a waiting time, and of the additional equipment required to keep this waiting time

within acceptable limits, cf. the last part of 12.6 and the conclusions of 12.7).
An iconoscope memory should therefore conserve the basic temporal sequence by providing the usual equipment for automatic sequential scanning
with the electron beam, but it should at the same time be capable of a rapid
switching (deflecting) of the electron beam to any desired point under special instruction.

(d) The delay organ $\boxed{dl}$ contains information in the form of transient
waves, and needs a feedback in order to become a (cyclical) memory. The
iconoscope on the other hand holds information in a static form (charges on a
dielectric plate), and is a memory per se. Its reliable storing ability is, however, not unlimited in time—it is a matter of seconds or minutes. What further measures does this necessitate?

It should be noted that M's main function is to store information which is
required while a problem is being solved, since it is then that there is a need
for the rapid accessibility, which is the main advantage of M over outside
storage (i.e. over R, cf. 2.9). Longer range storage—e.g. of certain function
tables (like ^{10}log, sin, or equations of state) or of standard logical instructions
(like interpolation rules) between problems, or of final results until they are
printed—should be definitely effected outside (i.e. in R, cf. again 2.9 and
[*not completed*]). Hence M should only be used for the duration of one problem and considering the expected high speed of the device this will in many
cases not be long enough to effect the reliability of M. In some problems,
however, it will be too long (cf. [*not completed*]) and then special measures
become necessary.

The obvious solution is this: Let Nt be a time of reliable storage in the
iconoscope. (Since Nt is probably a second to 15 minutes, therefore t, one
microsecond gives N of the order of 10^6 to 10^9. For $N \cong 10^9$ this situation
will hardly ever arise.) Then two iconoscopes should be used instead of one,
so that one should always be empty while the other is in use, and after N
periods t the latter should transfer its information to the former and then
clear, etc. If M consists of a greater number of iconoscopes, say k, this
scheme of *renewal* requires k + 1, and not k iconoscopes. Indeed, let I_0, I_1,
..., I_k be these iconoscopes. Let at a given moment I_i be empty, and I_0, ...,
I_{i-1}, I_{i+1}, ..., I_k in use. After N k+1 periods t I_{i+1} should transfer its information to I_i and then clear (for i = k replace i+1 by 0). Thus I_{i+1} takes over
the role of I_i. Hence if we begin with I_0, then this process goes through a
complete cycle I_1, I_2, ..., I_k and back to I_0, in k + 1 steps of duration N
k+1 t each i.e. of total duration Nt. Thus all I_0, I_1, ..., I_k are satisfactorily
renewed. A more detailed plan of these arrangements would have to be based

on a knowledge of the precise orders of magnitude of N and k. We need not do this here. We only wish to emphasize this point: All these considerations bring a dynamical and cyclical element into the use of the intrinsically static iconoscope—it forces us to treat them in a manner somewhat comparable to the manner in which a delay (cyclical memory) treats the single memory units.

From (a)–(d) we conclude this: It is very probable that in the end the iconoscope memory will prove superior to the delay memory. However this may require some further development in several respects, and for various reasons the actual use of the iconoscope memory will not be as radically different from that of a delay memory, as one might at first think. Indeed, (c) and (d) show that the two have a good deal in common. For these reasons it seems reasonable to continue our analysis on the basis of a delay memory although the importance of the iconoscope memory is fully realized.

13.0 Organization of M

13.1 We return to the discussion of a delay memory based on the analysis and the conclusions of 12.6 and 12.7. It is best to start by considering Figure 19 again, and the alternatives which it exhibits. We know from 12.7 that we must think in terms of $256 = 2^8$ organs $\boxed{\text{dl}}$, of capacity $1,024 = 2^{10}$ each. For a while it will not be necessary to decide which of the two alternatives Figure 19 (a) and (b) (or which combination of both) will be used. (For the decision of [*not completed*].) Consequently we can replace Figure 19 by the simpler Figure 18.

The next task is, then, to discuss the terminal organs A and SG. A is a 4 stage amplifier, about which more was said in 12.5. The function of A is solely to restore the pulse emerging from $\boxed{\text{dl}}$ to the shape and intensity with which it originally entered $\boxed{\text{dl}}$. Hence it should really be considered a part of $\boxed{\text{dl}}$ proper, and there is no occasion to analyze it in terms of E-elements. SG, on the other hand, is a switching and gating organ and we should build it up from E-elements. We therefore proceed to do this.

13.2 The purpose of SG is this: At those moments (i.e. periods τ) when other parts of the device (i.e. CC, CA and perhaps I, O) are to send information into the $\boxed{\text{dl}}$ to which this SG is attached, or when they are to receive information from it, SG must establish the necessary connections—at such moments we say that SG is *on*. At those moments when neither of these things is required, SG must route the output of its $\boxed{\text{dl}}$ back into the input of its (or its other) $\boxed{\text{dl}}$, according to the approximate alternative of Figure 19; at such moments we say that SG is *off*. In order to achieve this it is clear-

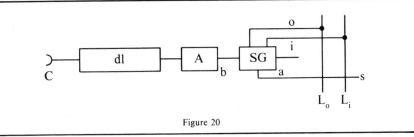

Figure 20

ly necessary to take two lines from C (and I, O) to this SG: One to carry the $\boxed{\text{dl}}$ output to C, and one to bring the $\boxed{\text{dl}}$ input from C. Since at any given time (i.e. period τ) only one SG will be called upon for these connections with C, i.e. be on (remember the principle of 5.6!) there need only be one such pair of connecting lines, which will do for all 256 SG's. We denote these two lines by L_o and L_i, respectively. Now the scheme of Figure 18 can be made more detailed, as shown in Figure 20.

As indicated, L_o is the line connecting the outputs of all SG's to C, and L_i is the line connecting C to the inputs of all SG's. When SG is off, its connections o, i with L_o, L_i are interrupted, its output goes to a, this being permanently connected to the input c of the proper $\boxed{\text{dl}}$, according to Figure 19, (a) or (b). When SG is on, its connections with a are interrupted, its output goes through o to L_o and so to C, while the pulses coming from C over L_i go into i which is now connected with a, so that these stimuli get now to a and from there to the proper $\boxed{\text{dl}}$ input (cf. above). The line s carries the stimuli which put SG on or off—clearly each SG must have its individual connection s (while L_o, L_i are common).

13.3 Before we consider the E-network of SG, one more point must be discussed. We allowed for only one state when SG is on, whereas there are actually two: First, when SG forwards information from M to C, second, when SG forwards information from C to M. In the first case the output of SG should be routed into L_o, and also into a, while no L_i connection is wanted. In the second case L_i should be connected to a (and hence to the proper $\boxed{\text{dl}}$ input by the corresponding permanent connection of a). This information takes away the place of the information already in M, which would have normally gone there (i.e. the output of SG which would have gone to a if SG had remained off), hence the output of SG should go nowhere, i.e. no L_o connection is wanted. (This is the process of *clearing*. For this treatment of clearing cf. [*not completed*].) To sum up: Our single arrangement for the on state differs from what is needed in either of these two cases. First case: a

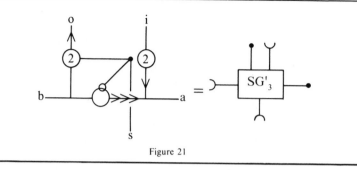

Figure 21

should be connected to the output of SG, and not to L_i. Second case: a should lead nowhere, not to L_o.

Both maladjustments are easily corrected. In the first case it suffices to connect L_o not only to the organ of C which is to receive its information, but also to L_i—in this manner the output of SG gets to a via L_o, the connection of L_o with L_i, and L_i. In the second case it suffices to connect L_o to nothing (except its i's)—in this manner the output of a goes into L_o, but then nowhere.

In this way the two above supplementary connections of L_o and L_i precise the originally unique on state of SG to be the first or the second case described above. Since only one SG is on at any one time (cf. 13.2) these supplementary connections are needed only once. Accordingly we place them into C, more specifically into CC, where they clearly belong. If we had allowed for two different on states of SG itself, then the it would have been necessary to locate the E-network, which establishes the two corresponding systems of connections, into SG. Since there are 256 SG's and only one CC, it is clear that our present arrangement saves much equipment.

13.4 We can now draw the E-network of SG, and also the E-network in CC which establishes the supplementary connections of L_o and L_i discussed in 13.3

Actually SG will have to be redrawn later (cf. [*not completed*]), we now give its preliminary form: SG[1] in Figure 21. When s is not stimulated the two ② are impassable to stimuli, while ◯ is, hence a stimulus entering at b goes on to a, while o and i are disconnected from b and a. When s is stimulated the two ② become passable, while ◯ is blocked, hence b is now connected to o and i to a. Hence SG[1] is on in the sense of 13.2 while s is stimulated, and it is off at all other times. The triple delay on ◯ is necessary for this reason: When SG[1] is on, a stimulus needs one period τ to get from b to o, i.e. to L_o (cf. 13.3 and the end of this section 13.4), and one to

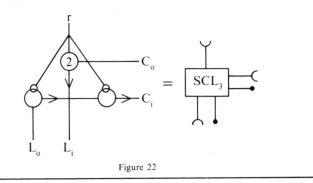

Figure 22

get from L_i, i.e. from i (cf. Figure 20), to a—that is, it takes 3τ from b to a. It is desirable that the timing should be the same when SG^1 is off, i.e. when the stimulus goes via ◯ from b to a—hence a triple delay is needed on ◯ .

The supplementary connections of L_o and L_i are given in Figure 22. When r is not stimulated the two ◯ are passable to stimuli; while ② is not, hence a stimulus entering at L_o is fed back into L_i and appears also at C_i, which is supposed to lead to C. When r is stimulated the two ◯ are blocked, while ② becomes passable, hence a stimulus entering at C_o, which is supposed to come from C, goes on to L_i, and L_o is isolated from all connections. Hence SCL produces the first state of 13.3 when r is not stimulated, and the second state when r is stimulated. We also note, that in the first case a stimulus passes from L_o to L_i with a delay of τ (cf. the timing question of SG^1, discussed above).

13.5 We must next give our attention to the line s of Figure 20 and 21: As we saw in the first part of 13.4, it is the stimulation of s which turns SG on. Hence, as was emphasized at the end of 13.2, each SG must have its own s—i.e. there must be 256 such lines s. Turning a desired SG on, then, amounts to stimulating its s. Hence it is at this point that the $\sim$250-way—precisely 256-way—switching problem commented upon in 12.7 presents itself.

More precisely: It is to be expected, that the order to turn on a certain SG—say No. k—will appear on two lines in CC reserved for this purpose, in this manner: One stimulus on the first line expresses the presence of the order as such, while a sequence of stimuli on the second line specifies the number k desired. k runs over 256 values, it is best to choose these as 0, 1, . . . , 255, in which case k is the general 8-digit binary integer. Then k will be represented by a sequence of 8 (possible) stimuli on the second line, which express (by their presence or absence), in their temporal succession, k's binary digits (1 or 0) from right to left. The stimulus expressing the order as such must appear on the first line (cf. above) in some definite time relation to these stimuli on the second line—as will be seen in [*not completed*], it comes immediately after the last digit.

Before going on, we note the difference between these 8 (binary) digit integers k and the 30 (binary) digit real numbers (lying between 0 and 1, or, with sign, between −1 and 1): the standard real numbers of 12.2. That we consider the former as integers, i.e. with the binary point at the right of the 8 digits, while in the latter the binary point is assumed to be to the left of the 30 digits, is mainly a matter of interpretation. (Cf. [*not completed*].) Their difference in lengths, however, is material: A standard real number constitutes the entire content of a 32 unit minor cycle, while an 8 digit k is only part of an order which makes up such a minor cycle. (Cf. [*not completed*].)

14.0 CC and M

14.1 Our next aim is to go deeper into the analysis of CC. Such an analysis, however, is dependent upon a precise knowledge of the system of orders used in controlling the device, since the function of CC is to receive these orders, to interpret them, and then either to carry them out, or to stimulate properly those organs which will carry them out. It is therefore our immediate task to provide a list of the orders which control the device, i.e. to describe the *code* to be used in the device, and to define the mathematical and logical meaning and the operational significance of its *code words*.

Before we can formulate this code, we must go through some general considerations concerning the functions of CC and its relation to M.

The orders which are received by C come from M, i.e. from the same place where the numerical material is stored. (Cf. 2.4 and 12.3 in particular (b).) The content of M consists of minor cycles (cf. 12.2 and 12.7), hence by the above each minor cycle must contain a distinguishing mark, which indicates whether it is a standard number or an order.

The orders which CC receives fall naturally into these four classes: (a) Orders for CC to instruct CA to carry out one of its ten specific operations (cf. 11.4). (b) Orders for CC to cause the transfer of a standard number from one place to another. (c) Orders for CC to transfer its own connection with M to a different point in M, with the purpose of getting its next order from there. (d) Orders controlling the operation of the input and the output of the device (i.e. 1 of 2.7 and 0 of 2.8).

Let us now consider these classes (a)–(d) separately. We cannot at this time add anything to the statements of 11.4 concerning (a). (Cf. however [*not completed*].) The discussion of (d) is also better delayed for (cf. [*not completed*]). We propose, however, to discuss (b) and (c) now.

14.2 Ad (b): These transfers can occur within M, or within CA, or between M and CA. The first kind can always be replaced by two operations of the last kind, i.e. all transfers within M can be routed through CA. We propose to do this, since this is in accord with the general principle of 5.6. (cf. also the discussion of the second question in 11.1), and in this way we eliminate all transfers of the first kind. Transfers of the second kind are obviously handled by the operating controls of CA. Hence those of the last kind alone remain. They fall obviously into two classes: Transfers from M to CA and transfers from CA to M. We may break up accordingly (b) into (b') and (b''), corresponding to these two operations.

14.3 Ad (c): In principle CC should be instructed after each order, where to find the next order that it is to carry out. We saw, however, that this is undesirable per se, and that it should be reserved for exceptional occasions, while as a normal routine CC should obey the orders in the temporal sequence, in which they naturally appear at the output of the DLA organ to which CC is connected. (Cf. the corresponding discussion for the iconoscope memory, (c) in 12.8.) There must, however, be orders available, which may be used at the exceptional occasions referred to, to instruct CC to transfer its connection to any other desired point in M. This is primarily a transfer of this connection to a different DLA organ (i.e. a $\boxed{\text{dl}}$ organ in the sense of 12.7). Since, however, the connection actually wanted must be with a definite minor cycle, the order in question must consist of two instructions: First, the connection of CC is to be transferred to a definite DLA organ. Second, CC is to wait there until a definite t-period, the one in which the desired minor cycle appears at the output of this DLA, and CC is to accept an order at this time only.

Apart from this, such a transfer order might provide, that after receiving and carrying out the order in the desired minor cycle, CC should return its connection to the DLA organ which contains the minor cycle that follows upon the one containing the transfer order, wait until this minor cycle appears at the output, and then continue to accept orders from there on in the natural temporal sequence. Alternatively, after receiving and carrying out the order in the desired minor cycle, CC should continue with that connection, and accept orders from there on in the natural temporal sequence. It is convenient to call a transfer of the first type a *transient* one, and one of the second type a *permanent* one.

It is clear that permanent transfers are frequently needed, hence the second type is certainly necessary. Transient transfers are undoubtedly required in connection with transferring standard numbers (orders (c') and (c″)), cf. the end of 14.2 and in more detail in 14.4 below). It seems very doubtful whether they are ever needed in true orders, particularly since such orders constitute only a small part of the contents of M (cf. (b) in 12.3), and a transient transfer order can always be expressed by two permanent transfer orders. We will therefore make all transfers permanent, except those connected with transferring standard numbers, as indicated above.

14.4 Ad (b) again: Such a transfer between CA and a definite minor cycle in M (in either direction, corresponding to (b') or (b″), cf. the end of 14.2) is similar to a transfer affecting CC in the sense of (c), since it requires establishing a connection with the desired DLA organ, and then waiting for the appearance of the desired minor cycle at the output. Indeed, since only one connection between M and CC (actually CC or CA, i.e. C) is possible at one time, such a number transfer requires abandoning the present connection of CC with M, and then establishing a new connection, exactly as if a transfer affecting CC in the sense of (c) were intended. Since, however, actually no such transfer of CC is desired, the connection of CC with its original DLA organ must be reestablished, after the number transfer has been carried out, and the waiting for the proper minor cycle (that one following in the natural temporal sequence upon the transfer order) is also necessary. I.e. this is a transient transfer, as indicated at the end of 14.3.

It should be noted, that during a transient transfer the place of the minor cycle which contained the transfer order, must be remembered, since CC will have to return to its successor. I.e. CC must be able to remember the number of the DLA organ which contains this minor cycle, and the number of τ periods after which the minor cycle will appear at the output. (Cf. for details [*not completed*].)

14.5 Some further remarks:

First: Every permanent transfer involves waiting for the desired minor cycle, i.e. in the average for half a transit through a DLA organ, 512 periods τ. A transient transfer involves two such waiting periods, which add up exactly to one transit through a DLA organ, 1,024 periods τ. One might shorten certain transient transfers by appropriate timing tricks, but this seems inadvisable, at least at this stage of the discussion, since the switching operation itself (i.e. changing the connection of CC) may consume a non-negligible fraction of a minor cycle and may therefore interfere with the timing.

Second: It is sometimes desirable to make a transfer from M to CA, or conversely, without any waiting time. In this case the minor cycle in M, which is involved in this transfer, should be the one immediately following (in time and in the same DLA organ) upon the one containing the transfer order. This obviously calls for an extra type of *immediate* transfers, in addition to the two types introduced in 14.3. This type will be discussed more fully in [*not completed*].

Third: The 256 DLA organs have number 0, 1, . . . , 255, i.e. all 8-digit binary numbers. It is desirable to give the 32 minor cycles in each DLA organ equally fixed numbers 0, 1, . . . , 31, i.e. all 5-digit binary numbers. Now the DLA organs are definite physical objects, hence their enumeration offers no difficulties. The minor cycles in a given DLA organ, on the other hand, are merely moving loci, at which certain combinations of 32 possible stimuli may be located. Alternatively, looking at the situation at the output end of the DLA organ, a minor cycle is a sequence of 32 periods τ, this sequence being considered to be periodically returning after every 1,024 periods τ. One might say that a minor cycle is a 32τ "hour" of a $1,024\tau$ "day," the "day" thus having 32 "hours." It is now convenient to fix one of these "hours," i.e. minor cycles, as zero or [*not completed*] and let it be at the same time at the outputs of all 256 DLA organs of M. We can then attribute each "hour," i.e. minor cycle, its number 0, 1, . . . , 31, by counting from there. We assume accordingly that such a convention is established—noting that the minor cycles of any given number appear at the same time at the outputs of all 256 DLA organs of M.

Thus each DLA organ has now a number $\mu = 0, 1, . . . , 255$ (or 8-digit binary), and each minor cycle in it has a number $p = 0, 1, . . . , 31$ (or 5-digit binary). A minor cycle is completely defined within M by specifying both numbers i, p. Due to these relationships we propose to call a DLA organ a *major cycle.*

Fourth: As the contents of a minor cycle make their transit across a DLA organ, i.e. a major cycle, the minor cycles number p clearly remains the same. When it reaches the output and is then cycled back into the input of a major cycle the number p is still not changed (since it will reach the output again after 1,024 periods τ, and we have synchronism in all DLA organs, and a $1,024\tau$ periodicity, cf. above), but μ changes to the number of the new major cycle. For individual cycling, the arrangement of Figure 19, (a), this means that μ, too, remains unchanged. For serial cycling, the arrangement of Figure 19, (b), this means that μ usually increased by 1, except that at the end of such a series of, say s major cycles it decreases by s − 1.

These observations about the fate of a minor cycle after it has appeared at the output of its major cycle apply as such when that major cycle is undisturbed, i.e. when it is off in the sense of 13.2. When it is on, in the same sense, but in the first case of 13.3, then our observations are obviously still valid—i.e. they hold as long as the minor cycle is not being cleared. When it is being cleared, i.e. in the second case of 13.3, then those observations apply to the minor cycle which replaces the one that has been cleared.

15.0 The code

15.1 The considerations of 14.0 provide the basis for a complete classification of the contents of M, i.e. they enumerate a system of successive disjunction which together give this classification. This classification will put us into the position to formulate the code which effects the logical control of CC, and hence of the entire device.

Let us therefore restate the pertinent definitions and disjunctions.

The contents of M are the memory units, each one being characterized by the presence or absence of a stimulus. It can be used to represent accordingly the binary digit 1 or 0, and we will at any rate designate its content by the binary digit $i = 1$ or 0 to which it corresponds in this manner. (Cf. 12.2 and 12.5 with 7.6.) These units are grouped together to form 32-unit minor cycles, and these minor cycles are the entities which will acquire direct significance in the code which we will introduce. (Cf. 12.2.) We denote the binary digits which make up the 32 units of a minor cycle, in their natural temporal sequence, by $i_0, i_1, i_2, \ldots, i_{31}$. The minor cycles with those units may be written $I = (i_0, i_1, i_2, \ldots, i_{31}) = (i_v)$.

Minor cycles fall into two classes: *Standard numbers* and *orders* (cf. 12.2 and 14.1). These two categories should be distinguished from each other by their respective first units (cf. 12.2) i.e. by the value of i_0. We agree accordingly that $i_0 = 0$ is to designate a standard number, and $i_0 = 1$ an order.

15.2 The remaining 31 units of a standard number express its binary digits and its s sign. It is in the nature of all arithmetical operation, specifically because of the role of carry digits, that the binary digits of the numbers which enter into them, must be fed in from right to left, i.e. those with the lowest positional values first. (This is so because the digits appear in a temporal succession and not simultaneously, cf. 7.1. The details are most simply evident in the discussion of the adder in 7.2.) The sign plays the role of the digit farthest left, i.e. of the highest positional value (cf. 8.1). Hence it comes last, i.e. $i_{31} = 0$ designates the $+$ sign, and $i_{31} = 1$ the $-$ sign. Finally by 9.2 the binary point follows immediately after the sign digit, and the number ξ, this represented must be moved mod 2 into the interval $-1, 1$. That is

$$\xi = i_{31}\, i_{30}\, i_{29} \ldots i_1 = \sum_{v=1}^{31} \; i_v\, 2^{v-31} \; (\text{mod } 2),\; -1 \leqq \xi < 1.$$

15.3 The remaining 31 units of an order, on the other hand, must express the nature of this order. The orders were classified in 14.1 into four classes (a)–(d), and these were subdivided further as follows: (a) in 11.4, (b) in 14.2, (b) and (c) in 14.3, 14.4, and the second remark in 14.5. Accordingly, the following complete list of orders obtains:

(a) Orders for CC to instruct CA to carry out one of its ten specific operations enumerated in 11.4. (This is (a) in 14.1.) We designate these operations by the numbers 0, 1, 2, . . . , 9, in the order in which they occur in 11.4, and thereby place ourselves into the position to refer to any one of them by its number w = 0, 1, 2, . . . , 9, which is best given as a 4-digit binary (cf., however, [*not completed*]). Regarding the origin of the numbers which enter (as variables) into these operations and the disposal of the result, this should be said: According to 11.4, the former come from I_{CA} and J_{CA} and the latter goes to O_{CA}, all in CA (cf. Figures 16, 17) J_{CA} is fed through I_{CA}, and I_{CA} is the original input and O_{CA} the final output of CA. Consequently these are the actual connecting links between M and CA. The feeding into I_{CA} will be described in (β), (γ), (α) below, the disposal from O_{CA} will be described in (δ), (α), (α) below.

Certain operations are so fast (they can be handled so as to consume only the duration of a minor cycle), that it is worth while to bypass O_{CA} when disposing of their result. (Cf. [*not completed*].)

The provisions for clearing I_{CA} and J_{CA} were described in 11.4. Regarding the clearing of O_{CA} this ought to be said: It would seem natural to clear each O_{CA} each time after its contents have been transferred into M (cf. below). There are, however, cases, when it is preferable not to transfer out from O_{CA}, and not to clear the contents of O_{CA}. Specifically: In the discussion of the operation s in 11.3 it turned out to be necessary to hold in this manner in O_{CA} the result of a previous operation $-$. Alternatively, the previous operation might also be $+$, i, j, or even x, cf. there. Another instance: If a multiplication xy is carried out, with an O_{CA} which contains, say, z at the beginning of the operation, then actually z + xy will form in O_{CA} (cf. the discussion of multiplication in 7.7). It may therefore be occasionally desirable to hold the result of an operation, which is followed by a multiplication, in O_{CA}. Formation of sums Σxy is one example of this.

We need therefore an additional digit c = 0, 1 to indicate whether O_{CA} should or should not be cleared after the operation. We let c = 0 express the former, and c = 1 the latter.

(β) Orders for CC to cause the transfer of a standard number from a definite minor cycle in M to CA. (This is (b) in 14.1, type (b') of 14.2.) The minor cycle is defined by the two indices u, p (cf. the third remark in 14.5). The transfer into CA is, more precisely, one into I_{CA} (cf. (a) above).

(γ) Orders for CC to cause the transfer of a standard number which follows immediately upon the order, into CA. (This is the immediate transfer of the second remark in 14.5 in the variant which corresponds to (β) above.) It is simplest to consider a minor cycle containing a standard number (the kind analyzed in 15.2) as such an order per se. (This modifies the statement loc. cit. somewhat: The standard number in question is not in the minor cycle following immediately upon a minor cycle which has just given an order to CC, then the number will automatically operate as an immediate transfer order of the type described. (Cf. also the pertinent remarks in (ϵ) and in (ζ) below.) The transfer into CA is again one into I_{CA} (cf. (a) or (β) above).

(δ) Orders for CC to cause the transfer of a standard number from CA to a definite minor cycle in M. (This is (b) in 14.1, type (b'') in 14.2.) The minor cycle in M is defined by the two indices u, p, as in (β) above. The transfer from CA is, more precisely, one from O_{CA}—this was discussed, together with the necessary explanations and qualifications, in (a) above.

(ϵ) Orders for CC to cause the transfer of a standard number from CA into the minor cycle which follows immediately upon the one containing this order. (This is the immediate transfer of the second remark in 14.5, in the variant which corresponds to (δ) above.) The transfer from CA is again one from O_{CA} (cf. (a) or (δ) above).

In this case the CC connection passes from this transfer order on to the next minor cycle, into which the standard number in question is just being sent. There would be no point in CC now obeying (γ), and sending this number back into CA—also, there might be timing difficulties. It is best, therefore, to except this case explicitly from the operation of (γ). I.e.: (γ) is invalid if it follows immediately upon an (ϵ).

(β) Orders for CC to cause the transfer of a standard number from CA into CA. (This is an operation of CA, the usefulness of which we recognized in 11.2 cf. also [*not completed*].) More precisely, from O_{CA} into I_{CA} (cf. (a) above).

(ϵ) Orders for CC to transfer its own connection with M to a definite minor cycle (elsewhere) in M. (This is (c) in 14.1.) The minor cycle in M is defined by the two indices u, p, as in (β) above.

Note, that a (β) could be replaced by a (ζ), considering (γ). The only difference is, that (ζ) is a permanent transfer, while (β) is a transient one. This may serve to place additional emphasis on the corresponding considerations of 14.3 and 14.4.

(η) Orders controlling the operation of the input and the output of the device (i.e. I of 2.7 and O of 2.8). (This is (d) in 14.1.) As indicated in 14.1, the discussion of these orders is better delayed (cf. [*not completed*]).

15.4 Let us now compare the number of digits necessary to express these orders with the number of available digits in a minor cycle 31, as stated at the beginning of 15.3.

To begin with we have in (α)–(η) 8 types of orders, to distinguish those from each other requires 3 digits. Next, the types (α)–(ζ) (we postpone (η), cf. above) have these requirements: (α) must specify the number w, i.e. 4 digits, plus the digit c—all together 5 digits. (β), as well as (δ) and (ζ), must specify the numbers μ and ρ, i.e. $8 + 5 = 13$ digits. (γ) is outside this category. (ϵ), as well as (θ), requires no further specifications.

Neither of these uses the 31 available digits very efficiently. Consequently we might consider putting several such orders into one minor cycle. On the other hand such a tendency to pool orders should be kept within very definite limits, for the following reasons.

First, pooling several orders into one minor cycle should be avoided, if it requires the simultaneous performance of several operations (i.e. violates the principle of 5.6). Second, it should also be avoided if it upsets the timing of the operations. Third, the entire matter is usually not important from the point of view of the total memory capacity. Indeed, it reduces the number of those minor cycles only, which are used for logical instructions, i.e. for the purpose (b) in 2.4, and those represent usually only a small fraction of the total capacity of M (cf. (b) in 12.3 and [*not completed*]). Hence the pooling of orders should rather be carried out from the point of view of simplifying the logical structure of the code.

15.5 Those considerations discourage pooling several orders of the type (α)—besides this would often not be logically possible either, without intervening orders of the types (β)–(ζ). Combining two orders of the types (β), (δ), (ζ) is also dubious from the above points of view, besides it would leave only $31 - 3 - 13 - 13 = 2$ digits free, and this (although it could be increased by various tricks to 3) is uncomfortably low: It is advisable to conserve some spare capacity in the logical part of the code (i.e. in the orders), since later on changes might be desirable. (E.g. it may become advisable to increase the capacity of M, i.e. the number 256 of major cycles, i.e. the number 8 of digits of u. For another reason cf. [*not completed*].)

The best chance lies in pooling an operation order (α) with orders controlling the transfer of its variables into CA or the transfer of its result out of CA. Both types may involve 13 digits orders (namely (β) or (δ)), hence we cannot count on pooling (α) with more than one such order (cf. the above estimate plus the 5 digits required by (α)!). Now one (α) usually requires transferring two variables into CA, hence the simplest systematical procedure consists in pooling (α) with the disposal of its result. I.e. (α) with (δ) or (ϵ) or (θ). It should be noted that every (δ), (ϵ), (θ), i.e. transfer from CA must be preceded by an (α), and every (β), (γ), i.e. transfer into CA, just be followed by an (α). Indeed, these transfers are always connected with an (α) operation, the only possible exception would be an M to M transfer, routed through (α) but even this involves an (α) operation (i or j in 11.4, cf. there and in 11.2). Consequently orders (δ), (ϵ) (θ) will always occur pooled with (α), and orders (β), (γ) will always occur alone. (α), too, may occasionally occur alone: If the result of the operation ordered by (α) is to be held in O_{ca} (cf. the last part of (α) in 15.3), then it will usually not be necessary or desirable to dispose of this result in any other way also (cf. the examples loc. cit.). We shall keep both possibilities open: there may or may not be an additional disposal of the result, and in the second case (α) will not be pooled with any disposal order. Orders (ζ) are of a sufficiently exceptional logical character, to justify that they too always occur alone.

Thus we have—if we disregard (γ), which is in reality a standard number—the 7 following types of orders: $(\alpha) + (\delta)$, $(\alpha) + (\beta)$, (α), (β), (ζ), (η). They require $5 + 13 = 18$. 5, 5, 5, 13, 13 digits (we disregard (η), which will be discussed later) plus 3 digits to distinguish the types from each other, plus one digit $(i_o = 1)$ to express that an order is involved. Hence the totals are 22, 9, 9, 9, 17, 17 digits. This is an average efficiency of 50% in utilizing the 32 digits of a minor cycle. This efficiency can be considered adequate, in view of the third remark of 15.4, and it leaves at the same time a comfortable spare capacity (cf. the beginning of 15.5).

15.6 We are now in the position to formulate our code. This formulation will be presented in the following manner:

We propose to characterize all possible minor cycles which may be used by the device. These are standard numbers and order, already enumerated and described in 15.1–15.5. In the table which follows we will specify the four following things for each possible minor cycle: (I) The *type*, i.e. its relationship to the classification (α)–(η) of 15.3, and to the pooling procedures of 15.5. (II) The *meaning*, as described in 15.1–15.5. (III) The *short symbol*, to

Table

I Type	II Meaning	III Short Symbol	IV Code Symbol
			Minor cycle $I = (i_y) =$ $(i_0 i_1 1_2 \ldots i_{31})$
Standard Number or Order (γ)	Storage for the number defined by $\xi = i_{31} . i_{30} i_{29} \ldots i_1 = \sum_{v=1}^{31} i_v 2 \pmod 2$ so that $-1 \leq \xi < 1$. i_{31} is the sign: 0 for $+$, 1 for $-$. If CC is connected to this minor cycle, then it operates as an order, causing the transfer of a standard number into I_{ca}. This does not apply however if this minor cycle follows immediately upon an order w$\rightarrow$A or wh$\rightarrow$A.	Nξ	$i_0 = 0$
Order $(\alpha) + (\delta)$	Order to carry out the operation w in CA and to dispose of the result. w is from the list of 11.4. These are the operations of 11.4, with their current numbers w and their symbols w:	w$\rightarrow\mu\rho$ or wh$\rightarrow\mu\rho$	$i_1 = 1$

w,decimal	w,binary	w	w,decimal	w,binary	w
0	0000	$+$	5	0101	i
1	0001	$-$	6	0110	j
2	0010	$\times$	7	0111	s
3	0011	$\div$	8	1000	db
4	0100	$\sqrt{}$	9	1001	bd

I Type	II Meaning	III Short Symbol
Order $(\alpha) + (\epsilon)$		w$\rightarrow$f or wh$\rightarrow$f
Order $(\alpha) + (\theta)$	h means that the result is to be held in O_{ca}. $\rightarrow\mu\rho$ means, that the result is to be transferred into the minor cycle ρ in the major cycle μ; $\rightarrow$f, that it is to be transferred into the minor cycle immediately following upon the order;	w$\rightarrow$A or wh$\rightarrow$A
Order (α)	$\rightarrow$A, that it is to be transferred into I_{ca}; no $\rightarrow$, that no disposal is wanted (apart from h).	wh
Order (β)	Order to transfer the number in the minor cycle in the major cycle μ into I_{ca}.	A$\leftarrow\mu\rho$
Order (ζ)	Order to connect CC with the minor cycle in the major cycle μ.	C$\leftarrow\mu\rho$

be used in verbal or written discussions of the code, and in particular in all further analyses of this paper, and when setting up problems for the device. (Cf. [*not completed*].) (IV) The code symbol, i.e. the 32 binary digits i_0, i_1, i_2, . . . , i_{31}, which correspond to the 32 units of the minor cycle in question. However, there will only be partial statements on this last point at this time, the precise description will be given later (cf. [*not completed*]).

Regarding the numbers (binary integers) which occur in these symbols, we observe this: These numbers are μ, ρ, w, c. We will denote their binary digits (in the usual, left to right, order) by u_7, . . . , u_0; p_4, . . . p_0; w_3, . . . , w_0; c.

Remark: Orders w (or wh) $\rightarrow \mu\rho$ (or f) transfer a standard number ξ', from CA into a minor cycle. If this minor cycle is of the type Nξ (i.e. $i_0 = 0$), then it should clear its 31 digits representing ξ and accept the 31 digits of ξ. If it is a minor cycle ending in $\mu\rho$ (i.e. $i_0 = 1$, order w $\rightarrow \mu\rho$ or wh $\rightarrow \mu\rho$ or A $\leftarrow \mu\rho$ or C $\leftarrow \mu\rho$), then it should clear only its 13 digits representing $\mu\rho$, and accept the last 13 digits of ξ!

Bibliography

Unpublished Sources

Archives. Unpublished materials in the following collections were examined during the research for this book:

The Association for Computing Machinery papers, Easton, Maryland, include sixty boxes of uncatalogued manuals, reports, and correspondence. A smaller collection of similar papers is available at ACM headquarters in New York City.

The Niels Bohr Library of the American Institute of Physics, New York City, contains transcripts of interviews with Franz Alt, Edward U. Condon, Richard Courant, Emanuel Piore, and Edward Teller.

The papers of the Moore School of Electrical Engineering, University of Pennsylvania, Philadelphia, Pennsylvania are cited as part of the larger collection comprising the University of Pennsylvania Archives (in this work abbreviated UPA). In addition to numerous reports, manuals, and other documents, the Moore School collection contains the 50,000-page trial transcript of *Honeywell* v. *Sperry Rand*: 36,000 documents, correspondences, and other materials entered as evidence, and 100 depositions and affidavits.

The National Archives, Washington, D.C., contain a variety of material relating to Eckert and Mauchly's work, including documents from the Ballistics Research Laboratory, the Army Ordnance Department, the National Bureau of Standards, the Census Bureau, the Air Force, the Army Map Service, and the National Research Council.

The National Bureau of Standards papers, Washington, D.C., include boxes of uncatalogued material and progress reports of NBS-funded research during the 1940s. NBS also has a complete collection of the *Projects and Publications of the National Applied Mathematics Laboratories.*

The Smithsonian History of Computing Project, the Museum of Science and Technology, Smithsonian Institution, Washington, D.C., contains transcripts of taped interviews with computer pioneers as well as progress reports, manuals, diagrams, and other documents. It includes a complete file of the Office of Naval Research's *Digital Computer Newsletter.*

The Sperry-Univac Archives, Blue Bell, Pennsylvania, contain the full collection of the *Honeywell* v. *Sperry Rand* material and, in addition, the Eckert-Mauchly and Remington Rand documents which were not used in the trial.

John von Neumann Papers, Library of Congress, Washington, D.C.

Private papers. The following individuals gave me access to their personal files: the late John William Mauchly; Herman H. Goldstine, Princeton, New Jersey; Margaret Fox, Computer Division, National Bureau of Standards, Gaithersburg, Maryland; Edmund C. Berkeley, Chief Research Consultant, Prudential Insurance Company, New York, New York; Warren Cordell, Research Analyst, A. C. Nielsen Company, Chicago, Illinois.

Interviews. I conducted a number of interviews that have proved invaluable to my research efforts. Some of the transcripts have been deposited with the Charles Babbage Institute at the University of Minnesota, Minneapolis. Those who were interviewed follow, in alphabetical order: Isaac Auerbach, Pennsauken, New Jersey, April 10, 1978; Edmund C. Berkeley, New York, March 29, 1978; John Grist Brainerd, Philadelphia, November 29, 1976, and March 23, 1977; Arthur W. Burks, Ann Arbor, Michigan, June 20, 1980; Carl C. Chambers, Philadelphia, November 30, 1977; Warren Cordell, Chicago, telephone interview, March 10, 1978; John Presper Eckert, Jr., Blue Bell, Pennsylvania, October 28, 1977, and January 23, 1980; Churchill Eisenhart, Gaithersburg, Maryland, January 19, 1978; George Eltgroth, New York, January 25, 1980; Margaret Fox, Gaithersburg, Maryland, April 20, 1977; Herman H. Goldstine, Princeton, New Jersey, November 1, 1976, and March 14, 1977; Morris Hanson, Rockville, Maryland, January 19, 1978; Betty Holberton, Gaithersburg, Maryland, April 20, 1977; Harry Huskey, Santa Cruz, California, June 7, 1978; John W. Mauchly, Ambler, Pennsylvania, October 22, 1976, March 28 and May 7, 1977, and March 31, 1978; Kay Mauchly, Ambler, Pennsylvania, January 23, 1980; Henry Rahmel, Belle Air, Florida, telephone interview, March 10, 1978; Mina Rees, New York, March 21, 1977; Irven Travis, Paoli, Pennsylvania, October 21, 1977; S. Reid Warren; Philadelphia, October 5, 1977; Philip Vincent, Landsdale, Pennsylvania, June 30, 1978.

Books and Articles

Alt, F. L. "A Bell Telephone Laboratories' Computing Machine," parts 1 and 2. *Mathematical Tables and Other Aids to Computation* 3 (1948): 1–13, 69–84.

———. "Archaeology of Computers—Reminiscences: 1945–1947." *Communications of ACM* 7 (1972): 693.

———. *Electronic Digital Computers.* New York, 1958.

Atanasoff, J. V. "Computing Machine for the Solution of Large Systems of Linear Algebraic Equations." In Brian Randell, ed. *The Origins of Digital Computers: Selected Papers.*

Auerbach, A., J. P. Eckert, Jr., R. Shaw, J. R. Weiner, and L. D. Wilson. "The BINAC." In *Proceedings of the IRE,* January 1952.

Baxter, James Phinney. *Scientists against Time.* Cambridge, Mass., 1946.

Belden, T. G., and M. R. Belden. *The Lengthening Shadow: The Life of Thomas J. Watson.* Boston, 1962.

Bell, C. G., and A. Newell. *Computer Structures: Readings and Examples.* New York, 1971.

Bergstein, H. "An Interview with Eckert and Mauchly." *Datamation,* April 1962.

Berkeley, E. C. "Electronic Machinery for Handling Information and Its Uses in Insurance." *Actuarial Society of America,* Transaction v, 48, part 1 (1947): 36–52.

———. *Giant Brains.* New York, 1949.

_____. "The Relations between Symbolic Logic and Large Scale Calculating Machines." *Science* 112 (October 6, 1950): 395.

Blachman, Nelson. *A Survey of Digital Computers.* Washington, D.C., 1953.

Bochner, S. "John von Neumann." *National Academy of Sciences Biographical Memoirs* 32 (1958): 438–457.

Booth, A. D., and K. H. V. Booth. *Automatic Digital Computers.* 3rd ed. London, 1965.

Bowden, B. V. *Faster Than Thought.* London, 1953.

Brainerd, John G. "Genesis of the ENIAC." *Technology and Culture* 17 (July 1976): 482–488.

_____. "Project PX—the ENIAC." *The Pennsylvania Gazette* 44 (1946): 16–32.

_____. "Stability of Oscillations in Systems Obeying Mathieu's Equation." *Journal of the Franklin Institute* 233 (1942): 135–142.

_____, and T. K. Sharpless. "The ENIAC." *Electrical Engineering* 67 (February 1948): 163–172.

Brainerd, John G., and C. N. Weygandt. "Solutions of Mathieu's Equations–I." *Philosophical Magazine* 30 (1940): 458.

Branscomb, Lewis. "E. U. Condon." *Physics Today* 27 (1974).

Brennan, Jean Ford. *The IBM Watson Laboratory at Columbia University.* New York, 1971.

Brown, Anthony Cave. *Bodyguard of Lies.* New York, 1975.

Burks, Arthur W. "Electronic Computing Circuits of the ENIAC." In *Proceedings of the Institute of Radio Engineers* 35 (1947): 756–767.

_____. "Super Electronic Computing Machine." *Electronic Industries* 5 (July 1948).

_____, H. H. Goldstine, and J. von Neumann. "Preliminary Discussion of the Logical Design of an Electronic Computing Instrument." In von Neumann, *Collected Works,* vol. 5, pp. 34–79.

Bush, Vannevar. *Pieces of the Action.* New York, 1970.

_____. "The Differential Analyzer: A New Machine for Solving Differential Equations." *Journal of the Franklin Institute* 212 (1931): 447–488.

Carpenter, B. E., and R. W. Doran. "The Other Turing Machine." *Computer Journal* 20 (August 1977): 269–279.

Chambers, Carl C., ed. "Theory and Techniques for the Design of Electronic Digital Computers: Lectures Delivered at the Moore School of Electrical Engineering, 8 July to 31 August 1946." Vols. 1–3. Mimeographed. Philadelphia, 1947.

Chase, G. C. "History of Mechanical Computing Machinery." In *Proceedings of the ACM,* May 1952, pp. 1–28.

Cochrane, Rexmond. *Measures for Progress: A History of the National Bureau of Standards.* Washington, D.C., 1966.

Comrie, L. J. "Modern Babbage Machines." *Bulletin, Office Machinery Users Association, Ltd.* London, 1932.

Crawford, P. O., Jr. "Automatic Control by Arithmetical Operations." M.Sc. thesis, Massachusetts Institute of Technology, Cambridge, Mass., 1942.

Davis, Martin. *Computability and Unsolvability.* New York, 1958.

Dubbey, J. M. "Charles Babbage and His Computer." *Institute of Mathematics and Its Applications* 9 (March 1973): 62–69.

Eames, Charles, and Ray Eames. *A Computer Perspective: A Sequence of 20th Century Ideas, Events, and Certificates from the History of the Information Machine.* Cambridge, Mass., 1973.

Eckert, J. Presper, Jr. "In the Beginning and to What End." *Computers and Chips.* Llandudno, Wales, 1970.

———, J. W. Mauchly, H. H. Goldstine, and J. G. Brainerd. *Description of the ENIAC and Comments on Electronic Digital Computing Machines.* National Defense Research Committee Report, November 1945.

Eckert, J. Presper, Jr., J. W. Mauchly, and J. R. Weiner. "An Octal System Automatic Computer." *Electrical Engineering* 68 (April 1949).

Eckert, Wallace J. *Punched Card Methods in Scientific Computation.* New York, 1940.

Ellis, N. D. "The Scientific Worker." Ph.D. dissertation, University of Leeds, England, 1969.

Emslie, A. G., H. B. Huntington, H. Shapiro, and A. E. Benfield. "Ultrasonic Delay Lines II." *Journal of the Franklin Institute* 245 (1948): 101–115.

Engineering Research Associates. *High-Speed Computing Devices.* New York, 1950.

Fernbach, S., and A. H. Taub, eds. *Computers and Their Role in the Physical Sciences.* New York, 1970.

Foy, N. *The IBM World.* London, 1974.

Frankel, S., and N. Metropolis. "Calculations in the Liquid-Drop Model of Fission." *Physical Review* 72 (1947): 914–925.

Fritz, W. Barkley. "A Survey of ENIAC Operations and Problems: 1946–1952." Memorandum, Ballistics Research Laboratory, Report No. 617, August 1952.

Gardner, W. D. "Will the Inventor of the First Digital Computer Please Stand Up?" *Datamation* 20 (February 2, 1974): 84–90.

Gibbons, Michael, and Phillip King. "The Development of Ovonic Switches: A Case Study of a Scientific Controversy." *Science Studies* 2 (London, 1972): 295–309.

Gluck, S. E. "The Electronic Discrete Variable Computer." *Electrical Engineering* 72 (1953): 159–162.

Goldstine, Herman H. *The Computer from Pascal to von Neumann.* Princeton, N.J., 1972.

———, and A. Goldstine. "The Electronic Numerical Integrator and Computer (ENIAC)." *Mathematical Tables and Other Aids to Computation* 2 (1949): 97–110.

Goldstine, Herman, and J. von Neumann. "Planning and Coding of Problems for an Electronic Computing Instrument" (1947). In von Neumann, *Collected Works,* vol. 5, pp. 80–151.

———. "On the Principles of Large-Scale Computing Machines." In von Neumann, *Collected Works,* vol. 5, pp. 1–32.

Goldstine, Herman, and E. P. Wigner. "Scientific Work of J. von Neumann." *Science* 125 (1957): 683–684.

Halmos, P. R. "The Legend of John von Neumann." *American Mathematical Monthly* 80 (1958): 382–394.

Hamming, R. W. "Controlling the Digital Computer." *Scientific Monthly* 85 (October 1957): 169–175.

Hartree, D. R. *Calculating Instruments and Machines.* Urbana, Ill., 1949.

———. *Calculating Machines—Report and Prospective Developments.* Cambridge, Mass., 1947.

———. "The ENIAC: An Electronic Calculating Engine." *Nature* 157 (April 20, 1946): 527.

———. "A Historical Survey of Digital Computing Machines." In *Proceedings of the Royal Society of London,* A 195, pp. 265–271. London, 1948.

Harvard University Computation Laboratory. *Description of a Magnetic Drum Calculator.* Cambridge, Mass., 1952.

_____. *Synthesis of Electronic Computing and Control Circuits.* Cambridge, Mass., 1951.

Heims, Steve J. *John Von Neumann and Norbert Wiener: From Mathematics to the Technologies of Life and Death.* Cambridge, Mass., 1980.

Hewlett, Richard G., and Francis Duncan. *A History of the U.S. Atomic Energy Commission,* vol 2. University Park, 1969.

Hughes, Thomas Parke. "ENIAC: Invention of a Computer." *Technikgeschichte* 42, no. 2, 1975.

Huskey, Harry D. "The Development of Automatic Computing." In *Proceedings of the First USA-Japan Computer Conference.* Tokyo, Japan, 1972.

Kneale, William, and Martha Kneale. *The Development of Logic.* Oxford, 1962.

Knight, Kenneth E. "A Study of Technological Innovation—The Evolution of Digital Computers." Ph.D. dissertation, Carnegie Institute of Technology, November 1963.

Knuth, D. E. *The Art of Computer Programming.* Reading, Mass., 1969.

_____. "Von Neumann's First Computer Program." *Computing Surveys,* vol. 2 (1970).

Larson, E. R. "Findings of Fact, Conclusions of Law and Order for Judgment," *Honeywell* v. *Sperry Rand and Illinois Scientific Development,* U.S. District Court, District of Minnesota, Fourth Division, October 19, 1973.

Lewis, C. I. *A Survey of Symbolic Logic.* Berkeley, Calif., 1918.

Lilley, S. "ENIAC, ASCC and ACE, Machines that Solve Complex Mathematical Problems." *Discovery* 8 (January 1947): 23–27.

Lowan, Arnold N. "The Computational Laboratory of NBS." *Scripta Mathematica* (March 1949): 33–63.

Lukoff, Herman. *From Dits to Bits: A Personal History of the Electronic Computer.* Portland, Oregon, 1979.

Matz, Adolph. "Electronics in Accounting." *Accounting Review* 21 (October 1946): 371–379.

Mauchly, John. "Mauchly on the Trials of Building ENIAC." *IEEE Spectrum,* April 1975.

_____. "Preparation of Problems for EDVAC-type Machines: Proceedings of a Symposium on Large Scale Digital Calculating Machinery, 7–10 January 1947." *Annals of the Computation Laboratory of Harvard University* 16 (1948): 203–207.

McCullough, W. S., and W. Pitts. "A Logical Calculus of the Ideas Immanent in Nervous Activity." *Bulletin of Mathematical Biophysics* 5 (1943): 115.

Metropolis, N. J. Howlett, and Gian Carlo Rota, eds. *A History of Computing in the Twentieth Century: A Collection of Essays.* New York, 1980.

Metropolis, N. J., and Jack Worlton. "A Trilogy on Errors in the History of Computing." In *Proceedings of the First USA-Japan Computer Conference.* Tokyo, Japan, 1972.

Michaels, F. Robert. "Tube Failures in ENIAC." *Electronics,* October 1947, pp. 116–119.

Mollenhoff, Georgia G. "John V. Atanasoff, Data Processing Pioneer." *Computerworld* 8:1 (March 13, March 20, March 27, 1979).

Morgenstern, Oskar. "The Collaboration between Oskar Morgenstern and John von Neumann on the Theory of Games." *Journal of Economic Literature,* 1976, pp. 805–816.

Murray, Francis J. *The Theory of Mathematical Machines.* New York, 1947.

Office of Naval Research. *Digital Computer Newsletter.* Washington, D.C., September 1949–December 1952.

Office of Naval Research, Civilian Personnel Division. *Civilian Scientists and Engineers in the Department of the Navy.* Washington, D.C., 1952.

———. "A Decade of Basic and Applied Science in the Navy," symposium sponsored by ONR, 1958.

Pylyshun, Z. W., ed. *Perspectives on the Computer Revolution.* Englewood Cliffs, N. J., 1970.

Rajchman, Jan. "The Selectron—A Tube for Selective Electrostatic Storage." In *Proceedings of a Symposium on Large-Scale Digital Calculating Machinery.* Cambridge, Mass., 1951.

Randell, Brian, ed. *The Origins of Digital Computers: Selected Papers.* 2nd ed. New York, 1973.

Redmond, Kent, and Thomas M. Smith. *Project Whirlwind: The History of a Pioneer Computer.* Bedford, Mass., 1980.

Richtmyer, R. D. "The Postwar Computer Developments." *American Mathematical Monthly* 72 (1965): 8–14.

Rodgers, William. *Think: A Biography of the Watsons and IBM.* New York, 1969.

Rosen, Saul. "Electronic Computers: A Historical Survey." *Computing Surveys,* March 1969.

Sammet, Jean. *Programming Languages: History and Fundamentals.* Englewood Cliffs, N. J., 1969.

Seeber, R. R. "Value of Super Calculators." *National Underwriter,* no. 4 (April 4, 1947).

Serrel, R., M. M. Astrahan, G. M. Patterson, and I. E. Pyne. "The Evolution of Computing Machines and Systems." *Proceedings IEEE.* 50 (May 1962): 1039–1058.

Shannon, C. E. "A Symbolic Analysis of Relay and Switching Circuits." *Transactions AIEE* 57 (1938).

———, and W. Weaver. *The Mathematical Theory of Communication.* Urbana, Ill., 1949.

Sharpless, T. K. "Mercury Delay Lines as a Memory Unit." In *Annals of the Computation Laboratory of Harvard University* 16: 103–109. Cambridge, Mass., 1948.

Shaw, R. F. "Arithmetic Operations in a Binary Computer." *Review of Scientific Instruments* 21 (August 1950): 687–693.

Smith, Charles V. L. *Electronic Digital Computers.* New York, 1959.

Smith, Thomas M. "Project Whirlwind: An Unorthodox Development Project." *Technology and Culture,* July 1976 pp. 447–464.

Sprague, Richard E. "A Western View of Computer History." *Communications of the ACM* 15 (July 1972).

Stevenson, M. G. "Bell Laboratories: A Pioneer in Computing Technology." *Bell Labs Record* 51 (December 1973): 344–351.

Stewart, Irwin. *Organizing Scientific Research for War.* Boston, 1948.

Stibitz, G. R. "The Relay Computer at Bell Laboratories." *Datamation,* April and May 1967, pp. 35–44, 44–49.

———, and J. A. Larrivee. *Mathematics and Computers.* New York, 1957.

Tomash, E., and A. A. Cohen, "The Birth of an ERA: Engineering Research Associates, Inc. 1946–1955." *Annals of the History of Computing* 1 (October 1979): 83–97.

Tropp, Henry. "The Effervescent Years: A Retrospective." *IEEE Spectrum* 11 (February 1974): 70–79.

Turing, A. M. "On Computable Numbers, with an Application to the Entscheidungs-problem." In *Proceedings of the London Mathematics Society* (2) 42 (1936): 230–267.

Ulam, Stanislaw. *Adventures of a Mathematician.* New York, 1976.

————, "John von Neumann, 1903–1957," *Bulletin of the American Mathematical Society* 64 (May 1958): 1–49.

von Neumann, John, *Collected Works.* 6 vols. Edited by A. H. Taub. New York, 1963.

————. "First Draft of a Report on the EDVAC." Mimeographed. University of Pennsylvania, June 30, 1945. See above, pp. 177–246.

————. *The Computer and the Brain.* New Haven, 1958.

————. "The Mathematician." *The Works of the Mind.* Edited by R. B. Heywood, 1: 180–196.

————. *The Theory of Self-Reproducing Automata.* Edited by Arthur Burks. Urbana, Ill., 1966.

————, and H. H. Goldstine. "Numerical Inverting of Matrices of High Order." *Bulletin of the American Mathematical Society* 53 (1947): 1021–1099.

Weaver, Warren. *Scene of Change: A Lifetime in American Science.* New York, 1970.

Weik, Martin H. "The ENIAC Story." *Ordnance* (1961), pp. 3–7.

————. *A Second Survey of Domestic Electronic Digital Computing Systems.* Ballistic Research Laboratories Report 1010, June 1957. Aberdeen, Md., 1957.

————. *A Survey of Domestic Electronic Digital Computing Systems.* Ballistic Research Laboratories Report No. 971, December 1951. Aberdeen, Md., 1955.

————. *A Third Survey of Domestic Electronic Digital Computing Systems.* Ballistic Research Laboratories Report 1115, March 1961. Aberdeen, Md.

Weiner, Norbert. *I Am a Mathematician.* Cambridge, Mass., 1956.

Weiss, Eric A. "Publications in Computing: An Informal Review." *Communications of the ACM* 15 (July 1972): 491–497.

Wilkes, Maurice V. *Automatic Digital Calculators.* London, 1956.

————. "Computers, Then and Now." *Journal of the ACM* 15 (1968): 1–7.

————, D. J. Wheeler, and S. Gill. *The Preparation of Programs for an Electronic Digital Computer.* Cambridge, Mass., 1951.

Wilkes, S. B. *Digital Computing Systems.* New York, 1959.

Williams, F. C., and T. Kilburn. "A Storage System for Use with Binary Digital Computers." In *Proceedings of the IEE,* vol. 96, pt. 2, no. 81 (1949).

Williams, F. C., T. Kilburn, G. C. Tootill. "Universal High-Speed Computers: A Small-Scale Experimental Machine." In *Proceedings IEE* 96 (1951).

Williams, Samuel B. "The Association for Computing Machinery." *Journal of the ACM* 1 (January 1954).

Notes

Introduction

1. E. R. Larson, "Findings of Fact, Conclusions of Law, and Order for Judgment," File No. 4-67, Civ. 138, *Honeywell Inc.* v. *Sperry Rand Corporation and Illinois Scientific Development, Inc.*, U.S. District Court, District of Minnesota, Fourth Division (19 October 1973).

Chapter 1 The ENIAC: Genesis of a Computer

1. *Honeywell* v. *Sperry Rand*, U. S. District Ct., Dist. Minn., 4th Div. (1973), p. 12494; Henry Tropp, "The Effervescent Years," *IEEE Spectrum*, February 1974; John Mauchly, "On the Trials of Building ENIAC," *IEEE Spectrum* 12 (April 1975): 70.
2. Mauchly, "On the Trials of Building ENIAC," p. 70.
3. *Honeywell* v. *Sperry Rand*, p. 12494.
4. John Mauchly, Fireside Chat, UNIVAC Conference in Rome, Italy, 1976, p.7, SUA.
5. Larson, "Findings of Fact, Conclusions of Law and Order for Judgment," *Honeywell* v. *Sperry Rand*, U.S. District Court, District of Minnesota, Fourth Division (19 October 1973).
6. Ibid.
7. Interview with John Mauchly by Nancy Stern, March 31, 1978.
8. See Vannevar Bush, "The Differential Analyzer: A New Machine for Solving Differential Equations," *Journal of the Franklin Institute* 212 (1931): 447–488.
9. John G. Brainerd, "Genesis of the ENIAC," *Technology and Culture* 17 (July 1976): 483.
10. Ibid., p. 484.
11. Interview with Nancy Stern, October 28, 1977.
12. Ibid.
13. Ibid.
14. Herman H. Goldstine, *The Computer from Pascal to von Neumann* (Princeton, 1972), pp. 148–149 (hereafter cited as *The Computer*).
15. Ibid, pp. 130–132.
16. BRL's increasing difficulty in providing firing tables is an oft-told story in the participants' published accounts of the ENIAC, including Goldstine, *The Computer*;

Mauchly, "On the Trials of Building ENIAC," *IEEE Spectrum*, April 1975; Arthur W. Burks, "Super Electronic Computing Machines," *Electronic Industries*, July 1946.

17. Arthur W. Burks, "Electronic Computing Circuits of the ENIAC," *Proceedings of the IRE* 35 (August 1947): 756.

18. Interview with Herman H. Goldstine by Nancy Stern, March 14, 1977.

19. War Department, Bureau of Public Relations, Press Branch, "Military Application of ENIAC Described," for release February 15, 1946.

20. John W. Mauchly, "The Use of High Speed Vacuum Tube Devices for Calculating," August 1942, UPA. The circumstances surrounding this issue have been provided by Mauchly in his court testimony, *Honeywell* v. *Sperry Rand*, p. 12129. See also Louis Serle Dederick's testimony, ibid., p. 16645. Dederick was associate director of BRL during the war.

21. See Goldstine's *The Computer*; Brainerd's "Genesis of the ENIAC," *Technology and Culture*, July 1976; U.S. War Department press release, "History of Development of Computing Devices," February 15, 1946, UPA; and interviews with Goldstine by Nancy Stern, November 1, 1976, and March 14, 1977.

22. Brainerd to Mauchly, January 12, 1943, UPA.

23. John G. Brainerd, "Report on an Electronic Diff. Analyzer," April 2, 1943, UPA. Goldstine provides a colorful account of the first meeting in *The Computer*, p. 149.

24. Brainerd to Pender, April 26, 1943, UPA.

25. University of Pennsylvania, Moore School of Electrical Engineering, "Estimate of cost for six-months' work (July 1–December 31, 1943) on project to develop electronic numerical integrator and computer for Ordnance Dept," May 17, 1943, UPA; Contract No. W-670-ORD-4926, The Trustees of the University of Pennsylvania and U.S. Army Ordnance Department, June 5, 1943, UPA.

26. Brainerd, "Genesis of the ENIAC," *Technology and Culture*, July 1976, pp. 482–488; Goldstine, *The Computer*, pp. 148–152. It is necessary to keep in mind the unconscious or even conscious tendency of principal participants to reconstruct selectively the details of events in a manner that emphasizes their own contributions. See also Thomas Parke Hughes, "ENIAC: Invention of a Computer," *Technikgeschichte* Bd. 42, Nr 2 (1975), p. 153.

27. "Report on an Electronic Diff. Analyzer," April 2, 1943.

28. "University of Pennsylvania, 'The ENIAC,' a Report Covering Work until December 31, 1943, submitted in accordance with Contract No. W-670-ORD-4926," p. I(6), UPA.

29. A. Hunter Dupree, *Science and the Federal Government* (Englewood Cliffs, N.J., 1963), p. 369.

30. Ibid., p. 371.

31. Irwin Stewart, *Organizing Scientific Research for War* (Boston, 1948); Vannevar Bush, *Pieces of the Action* (New York, 1970); Warren Weaver, *Scenes of Change* (New York, 1970); and James Phinney Baxter, *Scientists against Time* (Cambridge, Mass., 1946), are works written by participants about these organizations. As in the case of participants writing computer history, they can hardly be viewed as objective.

32. Thomas S. Kuhn, *The Structure of Scientific Revolutions*, 2nd ed. (Chicago, 1970), refers to this as commitment to "normal science," although in this context "normal technology" would be more appropriate.

33. James B. Conant, *My Several Lives* (New York, 1970), p. 236.

34. Warren Weaver to George Stibitz, March 13, 1942, requesting reports from RCA, BTL, MIT, and Kodak, National Archives, Washington, D.C.

35. The term "gatekeepers" appears in the literature of the sociology of science, e.g., Diana Crane, *Invisible Colleges* (Chicago, 1972). David O. Edge and Michael J. Mulkay, in *Astronomy Transformed: The Emergence of Radio Astronomy in Britain* (New York, 1976), use "leadership" as a synonym for gatekeeping, p. 295: "It is convenient to distinguish two . . . 'styles' of leadership. One common to all established leaders and groups, consists of administrative duties and 'supportive' tasks."

36. Interview with Stibitz and Andrews by Tropp, March 2, 1972, History of Computing Project, National Museum of Science and Technology, Smithsonian Institution, Washington, D.C. (hereafter cited as SHCP).

37. The Radiation Laboratory contracted with the Moore School in 1942 for the building of, among other things, delay lines, a project on which J. Presper Eckert worked.

38. Brainerd to Johnson, April 12, 1943, UPA.

39. J. Presper Eckert, deposition taken June 3, 1969, for *Honeywell* v. *Sperry Rand*, UPA.

40. Hazen's diary, April 14, 1943, subject: Conversation with Dr. Thomas Johnson, UPA.

41. V. Bush and S. H. Caldwell, "A New Type of Differential Analyzer," *Journal of the Franklin Institute* 240 (October 1945): 255–326; S. H. Caldwell, "Educated Machinery," *Technology Review* 48 (November 1945): 31–34.

42. Edge and Mulkay, *Astronomy Transformed*, p. 325, suggest that leaders, or gatekeepers, in general, play a role similar to that of Hazen and the NDRC: "This supportive style [of leadership] involved the conscious adoption of a policy of coordinating the wide range of topics made possible by commitment to multipurpose techniques, and of ordering priorities by strategic decisions on the allocation of resources."

43. Caldwell to Hazen, October 23, 1943, UPA.

44. Gillon to Hazen, October 7, 1943, UPA. See also Thomas M. Smith, "Project Whirlwind: An Unorthodox Development Project," *Technology and Culture* 17 (July 1976): 451.

45. George R. Stibitz to Warren Weaver, "Subject: Comments by Colonel Gillon on Differential Analyzer," November 6, 1943, UPA.

46. Brainerd's testimony, *Honeywell* v. *Sperry Rand*, pp. 6152–6155.

47. Interview with Harold Hazen by R. R. Mertz, December 15, 1970, p. II-24, SHCP.

48. Rajchman to Brainerd May 22, 1943 (see also May 29), UPA.

49. Kent C. Redmond and Thomas M. Smith, *Project Whirlwind: The History of a Pioneer Computer* (Bedford, Mass., 1980), make similar observations concerning the significance of administrators in research and development projects.

50. For a discussion of this competition, see Eckert's testimony in *Honeywell* v. *Sperry Rand*, p. 17711.

51. Gillon to Goldstine, October 9, 1943, Goldstine's private papers. Gillon's own West Point and MIT education suggests that his motives could have been closely tied to the wartime career officer's belief that the Army could make its own technical decisions without advice from NDRC.

52. Gillon to Goldstine, May 8, 1944, Goldstine's private papers.

53. Goldstine to Gillon, November 14, 1944, Goldstine's private papers.

54. Redmond and Smith, *Project Whirlwind*, p. 12.

Chapter 2 ENIAC Research and Development

1. "The ENIAC: Report Covering Work until June 30, 1944: Submitted in Accordance with Contract W-670-ORD-4926," UPA.

2. John W. Mauchly, "The Use of High Speed Vacuum Tube Devices for Calculating," unpublished memorandum, August 1942, UPA.

3. Arthur W. Burks, "From ENIAC to the Stored-Program Computer: Two Revolutions in Computers," *A History of Computing in the Twentieth Century*, edited by N. Metropolis, J. Howlett, and Gian-Carlo Rota (New York, 1980), pp. 315–344. This is a revised and expanded version of a paper presented at the International Research Conference on the History of Computing, Los Alamos, New Mexico, June 1976.

4. Goldstine, *The Computer*, p. 158.

5. Brainerd, "Report on an Electronic Diff. Analyzer," April 2, 1943, p. 1, UPA.

6. "Reports for Project PX," undated, UPA, lists all relevant existing technologies and engineers assigned to research them. Derek de Solla Price's contention that research is a significant part of the technicians' tasks, more important for them than for scientists, appears true of early electronic digital computer history. He states in "The Difference between Science and Technology," *Science since Babylon* (New Haven, 1975), p. 127: "One might indeed say that the scientist wants to write but not read and the technologist wants to read but not write."

7. "Report for Project PX: The NCR Thyratron Counter," September 1943, UPA; PX Report, "Dyadic Counters," November 15, 1943, UPA.

8. "Positive Action Ring Counter: Report for Project PX," August 17, 1943, UPA. This report was accepted as the final version in the December 1943 Progress Report.

9. Goldstine, *The Computer*, p. 158.

10. H. H. Goldstine and Adele Goldstine, "The Electronic Numerical Integrator and Computer (ENIAC)," *Mathematical Tables and Other Aids to Computation* 2 (1946): 97–110.

11. Nicholas Metropolis and Jack Worlton, "A Trilogy on Errors in the History of Computing," *Proceedings, First USA-Japan Conference* (Tokyo, 1972); Burks, "From ENIAC to the Stored-Program Computer," in *A History of Computing in the Twentieth Century*, edited by Metropolis et al.

12. "ENIAC Progress Report," December 31, 1943, UPA.

13. John Presper Eckert, "Disclosure of Magnetic Calculating Machine," January 1944, UPA.

14. "ENIAC Progress Report," December 31, 1943.

15. J. McPherson to McDowell, "IBM to furnish gang summary punch and reproducer for ENIAC," April 27, 1944, UPA.

16. "ENIAC Progress Report," June 1944.

17. Ibid.

18. Memorandum, J. Presper Eckert to ENIAC staff, July 1944, UPA.

19. Efforts to determine the optimum voltage necessary to increase the tube life revealed that failures resulted from open heaters and damaged cathodes. The failure rate was higher in tubes with folded filaments than in tubes with twisted filaments. F. R. Michael, "Tube Failures in ENIAC," *Electronics* 20 (October 1947): 116–119.

20. Interview by Nancy Stern, October 28, 1977, p. 29.

21. Burks, "From ENIAC to the Stored-Program Computer," *A History of Computing in the Twentieth Century*, edited by Metropolis et al., p. 314.

22. Brian Randell, ed. *The Origins of Digital Computers* (New York, 1973), p. 288. See also testimony of John V. Atanasoff, *Honeywell* v. *Sperry Rand*, p. 2396.

23. Goldstine, *The Computer*, p. 125.

24. "Findings of Fact, Conclusions of Law, and Order for Judgment," *Honeywell* v. *Sperry Rand*, p. 12.

25. Ibid, p. 47.

26. Mauchly's testimony, *Honeywell* v. *Sperry Rand*, p. 12159: In January 1941 "I was trying to get something within my possible budget. This is why I was working with ring counters which were gas tubes rather than vacuum tubes."

27. Mauchly to John V. Atanasoff, January 4, 1941, UPA.

28. John W. Mauchly, "The ENIAC," *A History of Computing in the Twentieth Century*, edited by Metropolis et al., p. 544.

29. Mauchly to Nancy Stern, January 29, 1979, p. 2.

30. Goldstine, *The Computer*, pp. 125–126.

31. *Honeywell* v. *Sperry Rand*, p. 12144.

32. Joseph A. Schumpeter, "The Creative Response in Economic History," *Journal of Economic History* 7 (May 1947): 152.

33. Goldstine, *The Computer,* p. 154.

34. See, specifically, the testimony of Goldstine and Brainerd.

35. In an interview on November 30, 1977, Carl Chambers called this a "systems" approach.

36. The intrinsic value in the ability to adapt or imitate has also been emphasized by Thorstein Veblen, *Imperial Germany and the Industrial Revolution* (New York, 1915).

37. Mauchly, "On the Trials of Building ENIAC," p. 74.

38. Mauchly, "The Use of High Speed Vacuum Tube Devices for Calculation," August 1942, UPA.

39. *Honeywell* v. *Sperry Rand*, pp. 12140–12144.

40. See the account of Samuel F. B. Morse's contribution to the telegraph in Dirk J. Struik, *Yankee Science in the Making* (New York, 1962), p. 332; see also the account of the work of James Watt and Matthew Boulton on the steam engine in D. S. L. Cardwell, *Turning Points in Western Technology* (New York, 1972), pp. 89–90.

41. Affidavit of Arthur W. Burks, *Honeywell* v. *Sperry Rand*, pp. 12, 18, UPA.

42. "Findings of Fact, Conclusions of Law, and Order for Judgment," *Honeywell* v. *Sperry Rand*, p. 18A.

43. IBM interoffice memo, J. W. Bryce, January 26, 1939, UPA.

44. "Report to the Services No. 57, Division 7 (Fire Control), National Defense Research Committee: RCA Computron," June 1943, UPA; C. Ehret, Director of Market Research, IBM, to John V. Atanasoff, January 16, 1942, UPA.

45. See Travis testimony, *Honeywell* v. *Sperry Rand*, vols. 41–42.

46. George Harrison, Chairman, Section D3, Instruments, NDRC, to Joseph Desch, NCR, February 4, 1942, UPA; see also, Jan Rajchman to G. Stibitz, April 20, 1943, UPA.

47. Colonel Paul Gillon to E. W. Engstrom, Director, RCA Laboratory, July 17, 1943, UPA, discusses a trip by Eckert and Mauchly to take place July 20, 1943, "to confer with Dr. Young on work currently underway on megacycle counters."

48. Brainerd to Pender, April 26, 1943, UPA.

49. Brainerd to Gillon, May 18, 1943, UPA.

50. Deposition, Jan A. Rajchman, September 17, 1969, p. 107, UPA. This deposition relates to *Honeywell* v. *Sperry Rand*.

51. Ibid., p. 107.

52. Ibid., p. 49.

53. Goldstine to Gillon, December 14, 1943, UPA.

54. Gillon to Goldstine, February 21, 1944, Goldstine's private papers.

55. Bush to Gillon, February 17, 1944, UPA.

56. Redmond and Smith, *Project Whirlwind*, pp. 5–6.

57. T. G. Belden and M. R. Belden, *The Lengthening Shadow: The Story of Thomas J. Watson* (Boston, 1962) attests to the fact that Watson's interest in both projects was related to his desire to assist academic institutions.

58. Interview by Larry Saphire, July 18, 1967, IBM Oral History Project in Computer Technology, Interview TC-3, TJW Research Laboratory, Yorktown, New York.

59. McPherson to McDowell, April 27, 1944: "IBM to furnish gang summary punch for ENIAC"; Gen. G. M. Barnes to J. M. Schackelford of IBM, May 29, 1944, on contract between Moore School and IBM to maintain input and output for ENIAC; J. G. Brainerd to A. H. Dickinson, June 30, 1944, regarding summary punch receptacles and punch equipment; IBM to J. P. Eckert, August 8, 1944: "IBM will supply machines," UPA.

60. Eckert's testimony, *Honeywell* v. *Sperry Rand*, p. 17324.

Chapter 3 ENIAC to EDVAC: From Confidence to Conflict

1. John W. Mauchly, "Notes on Electrical Calculating Devices," August 1941, unpublished report, UPA.

2. Simon to Herrstrom, September 2, 1944, UPA.

3. J. Presper Eckert, Chief Engineer, to Moore School Engineers, September 17, 1944, UPA.

4. Sharpless to Eckert, October 2, 1944, UPA.

5. *Honeywell* v. *Sperry Rand*, p. 5246.

6. University Policy on Patents on Inventions and Discoveries, University of Pennsylvania catalogue, 1944.

7. George A. Smith of Busser and Harding to Harold Pender, February 27, 1945, UPA, pp. 3–4.

8. *Who's Who in Engineering*, 1964.

9. That Pender's sympathy for Eckert and Mauchly resulted from his own patent problems was suggested in interviews with both Herman H. Goldstine, March 15, 1977, and John Brainerd, May 23, 1977, by Nancy Stern.

10. Pender to President George McClelland, March 10, 1945, and to Dr. Lukens, Chairman, University of Pennsylvania Patent Committee, March 10, 1945, UPA; McClelland to J. Presper Eckert, Jr., and John W. Mauchly, March 15, 1945, UPA.

11. Page 30.

12. James Ridgeway, *The Closed Corporation: American Universities in Crisis* (New York, 1968).

13. That some members of the Moore School, specifically, were eager to maintain government funding is evident in John G. Brainerd to Harold Pender, April 6, 1945, UPA; see also Reid Warren, Jr., "Outline of a Research Program for the Moore School of Electrical Engineering," December 1945, UPA.

14. *Honeywell* v. *Sperry Rand*, pp. 6193–6195.

15. Interview by Stern, October 28, 1977.

16. Ibid. Eckert indicated that the main reason for pursuing the patent matter in September 1944 was the Army Ordnance Department's eagerness to have a patent issued. In such cases, it is normally the research institution's place to file on behalf of the inventors.

17. The reason for Warren's selection were suggested by Eckert, Travis, and Warren himself, in interviews by Stern on October 28, 21, and 4, 1977, respectively.

18. Weaver to Brainerd, February 21, 1945, UPA.

19. On March 1, 1945, Brainerd notified Weaver that an Applied Mathematics Panel request would need to be made to the Ordnance Department since the ENIAC was classified.

20. John Mauchly, J. Presper Eckert, Jr., to S. Reid Warren, Jr., November 13, 1945, UPA.

21. J. G. Brainerd, J. P. Eckert, Jr., H. H. Goldstine, J. W. Mauchly, "Description of the ENIAC and Comments on Electronic Digital Computing Machines," submitted to Applied Mathematics Panel, November 30, 1945, UPA.

22. Goldstine and Goldstine, "The Electronic Numerical Integrator and Calculator," *Mathematical Tables and Other Aids to Computation* 2: 97–110; Burks, "Electronic Computing Circuits of the ENIAC," *Proceedings of the IRE* 35: 756–767.

23. *Honeywell* v. *Sperry Rand*, p. 17388A.

24. National Research Council, Committee on Mathematical Tables and Other Aids to Calculations, Subcommittee Z on Calculating Machines and Mechanical Computation.

25. Brainerd to Gillon, September 29, 1945, UPA: "We think it would be a good idea to present at such a gathering . . . However, if we do present a paper we would need clearance from you and the purpose of this letter is to ask for such clearance."

26. Eckert's testimony in *Honeywell* v. *Sperry Rand*, p. 17386, corroborates Mauchly's position.

27. Warren to Brainerd, October 9, 1945, UPA.

28. Moore School memorandum, October 16, 1945: "Proposed Presentation at M.I.T., October 30, 1945," UPA: "The paper described by the outline below will be written by Eckert, Mauchly and Goldstine in accordance with expediency—each will write what he is best prepared to write."

29. *Honeywell* v. *Sperry Rand*, p. 12492.

30. Unpublished memorandum, p. 1, UPA.

31. Goldstine, *The Computer*, pp. 155–156.

32. *Honeywell* v. *Sperry Rand*, p. 6455.

33. Eckert highlighted these aspects of the personality clash between Mauchly and Brainerd in an interview with Stern, October 28, 1977. Eckert suggested as well that Mauchly's quick mind and ability to motivate others both in the classroom and in the laboratory were attributes which differentiated him from men like Brainerd.

34. *Honeywell* v. *Sperry Rand*, p. 11922.

35. Interview with Stern, October 28, 1977.

36. Goldstine to Simon, August 11, 1944, Goldstine's private papers.

37. Brainerd to Gillon, September 13, 1944, UPA.

38. Supplement No. 4 to Contract W-670-ORD-4926, October 27, 1944. The first report on the EDVAC project, called Project PY, indicated the terms: "PY Summary Report No. 1," March 31, 1945, UPA: "By the terms of this Supplement the University agreed to carry out research and development of apparatus which may be combined into an Electronic Discrete Variable Computer, and to submit reports to the U.S. Army Ordnance Dept., describing this work."

39. See Goldstine, *The Computer*, pp. 184–210.

40. See testimony by Eckert, Brainerd, and Mauchly, *Honeywell* v. *Sperry Rand*.

41. Engineering Research Associates, *High Speed Computing Devices* (New York, 1950), pp. 341–354.

42. Goldstine to Gillon, May 26, August 21, December 14, 1944, UPA.

43. Pender to William DuBarry, April 19, May 12, 1945, UPA. IBM Engineering Lab. Dev. Work Order, June 9, 1945, UPA.

44. Information on the use of the ENIAC for this test run was taken primarily from the trial testimony of Edward Teller, Nicholas Metropolis, and Stanley Frankel. See also Goldstine, *The Computer*, pp. 214–215, 225–226.

45. *Honeywell* v. *Sperry Rand*, pp. 6698–6699.

46. Goldstine to Gillon, July 10, 1945, UPA; Dederick to Goldstine, November 15, 1945, UPA.

47. See Metropolis testimony.

48. See Frankel testimony, *Honeywell* v. *Sperry Rand*.

49. Frankel and Metropolis to Goldstine, February 4, 1946, UPA.

50. Norris Bradbury to General G. M. Barnes and Col. Gillon, quoted in Goldstine, *The Computer*, p. 215.

51. S. Frankel and N. Metropolis, "Calculations in the Liquid-Drop Model of Fission," *Physical Review* 72 (1947): 914–925.

52. Press Release, War Department, Bureau of Public Relations, "For Release in Morning Papers, Sat., Feb. 16, 1946, for Radio Broadcast after 7:00 PM EST, Feb. 15, 1946," UPA.

Chapter 4 John von Neumann and the Moore School Computers

1. Material concerning von Neumann's early life is largely from Solomon Bochner, "The Legend of John von Neumann," *National Academy of Sciences Biographical Memoirs*, 1957; P. R. Halmos, "The Legend of John von Neumann," *American Mathematical Monthly*, April 1958, pp. 382–402; and Stanislaw Ulam, "John von Neumann, 1903–1957," *Bulletin of the American Mathematical Society*, May 1958. See also Goldstine, *The Computer*; Arthur W. Burks, "Introduction" to John von Neumann, *The Theory of Self-Reproducing Automata* (Urbana, Ill., 1966); Klara von Neumann's introduction to John von Neumann, *The Computer and the Brain* (New Haven, 1958); and Steve Heims, *John von Neumann and Norbert Wiener: From Mathematics to the Technologies of Life and Death* (Cambridge, Mass., 1980). In addition, Herman Goldstine has been very helpful in supplying information and anecdotes on von Neumann's early years.

2. For the length and breadth of his mathematical papers, see John von Neumann, *Collected Works*, edited by A. H. Taub, 6 vols. (New York, 1963).

3. Constance Reid, *Hilbert* (New York, 1970).

4. Stanislaw Ulam, *Adventures of a Mathematician* (New York, 1976), p. 245.

5. Halmos, "The Legend of John von Neumann," p. 391.

6. Ibid.

7. Bochner, "John von Neumann," p. 446.

8. Ulam, "John von Neumann, 1903–1957," p. 20.

9. Halmos, "The Legend of John von Neumann," p. 391.

10. Ulam, *Adventures of a Mathematician*, p. 245.

11. Goldstine, *The Computer*, p. 181.

12. Burks, introduction to von Neumann, *Theory of Self-Reproducing Automata*, p. 2.

13. Fry, "Industrial Mathematics," p. 38.

14. Von Neumann, "The Mathematician," *Collected Works*, vol. 1.

15. Von Neumann to Weaver, January 14, 1944, UPA.

16. Interview with Mina Rees by Uta Merzbach, March 19, 1969, SHCP, p. 9.

17. Warren Weaver to Prof. Chaffee, Harvard University, March 22, 1944; John von Neumann (hereafter JvN) Papers, Library of Congress, Washington, D.C.; Weaver to von Neumann, March 22, 1944, JvN Papers; von Neumann to Weaver, June 28, 1944, JvN Papers.

18. Goldstine, *The Computer*, p. 182.

19. Ibid., p. 179

20. Warren Weaver wrote to J. Grist Brainerd, ENIAC project supervisor, February 21, 1945, expressing, for the first time, interest in the electronic computer at the Moore School.

21. Granted as Supplement No. 4 to Contract W-670-ORD-4926, October 27, 1944. "PY Summary Report No. 1," March 31, 1945, indicates the terms of that supplement (PY was the name for EDVAC).

22. "Notes on Meeting with Dr. von Neumann," March 14 and 23, 1945, UPA.

23. Goldstine to Gillon, December 14, 1944, UPA.

24. Von Neumann to Goldstine, February 12, 1945, Goldstine's private papers.

25. "ENIAC Progress Report," December 31, 1943, UPA.

26. Eckert, "Disclosure of Magnetic Calculating Machine," January 1944, UPA.

27. The distribution list was entitled, "Topics of von Neumann's Report, Logical Analysis of EDVAC," June 25, 1945, UPA.

28. See von Neumann, *The Computer and the Brain*.

29. "Preliminary Discussion of the Logical Design of an Electronic Computing Instrument," coauthored by Burks, Goldstine, and von Neumann at IAS in June 1946, was a more detailed report that further linked von Neumann's name with the stored-program concept; reprinted in von Neumann, *Collected Works*, vol. 5.

30. Goldstine, *The Computer*, pp. 191.

31. Burks, introduction to von Neumann, *Theory of Self-Reproducing Automata*, pp. 8–9.

32. Metropolis and Worlton, "A Trilogy on Errors in the History of Computing," *Proceedings, First USA-Japan Computer Conference*, p. 687.

33. Harry Huskey, "The Development of Automatic Computing, "*Proceedings, First USA-Japan Computer Conference*, p. 702.

34. "PY Summary Report No. 2," July 10, 1945, prepared by J. W. Mauchly, J. Presper Eckert, Jr., and S. Reid Warren, Jr., p.2, UPA.

35. Burks, "From ENIAC to the Stored-Program Computer," *A History of Computing in the Twentieth Century*, edited by Metropolis et al.

36. Eckert's testimony, *Honeywell* v. *Sperry Rand*, pp. 17412–17741.

37. John Mauchly, "Stored Programs in the ENIAC, BINAC and EDVAC," *Datamation,* October 1979. This article was written as a response to Nancy Stern, "The ENIAC," *Datamation,* May 1979.

38. Contract, John von Neumann and IBM, October 1951, JvN Papers.

39. Von Neumann to Stanley Frankel, October 29, 1946, JvN Papers.

40. Thornton C. Fry, "Industrial Mathematics," *American Mathematical Monthly* 48 (1941): 1038.

41. The sociology of science is filled with statistical analyses which demonstrate that productivity and achievement in science are directly related to the number of papers published. See, for example, Derek de Solla Price, "The Difference between Science and Technology," *Science since Babylon* (New Haven, 1975), p. 127.

42. Burks, "From ENIAC to the Stored-Program Computer," *A History of Computing in the Twentieth Century*, edited by Metropolis et al.

43. Von Neumann, *The Computer and the Brain*.

44. Von Neumann, "First Draft of a Report on the EDVAC," June 30, 1945: "It is clear that a very high speed computing device should ideally have vacuum tube elements . . . A consistent use of the binary system is also likely to simplify the operations of multiplication and division considerably."

45. See H. H. Goldstine and J. von Neumann, "Planning and Coding of Problems for an Electronic Computing Instrument," April 1, 1947, and Burks, Goldstine, and

von Neumann, "Preliminary Discussion of the Logical Design of an Electronic Computing Instrument," in von Neumann, *Collected Works*, vol. 5.

46. Wiener to von Neumann, March 24, 1945, JvN Papers.

47. As early as February 1, 1945, von Neumann was considering the staffing of such a project; von Neumann to Wiener, JvN Papers: "After some discussions with Cunningham and Goldstine, I think it would be desirable to add Eckert and Mauchly of Pa. and Chandrasekhar to our group and possibly George Stibitz."

48. D. V. Widder, Department of Mathematics, Harvard University, to von Neumann, November 26, 1945, JvN Papers; Robert Hutchins, Chancellor, University of Chicago, to von Neumann, November 24, 1945, JvN Papers; George R. Harrison, Dean, MIT, to von Neumann, November 23, 1945, JvN Papers.

49. Von Neumann to Harrison, August 28, 1945, JvN Papers: "I realize the inherent suitability of MIT for such projects but at the same time it is clear that I should wait to see what the Institute for Advanced Study can create in this direction." See also Weiner to von Neumann, March 24, 1945, and letters cited in note 48 above.

50. Von Neumann to Julian Huxley, Executive Secretary, UNESCO, March 28, 1946, JvN Papers.

51. Dean E. Wooldridge, President, Ramo-Wooldridge Corp. to von Neumann, December 18, 1953, JvN Papers; W. C. Asbury, Vice President, Standard Oil Development Corp., to von Neumann, June 19, 1947, JvN Papers; IBM to John von Neumann, October 5, 1951, JvN Papers.

52. "Minutes of November 12, 1945, at RCA," JvN Papers.

53. F. Reichelderfer to V. Zworykin, November 25, 1945, JvN Papers.

54. Reichelderfer to von Neumann, December 29, 1945, JvN Papers.

55. Sidney Shallet, "Electronics to Aid Weather Forecasting," *New York Times*, January 10, 1946. The agency or person who actually contacted the press on this matter has not been identified.

56. Mauchly's diary, January 14, 1946, UPA.

57. F. W. Reichelderfer, interoffice memo, January 24, 1946, subj.: "Publicity on Electronic Weather Calculator," JvN Papers.

58. Von Neumann to Eckert, November 27, 1945, and March 6, 1946, JvN Papers.

59. Eckert's testimony, *Honeywell* v. *Sperry Rand*, p. 17468.

60. Interview with Eckert by Stern, January 23, 1980, side 3, pp. 31–32.

Chapter 5 Transition to the Private Sector

1. Goldstine, *The Computer*, pp. 228–229.

2. Arthur W. Burks, "Who Invented the General-Purpose Electronic Digital Computer?" edited transcript of a talk given at the University of Michigan, April 2, 1974, p. 8. Quoted by permission of the author.

3. War Department, Bureau of Public Relations, Press Branch, UPA.

4. D. Hartree, "The ENIAC: An Electronic Calculating Engine," *Nature* 157 (April 20, 1946): 527 and 158 (October 12, 1946): 500.

5. A. P. Malyshev, Government Purchasing Commission of the Soviet Union in the USA, to the Moore School, April 5, 1946, UPA; Army Ordnance to Dean Pender, May 12, 1946, UPA.

6. Interview with Irven Travis by Stern, October 21, 1977.

7. Ibid.; see also interview with S. Reid Warren by Stern, October 5, 1977.

8. Interview with Eckert by Stern, October 28, 1977.

9. See Travis testimony, *Honeywell* v. *Sperry Rand*, vol. 41.

10. Ibid., p. 6570.

11. John von Neumann to Marston Morse, April 1, 1946, JvN Papers.

12. See Chambers's testimony, *Honeywell* v. *Sperry Rand*.

13. "Minutes, Research Meeting—15 March 1946," UPA.

14. Dean Pender to Eckert and Mauchly, March 22, 1946, "Subject: Conditions for continuance of employment on the research program at the Moore School," UPA.

15. Eckert's and Mauchly's testimony, *Honeywell* v. *Sperry Rand*; interviews by Stern with Mauchly, May 6, 1977, and Eckert, October 28, 1977. See also interviews by Stern with Travis, October 21; Warren, October 5; and Brainerd, March 23, 1977.

16. Dean Pender to Eckert and Mauchly, April 9, 1946, UPA.

17. Von Neumann to Eckert, December 15, 1945, UPA; Eckert to von Neumann, March 15, 1946, UPA.

18. See interviews by Stern with Mauchly, May 6, and Eckert, October 28, 1977. See also Mauchly to Everett Kimball, April 26, 1946, UPA. In his interview of October 28, 1977, Eckert expressed some remorse over his decision not to go with IBM.

19. Chuan Chu to Irven Travis, April 12, 1946, UPA. Interview with Travis by Stern, October 21, 1977.

20. Minutes, "Committee on Course: Theory and Techniques of Electronic Digital Computers," June 10, 1946, UPA.

21. "Theory and Techniques for the Design of Electronic Digital Computers," lectures given at the Moore School, July 8 to August 31, 1946, UPA.

22. M. V. Wilkes, *Automatic Digital Calculators* (London, 1956); M. V. Wilkes, D. J. Wheeler, and S. Gill, *The Preparation of Programs for an Electronic Digital Computer* (Cambridge, Mass., 1951).

23. Samuel H. Caldwell, "Publication, Classification and Patents," Harvard Symposium on Large-Scale Digital Calculating Machinery, January 1947.

24. "Disclosure of John von Neumann's First Draft of a Report on the EDVAC," April 2, 1946, UPA.

25. J. Warshaw, "Report on Trip to Patent Branch, Legal Division, Office of the Chief of Ordnance," April 3, 1947, p. 1, UPA.

26. Ibid.

27. Ibid.

28. War Department, Office of Chief of Ordnance, to Herman Goldstine, March 24, 1947, UPA.

29. Ibid., p. 1.

30. "Minutes of Conference held at the Moore School of Electrical Engineering on 8 April 1947," Mr. Church (attorney), UPA.

31. Ibid.

32. Jerome Ravetz, *Scientific Knowledge and Its Social Problems* (New York, 1971), p. 54.

33. Goldstine, *The Computer*, p. 225.

34. Ibid., p. 319.

35. John T. Wilson, "A Dilemma of American Science and Higher Educational Policy: The Support of Individuals and Fields versus the Support of Universities," *Minerva*, 1971, p. 173. ONR evolved out of the Navy's Office of Research and Invention in 1946.

36. See Redmond and Smith, *Project Whirlwind*; see also *Digital Computer Newsletter*, Office of Naval Research, September 1, 1949, NBS Archives.

37. HR 1452, "National Standardizing Bureau," 56 Cong., 1st sess., May 14, 1900, quoted in C. Cochrane, *Measures for Progress: A History of the National Bureau of Standards* (Washington, D.C., 1966), p. 1. This is also part of the inscription which appears over the new bureau laboratories at Gaithersburg, Maryland.

38. A. Hunter Dupree, *Science and the Federal Government* (Cambridge, Mass., 1957), pp. 271–277; Philip Morse, "E. U. Condon," *National Academy of Sciences Biographical Memoirs*, 1974, 48: 137–138.

39. Cochrane, *Measures for Progress*, p. 433, citing a letter from Vannevar Bush to Gano Dunn. See also p. 362.

40. Morse, "E. U. Condon," *NAS Memoirs* 48: 137.

41. Cochrane, *Measure for Progress*, pp. 440–441. See also Lewis Branscomb, "E. U. Condon," *Physics Today* 27 (1974): 69.

42. Branscomb, p. 69.

43. Daniel Greenberg, *The Politics of Pure Science* (New York, 1967), p. 84: "But even when university status was provided for the great wartime laboratories, there were scientists who felt that any concession to the ways of the military was unbearable." See also, Morse, "E. U. Condon," *NAS Memoirs* 48: 137: "The many physicists who were concerned with the military control of nuclear weapons looked to him for support." For Condon's postwar position on this issue, see E. U. Condon, "Science and Our Future," *Science*, April 5, 1946.

44. Cochrane, *Measures for Progress*, p. 450, on Wallace's attitude toward small business: "A strong friend of small business was now in power. Expansion of technology and other assistance for small firms from $300,000 to $4,500,000 income per year was initiated. He intended the Bureau to assist in the aid to business."

45. Transcript of an interview with E. U. Condon by Charles Weiner, April 27, 1968, American Institute of Physics, New York. It is interesting to note that Condon had done some prewar development work for Westinghouse on a digital computer called the Nimitron, p. 51: "In fact, the Nimitron was patented, and one of the patent claims that was given Westinghouse was 'any electrical means of representing a number as the sum of integral multiples of powers of another number.' So it was the complicated game of representing numbers digitally in a computing circuit. None of us had sense enough to do anything with it, so the patent never amounted to anything."

46. Morse, "E. U. Condon," *NAS Memoirs* 48: 137.

47. See James L. McPherson's deposition in *Honeywell* v. *Sperry Rand*, p. 101; see also interview with Mauchly by Stern, May 7, 1977.

48. See Mauchly interview; also Randell, ed., *Origins*, pp. 125–126.

49. This transfer may well have caused additional conflict between Eckert and Mauchly and the Moore School. Irven Travis noted, however, in an interview by Stern, October 21, 1977, that the Moore School was not interested in pursuing additional computer contracts at that time.

50. "U. S. Bureau of the Census Acquisition and Use of Automatic Data Processing: 1946 to 1957," report prepared for General Accounting Office, Survey of Automatic Data Processing Systems, December 13, 1957, p. 1, National Archives.

51. Census Bureau to NBS, March 28, 1946, National Archives.

52. Interview with Mauchly by Stern, May 6, 1977.

53. Minutes, March 28, 1946, of a meeting of NBS and Census Bureau, National Archives.

54. J. H. Curtiss, "The National Applied Mathematics Laboratories of the National Bureau of Standards," April 1, 1953, NBS Archives.

55. Ibid.; see also interview with Mina Rees, SHCP, "Those of us who were responsible for basic policy in the support of methods, identified this [numerical analysis] as a field where there was no question that stimulation was needed in order to use the machines."

56. J. H. Curtiss lecture, "Lectures on Theory and Techniques for the Design of Electronic Digital Computers," Moore School, p. 29-3, UPA.

57. Gillon to Pender, May 20, 1946, UPA.

58. Mauchly to Everett Kimball, April 23, 1946, UPA.

59. "History of the National Bureau of Standards Program for the Development and Construction of Large-Scale Electronic Calculating Machines," p. 2, NBS Archives.

60. George R. Stibitz to John H. Curtiss, May 25, 1946, UPA.

61. Ibid., p. 2; "History of NBS Program," p. 4; J. C. Capt to Curtiss, June 12, 1946, National Archives.

62. "History of the NBS Program," p. 4; Capt to Curtiss, p. 15.

63. "Background and Current Situation Relating to the Formation of an Electronic Calculator Company, June 4, 1946 (subsequently called Electronic Control Company)," UPA.

64. NBS Contract DA-2, UPA. The contract was approved and signed by the Secretary of Commerce on October 24, 1946.

65. NBS DA-2 Progress Report: "On the National Bureau of Standards Program for the Construction of Electronic Digital Computing Machines for the Office of Naval Research and the Bureau of Census," November 21, 1946, prepared by John Curtiss and Edward Cannon, NBS Archives; John Curtiss to Electronic Control Company, March 28, 1947, UPA.

66. Mauchly, interoffice memo, May 24, 1947, UPA.

67. Ibid.

68. On March 13, 1947, Mauchly requested a delay to June 15 and then on June 6 a delay to August 1. The due date was again extended to November. Mauchly to NBS, March 13, June 6, 1946, UPA.

69. "Proposed Electronic Calculator Company: Rough Tentative Statement of Requirements," June 14, 1946, UPA.

70. NBS Contract DA-2 Progress Report, November 21, 1946, p. 3, NBS Archives.

71. Eckert-Mauchly Computer Corporation (hereafter EMCC) to NBS, May 24, 1950, UPA.

72. J. H. Curtiss, "A Federal Program in Applied Mathematics," *Science* 107 (March 12, 1948). J. H. Curtiss, "The National Applied Mathematics Laboratories of the National Bureau of Standards," Department of Commerce, April 1, 1953, p. 10, NBS Archives.

73. Curtiss to Electronic Control Company, November 12, 1946, UPA.

74. NBS DA-2 Progress Report, November 21, 1946, p. 4, NBS Archives.

75. John von Neumann, Chairman, NRC Subcommittee, to NBS, March 16, 1948, "Cover Letter of Memorandum on High-Speed Computation by the Subcommittee Appointed to Consider Several High Speed Computing Machine Proposals for the National Bureau of Standards," National Archives.

76. Ibid., p. 1.

77. "History of the National Bureau of Standards Program for the Development and Construction of Large-Scale Electronic Computing Machines," p. 6.

78. Ibid., p. 7: "A second source of delay [of Bureau projects] arose from the attempt of the Bureau to obtain information concerning the features of all designs for automatic electronic digital computers, the work on which had been wholly or in part supported by government funds. In order to arrange that the evaluation of designs would be broadly based, it was considered feasible to have the Committee on High-Speed Calculating Machines of NRC participate in the evaluation."

79. John Curtiss to Electronic Control Company, October 20, 1947, Sperry-Univac Archives, Blue Bell, Pa. (hereafter cited as SUA).

80. Von Neumann to NBS, March 16, 1948, National Archives: "It was expected that they [the subcommittee] would in particular read and form an opinion on the reports that will be submitted to the Bureau of Standards by organizations which are interested in taking contracts for the construction of the machines involved."

81. "History of NBS Program," p. 7.

82. Aiken, Caldwell, Stibitz, and von Neumann, "Memorandum to the N.R.C. Committee on High-Speed Computing by the Subcommittee Appointed to Consider Several High Speed Computing Machine Proposals for the National Bureau of Standards," March 16, 1948, p. 3.

83. Ibid., pp. 3–4.

84. Edward Cannon, "Evaluation of the Mathematical Performance Characteristics of Proposed Electronic Computing Machines," Machine Development Laboratory, NBS Report No. 1, p. 9, NBS Archives.

85. "History of NBS Program," pp. 7–8.

86. Cannon's testimony, *Honeywell* v. *Sperry Rand*, p. 17935.

87. Ibid.

88. Minutes, March 22, 1948, NBS; EMCC interoffice memo, May 4, 1948, SUA.

89. Mauchly, EMCC interoffice memo, February 5, 1948, SUA.

90. EMCC interoffice memo, March 1, 1948, UPA.

91. See EMCC interoffice memos in August 1948, SUA.

92. Harry Huskey to Mauchly, April 12, 1948, UPA.

93. Mauchly, EMCC interoffice memo, March 31, 1948, SUA.

94. Huskey to Mauchly, April 12, 1948, SUA.

95. Mauchly, EMCC interoffice memo, May 4, 1948, SUA.

96. Department of Commerce, "Committee on Use of Mechanical Equipment," minutes of meeting of April 7, 1948, dated April 8, 1948, National Archives, p. 2.

97. Interview with Mauchly by Stern, May 7, 1977; with Eckert, October 28, 1977.

98. Interview with Mauchly, May 7, 1977.

99. Mauchly, EMCC interoffice memo, March 31, 1948, SUA.

100. Agreement of Sale, December 22, 1947, signed by Eckert and Mauchly, SUA; interviews with Mauchly, May 7, 1977, and Eckert, October 28, 1977.

101. Mauchly, interoffice memos, May 24 and 31, 1947, UPA.

Chapter 6 The BINAC: A Controversial Milestone

1. Only a few published works focus on developments during this era; see Randell, ed., *The Origins of Digital Computers*, Goldstine, *The Computer from Pascal to von Neumann*, and *A History of Computing in the Twentieth Century*, edited by Metropolis et al. Two sources contain periodic progress reports of government-supported computer projects: *Digital Computer Newsletter*, published by the Mathematical Sciences Division of the Office of Naval Research, which began producing monthly reports in 1949, and *Projects and Publications* of the National Applied Mathematics Laboratories of the National Bureau of Standards, which began publishing quarterly reports in 1948.

2. See Redmond and Smith, *Project Whirlwind*.

3. E. Tomash and A. A. Cohen, "The Birth of an ERA: Engineering Research Associates, Inc., 1946–1955," *Annals of the History of Computing*, vol. 1, no. 2 (October 1979), pp. 83–97.

4. See Simon Lavington, *Early British Computers* (Bedford, Mass., 1980).

5. Richard E. Sprague, "A Western View of Computer History," *Communications of the ACM* 15 (July 1971): 686.

6. G. Gore of Northrop to John W. Mauchly, April 18, 1947, UPA.

7. R. Rawlins of Northrop to ECC, June 25, 1947, UPA.

8. BINAC Contract, October 8, 1947, UPA.

9. Ibid.

10. *Digital Computer Newsletter*, vol. 1, no. 2 (September 3, 1949); Engineering Research Associates, *High-Speed Computing Devices* (New York, 1950), pp. 203, 214, 348.

11. Jerry Mendelson, "More Thoughts on BINAC," *Annals of the History of Computing* 2 (January 1980): 86.

12. Electronic Control Company interoffice memo, November 18, 1947; Electronic Control Company, "BINAC Instruction Code," undated, UPA.

13. E. C. Berkeley, *Giant Brains or Machines That Think* (New York, 1949), p. 179; also quoted in the "BINAC Press Release," August 22, 1949, UPA.

14. A. Auerbach, J. P. Eckert, Jr., R. Shaw, J. R. Weiner, L. D. Wilson, "The BINAC," *Proceedings of the IRE*, January 1952, p. 12. Al Auerbach, an engineer at ECC, should not to be confused with Isaac Auerbach, who also worked for Eckert and Mauchly and is mentioned in note 57 below.

15. Interview with Eckert by Stern, January 23, 1980.

16. "BINAC Press Release," August 22, 1949, UPA.

17. G. Eltgroth, EMCC, to A. V. Astin, Chief, Electronics Division, NBS, August 25, 1949, UPA.

18. G. V. Eltgroth, EMCC interoffice memo, "To: Messrs. Bosin, Brown, Eckert and Mauchly, Re: Contract Price Adjustment—Northrop Aircraft Inc., Dec. 7, 1949," SUA.

19. EMCC interoffice memo, July 20, 1948, UPA.

20. EMCC interoffice memo, December 7, 1949, UPA.

21. Ibid.

22. M. V. Wilkes, "Progress in High-Speed Calculating Machine Design," *Nature* 164 (1949): 341–343; M. V. Wilkes and W. Renwick, "The EDSAC," in Randell, ed., *Origins*, pp. 389–394.

23. Because of the various controversies surrounding the BINAC, many authors have either ignored it or minimized its significance. See, for example, Saul Rosen, "Electronic Computers: An Historical Survey," *Computing Surveys*, vol. 1, no. 1 (March 1969), stating only the following: "The BINAC apparently never worked satisfactorily."

24. R. Baker to F. Bell, May 11, 15, June 12, 1949, UPA.

25. F. C. Bell to E. W. Cannon, July 18, 1949, SUA.

26. F. Bell to G. Gore, August 17, 1949, SUA.

27. L. A. Ohlinger to J. W. Northrop, February 14, 1950, "Subject: BINAC Chronological History," UPA.

28. Ibid.

29. Byron Phelps, "Notes on Eckert-Mauchly Demonstration," August 19, 1949, p. 2, UPA.

30. It took the Ballistics Research Laboratory nine months to dismantle, move, and reassemble the ENIAC. Goldstine, in *The Computer*, pp. 234–235, states: "The ENIAC was 'turned off' on 9 November 1946 to ready it for the move to Aberdeen; it was not started up again until 29 July 1947."

31. L. A. Ohlinger to Northrop, February 14, 1950, UPA.

32. Sprague, "A Western View of Computer History," p. 689.

33. Interview with Donald Eckdahl by Henry Tropp, September 12, 1972, SHCP: "It [BINAC] ran but it had severe maintenance problems."

34. Ibid.

35. Nancy Stern, "The BINAC: A Case Study in the History of Technology," *Annals of the History of Computing* 1 (July 1979): 9–20.

36. Jerry Mendelson, "More Thoughts on BINAC," *Annals of the History of Computing* 2 (January 1980): 85.

37. Ibid., p. 86.

38. Florence R. Anderson, "BINAC at Northrop," *Annals of the History of Computing* 2 (January 1980): 83.

39. Ibid.

40. R. Rawlins to EMCC, June 25, 1947, SUA.

41. Contract, signed by George Gore, Secretary, Northrop Corporation, and John Mauchly and J. Presper Eckert, Jr., Electronic Control Company, October 15, 1947, UPA.

42. Baker to Bell, January 7, 1949, SUA.

43. Interview with Jerry Mendelson, on January 3, 1972, p. 12, SHCP.

44. Interview with Mauchly by Stern, May 7, 1977.

45. Eltgroth, EMCC interoffice memo, May 27, 1949, p. 2, UPA: "On behalf of Eckert-Mauchly Computer Corporation, it was pointed out that our engineering personnel are so heavily committed as to make it impossible to rescue Northrop from any dilemma in which they might find themselves as a result of attempting to maintain and operate the BINAC on their own premises with personnel not too familiar with the instruments. It was clear that Bell regarded this with mild aspersion. He revealed that Northrop has a digital computer section of perhaps 30 people who have had both design and operating experience on electronic digital computers."

46. President Mauchly to the Executive Committee, EMCC interoffice memo, August 18, 1948, SUA.

47. Baker to Bell, August 7, 1949, SUA.

48. EMCC interoffice memo, June 29, 1948, UPA.

49. Bell to Cannon, July 18, 1949, UPA.

50. Interview with Jerry Mendelson, pp. 13–14, SHCP.

51. NBS report to Edgar F. Hoppe and Edward J. Hickey, Investigative Staff, House Appropriations Committee, from A. V. Astin, Chief, Electronics and Ordnance Division, November 18, 1949, "Status of Work on Automatic Electronic Computing Machine," National Archives.

52. See John W. Mauchly to E. Mauchly, Vice President, Woolworth Corp., January 24, 1948, UPA, which outlines the types of contracts EMCC was hoping to obtain.

53. *Projects and Publications of the National Applied Mathematics Laboratories*, June 1948, p. 3, NBS Archives.

54. See J. H. Curtiss, "A Federal Program in Applied Mathematics," *Science* 107 (March 12, 1948); "History of the National Bureau of Standards Program for the Development and Construction of Large-Scale Electronic Computing Machines," undated NBS publication, NBS Archives.

55. EMCC interoffice memo, August 18, 1948, UPA.

56. EMCC interoffice memo, August 28, 1948, UPA.

57. Mauchly to Executive Committee, EMCC interoffice memo, August 18, 1948, UPA: "Ike Auerbach has, during the past few months, maintained that we could produce additional BINAC computers within six months from the time at which the Northrop BINAC was delivered."

Chapter 7 The UNIVAC and Beyond

1. Interview with E. G. Andrews by Henry S. Tropp, March 2, 1972, SHCP, p. 39.

2. Interview with Edmund C. Berkeley by Stern, March 29, 1978.

3. E. C. Berkeley, memorandum for Mr. H. J. Volk, December 18, 1947, "Subject: New Machines to Handle Information—Path of Development," Edmund Berkeley's personal papers, New York, N.Y. Volk, second vice president and Berkeley's superior, was transferred and replaced by Bruce Gerhard, who deemed Berkeley's outspoken political views inappropriate for Prudential's image.

4. "An Internal History of Prudential," undated, Prudential Archives, Newark, New Jersey; John W. Mauchly to Edmund C. Berkeley, March 28, 1947, UPA.

5. Berkeley, memo to Electronic Control Company, January 19, 1947, UPA.

6. Mauchly to Berkeley, March 28, 1947, Berkeley's personal papers, New York.

7. Ibid.

8. Description of UNIVAC system, January 1949, UPA.

9. Mauchly, Electronic Control Company interoffice memo, May 28, 1947, SUA.

10. ECC and Prudential, Letter of Agreement, August 4, 1947, UPA.

11. Ibid.

12. Prudential to Electronic Control Company, March 1, 1948, UPA.

13. Prudential contract, December 8, 1948, UPA.

14. EMCC interoffice memo, August 17, 1949, UPA.

15. Prudential contract, December 8, 1948, UPA.

16. EMCC interoffice memo, July 8, 1949, SUA.

17. EMCC interoffice memo, September 27, 1948, p. 3, SUA: " . . . Prudential evidenced tremendous enthusiasm for the UNIVAC system and rejected in no uncertain terms a suggestion by us that they hold off their decision until someone else's UNIVAC is in operation and subject to their inspection . . . Mr. Gerhard then brought up what he considered were the most serious points of misunderstanding. He declared that the Prudential was considerably disturbed upon receipt of the proposed contract to find a new schedule of prices . . . It was then decided that this corporation was morally obligated to revert to the figures in question . . . It appears that adherence to the higher schedule would have caused a complete breakdown of negotiations."

18. A. C. Nielsen, Jr., to J. H. Curtiss, October 23, 1946, Warren Cordell's private papers, Chicago, Illinois. Cordell was an A. C. Nielsen executive.

19. Curtiss to Nielsen, October 29, 1946, Cordell's private papers.

20. Nielsen interoffice memo, December 12, 1946, Cordell's private papers.

21. Ibid.

22. P. V. Jester, vice president, A. C. Nielsen Company to J. W. Mauchly, December 2, 1946, Cordell's private papers.

23. EMCC to A. C. Nielsen, Jr., January 4, 1947, UPA.

24. Contract between Electronic Control Company and A. C. Nielsen Company, February 13, 1947, UPA.

25. Art Nielsen to Henry Rahmel, May 28, 1947, Cordell's private papers.

26. Nielsen to Cordell, December 30, 1947, Cordell's private papers: "Similarly Henry [Rahmel] is studying the possibility of stock participation in the new Mauchly and Eckert corporation." In an interview on March 31, 1978, John Mauchly indicated that Nielsen was interested in acquiring controlling interest in EMCC.

27. Nielsen to Rahmel, May 28, 1947, Cordell's private papers.

28. Agreement between EMCC and A. C. Nielsen Company, April 23, 1948, UPA.

29. Gene Clute of EMCC to Henry Rahmel of A. C. Nielsen, May 21, 1948, UPA.

30. Mauchly to Rahmel, September 30, 1948, UPA.

31. John W. Mauchly to E. C. Mauchly, Woolworth Corporation, January 24, 1948, UPA.

32. EMCC interoffice memo, May 4, 1948, SUA.

33. Ibid., March 31, 1948, UPA.

34. Interview with Mauchly by Stern, March 31, 1978.

35. Contract between American Totalisator and EMCC, August 6, 1948, Board of Directors meeting of EMCC, August 6, 1948, UPA.

36. "President's Report to the Stockholders of EMCC," December 15, 1949, UPA.

37. "Minutes, Board of Directors Meeting, EMCC"; *Baltimore Sun*, October 29, 1949, p. 1.

38. Mauchly, "On the Trials of Building ENIAC," *IEEE Spectrum* 12 (April 1975): 70–76. Saul Rosen, "Electronic Computers: An Historical Survey," *Computing Surveys*, vol. 1, no. 1 (March 1969).

39. EMCC, President's Report to Shareholders, December 31, 1949, UPA.

40. Minutes of the December 29, 1949, Meeting of EMCC, UPA: "Loan from Reconstruction Finance Corp. for $800,000 requested . . . A loan from the Research and Development Co. also was requested."

41. Minutes of the December 29, 1949, meeting at EMCC, UPA, attests to NCR's and Remington Rand's interest: "He [T. Wistar Brown, sales manager of EMCC] also reported that the National Cash Register Company had sent a staff of 7 people to visit and investigate Eckert-Mauchly on December 20, 1949. He said that they were not awaiting a report from their general counsel and that Mr. Carl Beust was expected on January 4, 1950, for a further discussion . . . Mr. Brown said that Remington Rand continued to be an excellent prospect but no date has been set for the next discussion with them." See also EMCC interoffice memo, December 22, 1949, UPA.

42. Ibid.

43. Ibid.

44. See Robert Bork, *The Antitrust Paradox: A Policy at War with Itself* (New York, 1978); interview with Mauchly by Stern, March 31, 1978.

45. Agreement, Remington Rand and EMCC, February 6, 1950, UPA.

46. A thorough analysis of how Remington Rand lost that commanding lead to IBM, within only a few years, would be an interesting research project.

47. *Business Week*, March 4, 1950.

48. From May 1948 to February 1949, UNIVAC system development costs totaled $156,000. "Current Assets of EMCC as of June 30, 1948," UPA.

49. EMCC to NBS, May 24, 1950, SUA.

50. Interview with Mauchly by Stern, March 31, 1978.

51. Telephone interviews with Henry Rahmel and Warren Cordell of A. C. Nielsen, by Nancy Stern, March 10, 1978; interview with Mauchly by Stern, March 31, 1978.

52. Interview with Mauchly by Stern, March 31, 1978.

53. ERA, *High-Speed Computing Devices*, p. 203.

54. Electronic Control Company, "UNIVAC Report," December 1947, UPA.

55. Electronic Control Company, "UNIVAC Progress Report," undated, UPA, p. 4.

56. Ibid.; EMCC, *UNIVAC System Report*, publication of the Remington Rand Company, 1951, UPA.

57. *ENIAC, EDVAC, UNIVAC [UNIVERSAL AUTOMATIC COMPUTER]*, a publication of Electronic Control Company, 1215 Walnut St., Philadelphia, Pa., undated, UPA.

58. John Mauchly to Edmund C. Berkeley, March 28, 1947, UPA.

59. *UNIVAC System Report*, 1951.

60. Ibid.; see also ERA, *High-Speed Computing Devices*, p. 203.

61. Calvin E. Bosin, treasurer, EMCC, to F. B. Gerhard, vice president, Prudential, August 17, 1949, p. 2, E. C. Berkeley's personal papers.

62. EMCC, *UNIVAC Report*, 1948, pp. 1–8, SUA.

63. ERA, *High-Speed Computing Devices*, p. 205.

64. ECC, "Report on UNIVAC," December, 1947, UPA.

65. EMCC, *UNIVAC System Report*, 1951, S-UA.

66. See "A Tentative Instruction Code for a Statistical EDVAC," May 7, 1947, UPA, for a discussion of programming philosophy. The software considerations relevant to computer technology in these early years would make an interesting research topic.

67. Remington Rand, Inc., "UNIVAC, SHORT CODE," Philadelphia, Pa., October 1952, SUA. Jean Sammet, *The History of Programming Languages* (Englewood Cliffs, N.J., 1969), p. 129.

68. G. V. Eltgroth, EMCC, to Robert Fulwider, Esq., marked "Personal and Confidential," February 8, 1950, UPA.

69. T. Wistar Brown, EMCC interoffice memo, March 31, 1948, UPA.

70. John W. Mauchly, EMCC interoffice memo, February 5, 1948, UPA.

71. Interview with Isaac Auerbach by Nancy Stern, April 10, 1978.

72. ONR Report prepared by Mina Rees, undated, UPA.

73. EMCC interoffice memo, January 19, 1949, UPA.

74. Ibid., p. 2: "Mr. Alexander expressed quite freely his unhappiness with this situation. He stated that he had given us a free hand up until this point and had certified all our engineering decisions and opinions . . . he considered the electrostatic memory highly experimental . . . He then made it clear that if he were to accept such a design change he would require the construction of a full-fledged prototype memory which would be tested by the Bureau."

75. *Honeywell* v. *Sperry Rand*, p. 6055.

76. Mauchly was also instrumental in forming the ACM. See Samuel B. Williams, "The Association for Computing Machinery," *Journal of the ACM*, vol. 1, no. 1 (January 1954), p. 2.

Chapter 8 In Retrospect

1. David F. Noble, *America by Design: Science, Technology, and the Rise of Corporate Capitalism* (New York, 1977), esp. pp. 98–99.

2. Ibid., p. xxvi: "The imperatives of the automatic market, professional specialization, and rationalized management, coupled with the corporate monopolization of technological intelligence, have contributed to the appearance of technology as an autonomous force in history. Insofar as social analysis merely replicates such a perception of reality without penetrating beneath the apparent technological necessity, it further contributes to the general mystification and reinforces the particular social relations which are thereby obscured. This study is an attempt to reintegrate the mystified conception of technology with the actual activities from which it has been abstracted."

3. Ibid., p. 321.

4. See "The Interaction of Science and Technology in the Industrial Age," *Technology and Culture* 17 (October 1976).

5. Thomas Parke Hughes, "The Science-Technology Interaction: A Case of High-Voltage Power Transmission Systems," *Technology and Culture* 17 (October 1976): 646.

6. Hughes, "ENIAC: Invention of a Computer," *Technikgeschichte* 42, no. 2 (1975), p. 148.

7. Hughes, "The Science-Technology Interaction," pp. 658–659.

8. Ibid., p. 651.

9. Some authors, particularly Goldstine, depict Mauchly as an unconventional scientist.

10. Edwin T. Layton, Jr., "American Ideologies of Science and Engineering," *Technology and Culture* 17 (October 1976): 688.

11. Ibid., pp. 691, 695.

12. Jacob Schmookler, *Invention and Economic Growth* (Cambridge, Mass., 1966), for example, p. vii: "This work is an attempt to analyze the effects of economic growth on technology by focusing on its effects on invention"; see also W. Paul Strassman, *Risk and Technological Innovation: American Manufacturing Methods During the 19th Century* (Ithaca, 1959). That facet of Marxism which borders on economic determinism could be classified within this category as well.

13. Joseph Schumpeter, *The Theory of Economic Development* (Cambridge, Mass., 1934), pp. 88–89.

14. William F. Ogburn, "How Technology Causes Social Change," *Technology and Social Change*, edited by Francis Allen (New York, 1957), pp. 12–26; such social histories also include the works of humanists like Lewis Mumford's *Technics and Civilization, The Myth of the Machine, Technics and Human Development, The Pentagon of Power.*

15. Smith, "Project Whirlwind," *Technology and Culture* 17: 459.

16. Goldstine, *The Computer*, pp. 125, 148.

17. Louis C. Hunter, "The Heroic Theory of Invention," *Technology and Social Change in America*, edited by Edwin T. Layton (New York, 1973), p. 46.

18. Ibid.

19. Goldstine, *The Computer*, p. 198.

20. Ibid., p. 196.

21. Ibid., pp. 191–192.

22. Ibid., p. 192.

23. Ibid., p. 197.

24. Maurice V. Wilkes, "Computers Then and Now," *Journal of the ACM* 15 (January 1968): 2.

25. Goldstine, *The Computer*, p. 239.

26. Ibid., p. 240.

27. RCA's work on the Selectron was an academic project undertaken in conjunction with the Institute for Advanced Study.

28. Henry Tropp, "The Effervescent Years," *IEEE Spectrum*, February 1974, p. 76.

29. Ibid., p. 76.

30. William Rodgers, *Think: A Biography of the Watsons and IBM* (New York, 1968), pp. 214–215.

31. Goldstine, *The Computer*, p. 329.

Index

costs of, 15, 42
criticisms of, 16, 17, 20, 105, 111
development history of, 7–23, 24, 34, 36–48
  passim, 63, 71–72, 77, 80, 81, 160,
  170
differential analyzer modified in, 18, 38,
  162
as electronic analog to desk calculator, 24,
  28
existing technology utilized in, 24–25, 26,
  28, 30, 33, 38, 45, 56
funding of, *see* funding
as general purpose machine, 3, 4
as group effort, 5, 21, 24, 34, 39
IBM devices used in, 26, 30, 33, 38, 45, 56,
  63
Los Alamos use of, 3, 62–63, 65, 70, 72
moved to Aberdeen BRL, 61–62, 167
naming of, 15
NDRC view of, 17–23, 44, 71, 105, 111
patent situation, 3–4, 33–34, 36–39, 47–57
  passim, 65, 75, 84, 89, 91, 96, 165 (*see
  also Honeywell* v. *Sperry Rand*)
programming limitations of, 28, 58, 75
reliability of, 15–16, 63
research and development for, 24–47
specifications for, 50–51
speed of, 20, 30, 33, 34, 76, 87, 151, 152
storage capacity of, 26, 58, 61, 63, 151 (*see
  also* input-output devices;
  storage/memory device[s])
technical feautres of, compared, 133
testing/test run of, 3, 4, 19, 58, 61–62, 63,
  65, 72
vacuum-tube use in, 25, 26, 30, 33, 38, 42,
  61, 119, 151, 167
youth of staff engaged on, 18, 23, 44, 50,
  105
"entrepreneur" defined, 37. *See also* industry;
  innovation
equations, solution of, 18, 63, 89
  Atanasoff's computer and, 4, 34, 167, 168
  BINAC and, 122, 128
  BRL's human computers for, 12, 14
  von Neumann's contributions to, 67, 70
exchange of ideas, 74, 81–88 *passim*, 92,
  95–96, 99 107, 112
  and adaptation of technology, 24–25, 30,
  33–34, 37–39, 168, 175
  inhibition of, 95, 109
  and "wartime cooperation," 33, 41–42, 44,
  71, 74
See also patent(s)

fire control, 17, 18, 41, 62
  and trajectory calculation, 12
  by ENIAC, 33, 87

"First Draft of a Report on the EDVAC" (von
  Neumann), *see* EDVAC
flip-flop circuits, *see* circuitry
Frankel, Stanley, 62, 63, 79
Fry, Thornton, 70, 79
function table, 33
funding
  EDVAC, 1, 89, 116
  ENIAC, 1, 12, 15, 17, 20, 23, 47, 84, 89
  by government, 1, 2, 12-17 *passim*, 20, 23,
    41, 47, 52–53, 71, 83, 84, 88–89, 98,
    99, 101–107, 111, 116, 117, 160–161
  for IAS project, 83, 92
  by private industry, 2, 18, 47, 116, 161, 175
  UNIVAC, 2, 123
  See also costs; research and development

General Accounting Office, 103
General Electric Company, 41, 89, 94
General Motors Corporation, 134
Gillon, Colonel Paul, 15, 20, 21–22, 42, 45,
  58, 61, 74, 84
Goldstine, Adele, 26, 63
Goldstine, Herman Heine, 34, 63, 74, 80, 94,
  163, 172, 175, 176
  on Eckert, 10, 37
  and EDVAC, 58, 59, 75–76, 96–97, 170
  and ENIAC, 12, 14–23 *passim*, 25–26, 30,
    47, 49, 54, 58, 61, 62–63, 71, 87
  on Mauchly and Atanasoff-Mauchly
    relations, 36, 56, 166, 167
  and science-engineering dichotomy,
    170–171
  on von Neumann and IAS, 70, 71–72, 74,
    76, 99, 170, 172
government, 94
  contraints imposed by, 2, 42, 63
  funding by, *see* funding
  research and development policies of, 14,
    16, 20, 41, 52–53, 88, 103–106
  See also Air Force, U.S.; Army Ordnance,
    U.S. Department of; Census, U.S.
    Bureau of; National Bureau of
    Standards; National Defense Research
    Committee; Navy, U.S.; Office of
    Scientific Research and Development;
    Weather Bureau, U.S.
Great Britain, *see* Britain
Groves, General Leslie R., 148, 149

Halladay, Henry, 3, 158–159
Halmos, P. R., 67
harmonic analyzer, 7, 34, 37
Harrison, George R., 41, 82
Hartree, Douglas, 88